Marketing
Professional
Services
A Handbook

Marketing Professional Services

Services
A Handbook

PATRICK FORSYTH

FINANCIAL TIMES
PITMAN PUBLISHING

DEDICATION

For all those 'professionals' with whom I have had
the pleasure (and occasionally the frustration!) of working,
and especially the early converts who first helped
to get me involved in this fascinating area.

Pitman Publishing
128 Long Acre, London WC2E 9AN

A Division of Longman Group UK Limited

First published in 1992
Reprinted 1992

© Longman Group UK Limited 1992

British Library Cataloguing in Publication Data
A CIP catalogue record for this book can be obtained
from the British Library

ISBN 0 273 03849 4

Phototypeset in Linotron Times Roman by
Northern Phototypesetting Co. Ltd, Bolton
Printed and bound in Great Britain by
Biddles Ltd, Guildford and King's Lynn

CONTENTS

ACKNOWLEDGEMENTS

I like to think that, as a consultant and trainer, I provide a Professional service (though there are those in other professional services who might feel it is more correctly written with a small p).

This book sets out to explain, in a practical way, how marketing – in other words the business obtaining process – works, and can be used, in professional services.

Any ability I have to do this comes, in part, from many years not only in consultancy, but also on the marketing side of consultancy, and especially from the experience of working with a number of different kinds of professional service firms, both large and small, and with a number of the professional bodies in the field. I have also drawn, probably both consciously and unconsciously, on a variety of other experiences, from books I have read, from training films I have seen, from courses I have attended and conversations with delegates on courses I have conducted (one always learns as much from leading a course as from attending it.) So, thanks are due to many different people who have, wittingly or not, contributed to my knowledge of the topic and my competence to put something of it over to others.

Special thanks are due to a number of individuals who have contributed to this work or its sources. In no order of priority these include David Senton, Peter Kirkby and Ian Collins, with whom I worked for many years; Robin Birn and Ruth Webber, who number among current associates with whom my own firm collaborates; Barbara Hale at the Institute of Chartered Accountants for permission to adopt and include certain material first published by that body; and Drummond Abrams who made useful comments and put up with reading a rather untidy manuscript.

Marketing is a dynamic process and as such there can be no complete, right approach; what works for one situation today may be inappropriate tomorrow. However, what we do – and what we find works – tomorrow may well be helpful in devising longer term approaches.

Thus, this book sets the scene for something one can spend a life-time learning – and still not have completely sewn up. Being conscious of how the process works helps one to go on learning, so I am particularly grateful to those of my colleagues in consultancy who, in the past, have made me conscious of the mechanisms involved in such skills and thus helped me develop the habit of going on learning.

PATRICK FORSYTH

FOREWORD

This book is aimed at those in professional services who wish to know about 'the process of obtaining the business', and especially all those who bear a responsibility – formally or otherwise, in whole or in part – for that process.

In this book professional services means both the 'Professions', capital 'P', namely accountants, surveyors, architects, solicitors and others; and a range of other professionals, lower case 'p', including consultants, designers and engineers. The book will also be relevant to those operating in different professional areas, for instance doctors and dentists in private clinics; and also to others who provide business services (with an element of advice) ranging from market research to public relations, and from insurance brokers to pensions consultants.

The common factor among these people is that they all provide a service; that the service includes an element of advice, which depends in turn on their professional expertise and, sometimes, objectivity; and that time is a basic resource of their business. While the book concentrates on those elements of marketing where the fundamental approaches are similar for all, the terminology used in each area of business is, of course, different. 'Customers' may be called clients or patients; the organisation may be called just that or perhaps the firm, and while many are partnerships, some are sole practitioners.

Within the text, certain examples are quoted specifically, otherwise the range of people involved internally are referred to collectively as professionals, those externally as clients, and organisations are referred to as firms. In addition it is worth noting that it is said that there are only two kinds of people, namely those who worry that the word 'he' means only men, and those who assume it means both men and women. I am among the latter, but mean no offence to those in the first category, who will, perhaps, only be satisfied when the English language comes up with a new word with the unequivocal meaning 'he or she'. Alas, there is no such word at the time of writing so let us all assume hereafter that, at least in this book, 'he' should be taken to mean 'he or she', as appropriate.

The title of this book includes the word 'handbook'. This is important.

It is not intended to be a textbook, in the least practical interpretation of that description. It is not even intended to be comprehensive in the sense of containing a complete review of everything that goes on in marketing, both theory and practice. Rather it sets out to demystify the process, and show *what* it is, *how* it applies to professional services, and *how* to plan, organise and implement marketing activities that will help build, and indeed grow, your business in the right way.

The book unashamedly concentrates therefore on key issues, not so much as I perceive them to be, but as I observe them to be through my contacts and work with a variety of professional service firms. The chapters are arranged in a logical sequence, which moves from definitions to planning to the utilisation of individual techniques; and the chapters are designed to enable the reader to dip into, or revisit, particular topics individually. In addition, certain practical 'action points' (based very much on observations of what successful firms do), and examples, are boxed in order to highlight and separate them from the bulk of the text.

The overall intention is to illustrate how a marketing orientation and an appropriate deployment of the techniques involved can positively sustain and improve business results.

Note:

There are still guidelines (or rules) in many of the professions as to what promotional practices are, or are not, acceptable or allowed. I have not attempted here to make reference to all these rules; they are, in any case, different for each profession, they vary geographically and they are changing, and will no doubt continue to do so.

Some of these guidelines affect the detail of what may be done (for example, for accountants in the UK, direct mail is allowed, but follow-up telephone calls to those who have been mailed is not – at least at the time of writing), so it is advisable to have whatever regulations may affect your firm in mind as you read on.

PREFACE

'You cannot sit on the lid of progress.
If you do, you will be blown to pieces.'

Henry Kissinger

Services are different. Special. Professional services especially so. But they are not especially protected from competitiveness. Like any other business they prosper only by attracting sufficient clients, and the right kind of work, at the right time and at the right rates.

Surely one of the ways in which professionals offering services are different is in not having to concern themselves with the whole grisly process of 'getting in the business'. Perhaps this was the case once upon a time.

Indeed, not so very long ago the idea of a book on the marketing of professional services would have been viewed with a mixture of amazement and horror. And in some people, elements of this remain. For example, not long ago, as I contemplated writing this book, my father, who has just retired and given up his dental practice, telephoned me. He was angry at the 'unprofessional action' of his successor. What had he done? He had hung a discreet sign outside the premises saying 'Dental Surgery'. This is actually minimal promotional activity by any standards.

In the past the professions enjoyed increasing prosperity in what most outsiders regarded as a highly protected environment. Profit growth was assured as the volume of work increased with the growth of the market; future planning was easy because so many of the inputs could be taken as fixed.

But in recent years, much of that certainty has disappeared. Two factors, inextricably linked, have in many countries changed the look of the professionals' world for ever. First, the ethical restrictions which prohibited certain, in some cases many, forms of promotional activity have been progressively relaxed and this process continues. Secondly, the certainty of work 'walking through the door' almost as and when required has gone – the professions are now as competitive as most other business fields, indeed more so than many.

The competitive pressures are there for all to see, and they show themselves in three main areas in many professions. The first is the area of 'professional' competition (i.e. that from other similar firms), especially with the larger firms taking different attitudes to their own growth. Secondly, there is competition from outside the particular profession, for example the work being done by banks, management consultants and others, which overlaps with that of accountants. Thirdly, there is more client pressure, reflected in a much greater demand for value for money, even to the extent of 'shopping around' for the best deal. And no matter how much repeat business is done, the proportion of total fees that needs to be sought out is growing, and the right way to convert prospects, referrals and enquiries – even new projects with existing clients – is becoming less certain and demands a more professional approach.

These trends continue. As the market for professional services grows (and many are long-term growth markets), the question of who gets that growth and, indeed, who books any new business, is influenced in turn by the continuing debate on professional ethics, which has to some degree slowed progress towards a true marketing approach in the UK and elsewhere, and by the degree of adoption of marketing techniques and how effectively this has been done.

In some professions at least, a good deal has been done over the past few years. Moving tentatively at first, professionals have dipped their toes in the marketing stream. At first marketing was equated with advertising. So they tried advertising. Soon it was realised that there were other possibilities, such as public relations and other promotional activity. More recently, direct mail has been included among those techniques that have been tried. And more professionals are being designated 'marketing partner', setting promotional budgets and are even being regarded as having a sales role. Whether this whole process is regarded as revolution or evolution, it has certainly changed the face of the professions for ever.

Looking back now, surrounded by a plethora of marketing activity, the days when none of this was necessary already seem a long time ago. Originally there was a strong feeling within the professions that what would result from all these changes was simply 'the situation as was, plus some advertising'. In fact, everything has changed. Attitudes and practices with regard to services, fees, the organisation of the firm, the promotional mix, training and even recruitment of staff have all been affected. Muted talk of 'practice development' has given way to a situation where marketing has become the watchword of many. But does marketing *really* apply to professional services?

If a professional firm is to survive and prosper, then patently it must organise its activities in such a way that the fees and revenues it can earn from the supply of its services exceed the costs of those services. Indeed, in many cases it must do more – it must produce sufficient growth both of profit and its range of interesting work so that it can provide the satisfaction necessary to attract and keep the level of first-class staff to supply the professional (and senior) staff of tomorrow, to provide a future for the firm as a whole. Therefore, the firm must be constantly aware of the need to offer services to clients which fulfil not only technical but also commercial needs; and to fulfil these needs better than the competition at cost-effective fee levels.

To do this the needs of the client and the market must be defined; the appropriate services for today (and tomorrow) must be developed; fee levels which are both competitive and profitable must be set; and the services available must be communicated to existing and prospective clients so that they are persuaded to buy them. Thus, the main marketing tactics of research, product/service development, pricing and promotion all have a part to play.

Of course, some marketing tactics which may be appropriate to other industries will be neither applicable nor effective. For example, in-store merchandising and door-to-door selling are of little use to the professions. However, no commercial company can usefully employ all the available marketing and promotional tactics. It is the company's or firm's decision as to which tactics are most appropriate or cost-effective. However, it is hard to identify any examples of a company where marketing has no application at all.

Marketing focuses the drive for growth and profit and stimulates the whole process of client satisfaction which is the motivation for so many professionals. Its adoption represents a major opportunity for the professions, yet, as a wise man once said, 'the trouble with opportunities is that they are so often disguised as hard work'.

Marketing is as much an art as a science. It needs to be applied both creatively and systematically. The process is not easy and represents a challenge to many in the professions. There is no one right way, since the adoption of marketing has been and remains an area of continuing change. So, while I believe that the ideas expressed here represent the best current practice as this book goes to press, they are unlikely to be the final word. All the professions exist in dynamic and exciting times. *

PATRICK FORSYTH

Touchstone Training and Consultancy
17 Clocktower Mews
Arlington Avenue
London N1 7BB

---

* One excellent way of keeping up-to-date is provided by the new journal *Practice Marketing*. Aimed specifically at the professions (and accountants and solicitors in particular), it provides an on-going practical review of marketing matters as they develop in the field. *Practice Marketing* is at Boskessy House, Cargreen, Saltash, Cornwall PL12 6PA (Tel. 0752 846672).

'A wise man will make more opportunities than he finds'

Francis Bacon (1561–1626) *Essays*,
'Of Ceremonies and Respects'.

1 BLUEPRINT FOR MARKETING SUCCESS
Introduction and definitions

'They say if you build a better
mousetrap than your neighbour,
people are going to come running.
They are like hell! It's marketing
that makes the difference.'

Ed Johnson

Many people, and not just those in professional services, are confused by
the word marketing. So we will start by looking at what it is not.

It is not a euphemism for advertising or selling. It is not, in fact, one
thing at all; much less one straightforward thing. It is the fault of those in
the business of marketing perhaps, but the word is used in at least three
different ways. For any business, marketing is:

- **a concept**, that of seeing the business through the eyes of the customers
  (clients) and ensuring profitability through providing them with value
  satisfaction;
- **a function**, the total management function that co-ordinates the above
  approach, anticipating the demands of the customers, identifying and
  satisfying their needs via the provision of the right products or services
  at the right price, time and place;
- **a series of techniques** which make the process possible, including advertising plus other promotional activity, sales and also market research,
  pricing and others.

All are relevant and important to professional services. The first implies
that everyone in the firm is involved, everyone needs to adopt the right

attitude and many will have specific roles to play. The second implies that someone within the firm wears 'the marketing hat'. This does not mean that one person is involved exclusively, but responsibility, and particularly the planning and initiation of activity, must lie specifically with someone. Perhaps, by definition, that person should be a good delegator!

The third implies not only that a considerable number of techniques, many of which are not the traditional stock-in-trade of the professional, are involved and must be understood, but also that they are used systematically, appropriately and co-ordinated together.

So marketing is not something that can be compartmentalised. The firm does not need a cupboard of marketing techniques to be opened only when time permits or when additional business is urgently required. There must be a marketing orientation in every aspect of the firm and everyone in it needs to be involved – continuously.

Marketing is not now viewed with the suspicion – even hostility – which once was the case. We are all now used to seeing advertisements for professional services, receiving direct mail shots, newsletters and invitations to attend client seminars. They have become part of the status quo.

Of course, responses, attitudes and results vary, but one factor, I would venture to suggest, is common to all. Everyone has discovered there is more to it than meets the eye. Marketing does not come in the form of 'magic dust' – a quick sprinkle and the firm grows and develops. If only it were that simple! An understanding of the many techniques and the co-ordination of them all is essential, and it takes time. However obvious it may sound, this cannot be overstressed. Implementation of marketing takes time. In a fee-paying business, where the same people are both the production resource and the promotional resource, how that time is made available, when and who does what, is crucial. Even for firms taking a real initiative with marketing it often remains a problem, seemingly with no easy answers.

So it is unlikely that we will ever reach a stage where there is no more for professional services to take on board about marketing, or indeed that everything that is being done is regarded as successful. Several times I have been asked to speak at conferences and, while the brief may have varied a little, in each case I have suggested the title 'So now we are marketing-oriented, but what do we do?' This has been accepted because it reflects, perhaps exactly, not only the way those particular firms had been seeing things, but also because it is precisely the stage so many firms have now reached.

They have a marketing partner (or even a marketing director). They have a budget. They are taking action. But there is unease in terms of whether it is all as well directed, and as well controlled, co-ordinated and executed as it could be. Having moved away from a situation where nothing much was done (or allowed), professionals have, in some cases, moved to a situation where what is done is, in part, what is easiest to arrange. Things are also, in part, done because it has become 'what we always do'. Like accountants sending out a newsletter after the Budget or architects copiously illustrating their proposals (of which, more later). This kind of thinking is dangerous in an activity that must, by definition; be creative, effective in the marketplace and which may well consume a significant budget.

Appropriate marketing action needs to be based on a wide apprecia-tion and analysis of the needs of the business and the situation in the market. It cannot, or rather must not, be ad hoc, with a little marketing activity being fitted in as and when time allows.

This review of the process starts therefore with the planning stage. Every business needs a plan (as many consultants and accountants surely tell their clients and then get paid for doing them) and a key element of such a plan is the marketing plan. Chapter 2 thus looks at the planning process and comments additionally on the need for a marketing view to be taken of the services offered and the fees charged. Promotional activity, covering everything from what letterhead the firm has, to adver-tising and public relations, and how it is planned and co-ordinated, is the subject of Chapters 3 and 4. Next, direct mail, likely to be an especially important technique for many professional services, is reviewed in detail, because it exemplifies the approach needed if any description of services is to be persuasive.

All these promotional elements are designed to provide the direct personal contact which, perhaps being best regarded as the final link in a persuasive chain, must be sales-oriented. So Chapter 6 looks at personal selling and ends with the proposition that 'selling starts when the cus-tomer says yes'. This simply means that selling must continue in parallel with executing the work, as existing clients are your best prospects for the future. The whole question of managing, expanding and developing client relationships is then examined in the last chapter.

All of this information, however, must be examined, and indeed mar-keting techniques used, with certain truths about the nature of profes-sional services firmly in mind.

What do we sell?

Well, it is certainly nothing very tangible. By their very nature professional services cannot be tested in advance. Clients are asked, literally, to sign on the dotted line, start paying money and *then* find out if the provider of the service is any good or not. Understandably, clients do not like this.

Thus, clients tend to view professional services in a particular way. They are well aware they are intangible, and consequently tend to judge them from all those aspects of the professional firm that *are* tangible. From the client's viewpoint suppliers are numerous, similar, and by no means the only sources of the services they provide. In fact, a client does not first choose a firm by the quality of its work – because he is not in a position to assess that for himself. He chooses on the indications of quality that he can see, and he may not even know which indications have affected his choice.

This starts with many, seemingly small, things, which have a disproportionate impact on the client – or rather, at this stage, the prospect – and include things ranging from the design of a business card to the way your switchboard responds to an incoming call. These influence the perception, and expectation of quality, to a considerable degree.

EXAMPLE
One firm of accountants produced an excellent booklet on some aspect of taxation. They advertised it, in their newsletter and elsewhere, and, confident of its usefulness, even made a charge for it. They received more orders than they anticipated and had to reprint, which delayed despatch to some customers. The switchboard operators, no doubt to sort calls and ease their busy life, asked each caller referring to the booklet 'Are you placing an order, or chasing an order?', thus in one brief – and well-intentioned – phrase telling callers that it was *expected* that orders needed chasing.

This well illustrates how fragile a thing this kind of initial image is. (See Chapter 3 for more details.)

To understand the importance of this factor you must bear in mind that the building up of whatever view a prospect forms is cumulative – the impact of many little things adding up. This makes the individual elements well worth paying attention to.

> ACTION
> Consider telephoning your own office occasionally (or asking
> someone to do it for you), to get some objective feedback about just
> how your clients, and prospective clients, are received.

Thus marketing, and promotional activity in particular, represent an important means of affecting client choice – you can actively put forward those indicators you feel will signal the nature and quality of your services. If the client sees quality signalled in the promotional effort, he may surmise that these standards of quality are consistent with the standards of the firm's services.

To market intelligently, therefore, one must be able to see oneself from without, from the client's point of view. Part of taking up the client's perspective is being able to think in terms of benefits rather than services. A client is not looking for the services the firm provides, he is looking for the benefits those services will bring him, in the same way as a person does not buy an electric drill because he wants an electric drill, but because he wants to be able to make holes. The 'benefit' he derives from the drill is the hole that it makes for him, its ability to help him put up shelves or whatever. In professional services, whatever the specific technical nature of what is being provided clients are looking for assistance in:

- solving problems;
- exploiting or developing opportunities; and may want
- objective advice to augment (perhaps temporarily) internal resources.

And all this is to achieve *their* ends. A company seeking a creative graphic design input for instance is not simply wanting a smart new brochure, they are wanting more business or perhaps the successful introduction of a new product. The benefits are seen in the improvement of the profitability.

Thus, benefits are what the client wants your services to do for him. It is important, therefore, to be able to identify the particular benefits which will interest a given client. Different clients may buy the same services for different reasons; that is, they may wish different benefits from the same service. The firm must therefore see what is important for the client and demonstrate by their words and actions that they have done this. The client must realise that you can fulfil his needs. This skill is necessary because the client is most unlikely to see things, at the outset, from the professional's point of view.

Because the client is limited in his ability to distinguish services in advance by their actual quality, a firm is under greater pressure to present the benefits it offers to actual clients. This requires marketing and promotional skills.

Where does business come from?

The answer is from a variety of sources, but they can be categorised as is shown in Figure 1.1.

- **Repeat** business implies doing similar work, on new projects, for clients you have worked for last year (or in the past).
- **Extension** business is where more work, whether more profitable, more extensive, different and so on is done with existing, or recent, clients. This links to what many call 'cross-selling', that is selling on through the range.
- **Referral** business comes from intermediaries or recommenders.

And, if the circle shown in Figure 1.1 represents the total amount of business required by the firm, or perhaps a department, then the area marked by a question mark is the proportion that has to be found – from scratch – to make up the total.

In professional services repeat business is often a major proportion of the work and it is clearly important to know just how this balance of work is made up, and, as we will see, marketing must be directed at existing (and past) clients, at intermediaries and at the broader market from which it is hoped to produce the new contacts.

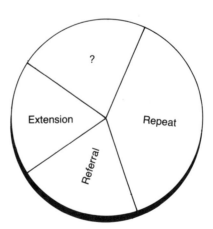

Figure 1.1   Where does business originate?

Competitiveness

This was mentioned in the preface, but is worth stressing again. Competition is broad. It includes direct competitors, in the way one surveying firm is competitive with another, similar firm. It also includes indirect competitors, as for example with an executive selection consultant who is in competition with headhunters, registers and even the classified columns in, say, *The Sunday Times*, where executives can advertise themselves, as well as other similar firms.

Competition is increasing too. This is partly due to (at the time of writing) any hardening of economic conditions; to firms increasing the effectiveness of their marketing efforts, making life harder for anyone lagging behind; and last, but by no means least, to the change that has taken place in recent years in client attitudes.

Once upon a time, many assignments were secured from clients who visited (for whatever reason) only you. They did not check you out alongside competing firms. What is more, once business was secured then, in many cases, the relationship was for life; or at least was long term. But, times change. Clients do not take these views these days. Far from seeing their professional advisers as unchallengeable, or omniscient even, in at least one profession the client speaks of the professional as:

'The man with his tongue in your ear,
his hand in your pocket,
and his faith in your gullibility.'

Times change that much.

Clients expect more and more. Higher quality (for the same cost?); time spent, for no charge, up front, to check out (the so-called 'beauty parade') competing firms at presentations and so on. They certainly expect a clearly demonstrated understanding of their situation, and are less and less prepared to pay for an expensive learning curve. And everything about the way you work needs to reflect these attitudes.

EXAMPLE
One firm of engineers is finding that more and more new client situations demand that presentations are made during the stage of discussion before work is booked. At senior level they are not bad at this, but standards drop off sharply further down the organisation. Conscious that poor presentations can lose business they protect their technical people from them, reckoning that 'it is uneconomic and difficult to train them in this

skill, and they don't want to do it'. But clients want to see the project team. Slick front men are seen as protecting not poor presenters, but poor quality engineers. The strike rate is lower than it should be, the marketing cost therefore higher, and – when business is booked – the senior people are sucked into doing far too much of the assignment, because they are the only people with whom the client has come to feel comfortable.

It is what the client demands that dictates how we run the business, and we ignore that at our peril.

(*Note*: In passing it is worth noting that there is no unwritten rule which says engineers (or anyone else with strong technical skills and background) cannot present well, though training can help.)

It is important never to underestimate the need to relate to clients' real attitudes today, and beware of thinking of them as they were. Yes, it was once easier, but waiting for those times to return is simply not one of the options in growing the business.

The constitution of the firm

It was mentioned earlier that many professional firms are partnerships. Partnerships have many undeniable advantages. One is perhaps that they are democratic in nature. This is, however, a two-edged sword. Democracy can be slow, and marketing action may need to be swift and decisive. Democracy can dilute effectiveness, a consensus can often lack edge – and we all know that the committee charged with designing the horse produced the camel.

EXAMPLE
As I write this I am still waiting for one partnership, for whom I have designed and written a new corporate brochure, to approve the text. This is three months after it was submitted! It is moving slowly round among the partners, and if something is changed (or queried) – and I am assured no significant changes are being made – it has to go round again to be sure 'everyone is happy with it'. When the project started it was described as 'urgent'.

At best it will be having an effect much later than it might, but at worst it will be diluted down to something 'acceptable to all'. The measure is not, in fact, whether all the partners like it, certainly an introspective view is of

little relevance; it is whether it will have a positive effect on clients and prospects.

This is a pity, because the original copy was good (in my, somewhat prejudiced, view), but this provides a by no means untypical example of the way partnerships work.

It is crucial that the necessary decision-making and communications processes exist within a partnership to allow, indeed encourage, the initiation of action as and when the market demands. The market has no inherent patience and will not wait, so if you are indecisive on marketing matters there is likely to be a competitor around who will take advantage of the fact.

All these factors influence the way marketing has to take place in the professional firm. We will return to specific instances where such influence is important, but you can usefully bear them in mind as you read on.

Finally, in this chapter, before moving on to review matters in a way which, necessarily, dissects the marketing process, there is some merit in us having a clear overview. Because successful marketing is dependent, to a major degree, on the interdependence of the elements and the continuity involved, we have to consider the whole and the parts together.

Figure 1.2 shows the process graphically. It is simplified to some extent, and the elements will be explained in more detail in subsequent chapters. The overall sequence is, however, clear. Planning should, in all logic, come first. Promotion is there to prompt enquiries; prospects who need personal persuasion to convert them to fee-paying clients. The sales process is the most variable element, involving many different sequences of meetings, proposals, presentations and follow-up depending on the individual circumstances, and 'doing the work' and 'client development' must run on in parallel.

None of this just happens, and the process of making it happen starts with the plan.

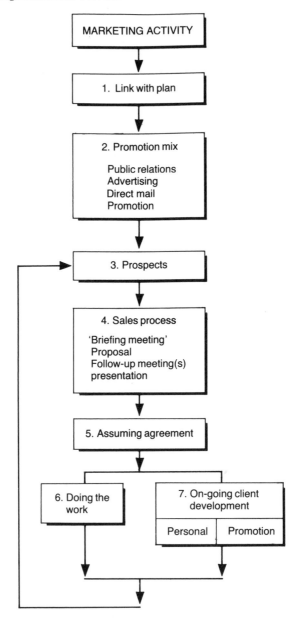

Figure 1.2   The marketing process

ACTION
One action which may help early on to persuade those senior
members of a firm whose commitment needs to be given before
action can flow easily, is to make information available in
manageable or palatable form. While it may be asking a good deal
to expect everyone to take in a large volume of information –
reading this book, for instance – circulating some information, in
the form of charts for example (which can also be used at a meeting
– as a visual aid), can begin to win others over.[1]

---

[1] One particularly palatable way of explaining something of what marketing is all about is
through my book *Everything you Need to Know About Marketing* (Kogan Page). This is a
humorous guide for the layman. (If a book about marketing cannot contain one,
unashamed, plug, what can?)

2 PLAN THE WORK, AND WORK THE PLAN
The marketing planning process

'Would you tell me, please, which way I ought to walk from here?'
'That depends a good deal on where you want to get to,' said the Cat.
'I don't much care where . . .' said Alice.
'Then it doesn't matter which way you walk,' said the Cat.
'So long as I get *somewhere*,' Alice added, as an explanation.
'Oh, you're sure to do that,' said the Cat, 'if you only walk long enough.'

Alice's Adventures in Wonderland, Lewis Carroll

You really do need a plan. But the planning process, which can seem daunting, need not be complex. As has been mentioned earlier, someone has to wear the 'marketing hat'. This really is a differentiating factor, and planning is one of that designated person's first responsibilities. Quite simply, firms who have someone firmly in charge of the process tend to do better than those who adopt an ad hoc approach.

ACTION
If no one in the firm currently wears the 'marketing hat', make an early decision to put this right. They do not need to do everything themselves, and whoever it is must be able to guarantee the support of others, but an initiator and co-ordinator is essential.

In any business where 'the people are the product' and the resource sold is, in a sense, time, there are conflicts. For most, the culture of the firm is one where doing client work (fee-earning work, that is) is good. Other, non-chargeable, tasks are to be avoided or minimised.

Figure 2.1 shows, in pie chart form, the split of tasks necessary in marketing activity. Of course, client work must predominate; but the other matters cannot be left to fit into any gaps. Marketing activity needs to take place at the right time. Continuity is vital. At worst, the firm can find itself in what is sometimes referred to as a 'feast and famine' situation. When all is going well and there is plenty of work in train, everyone is too busy for marketing; as projects finish an urgent need is recognised for marketing, time is spent on it and – if successful – new work and projects are secured. On this basis the sales graph can look like a switchback ride at a funfair. This is less than ideal. Time cannot be held in stock, and the revenue any time not utilised could have represented is gone, for ever. These peaks and troughs will jeopardise everything from cash flow to profitability.

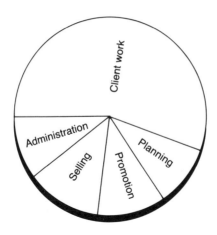

Figure 2.1   Deployment of time

So, it is important to have a systematic approach to planning, and this demands a degree of formality. The formality need not be inappropriately time-consuming, though it does mean that the right people must set aside sufficient time, at the right moments, to discuss, analyse and make the necessary decisions.

The plan itself may usefully be a document of some length, or, in the smaller firm, it may be a series of notes and key action points following a series of formats (such as those which appear throughout this chapter). In either case, it is important and it should be there, not least, to prompt action.

Thus, if the detail of the process we now outline seems too much, you may well decide to distil it down to the key elements appropriate to your business. However, even the sole practitioner should not avoid the exercise completely. And remember, if no plan exists, then putting together the first one is inevitably more time-consuming than the on-going process of updating a rolling plan.

Planning will affect many aspects of the firm and its operation. Again, it may be helpful to start with an overview. Figure 2.2 illustrates the continuous nature of the planning process (and relates closely, of course, to Figure 1.2 on page 6), and can usefully be borne in mind as you read on. The points made in the attendant commentary will be expanded on in the course of the chapter. Now, to the detail. (Figure 2.2 is repeated as a form and starts a series of formats, covering the whole process.)

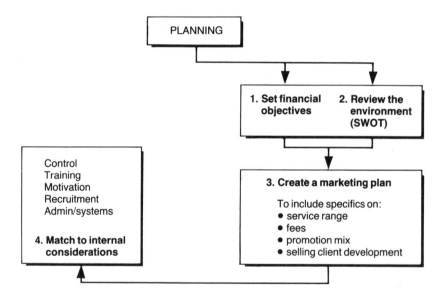

Figure 2.2   The continuous nature of the planning process

Planning activity – commentary on Figure 2.2
The following should be read referring to the numbered sequence on the chart.

1. To an extent we can take this as read in a publication on marketing. There will no doubt be financial objectives. Sometimes these tend to

be set in isolation sometimes to a formula (so many people, chargeable hours, additions leading to total fees sought) rather than with an eye on intentions, the market and so on. So stages 1 and 2 are shown as occurring in parallel in the chart.

2. The key here is to review, not just to extrapolate. The classic SWOT analysis (strengths and weaknesses, and opportunities and threats), the internal and external factors, works as well as anything. What is known and what must be found out, if not with formal market research, then at least with a truly objective eye on the facts.

3. The plan must be formal, in writing (though manageable), circulated to *all* those it affects, based on consultation, and research where necessary, not just on one person's view, and designed overall to be used and to prompt action.

SET DEADLINES?

4. These links are crucial and sometimes overlooked. For example, if a new area of work is developed, or a new industry approached, what are the staff implications for recruitment, training etc?

The marketing plan

Any firm approaching the construction of a marketing plan must recognise that the initial stages can only be the responsibility of the senior people in the firm. The importance of the strategic choices which must be made cannot be delegated. Equally, to ignore the strategic stage and simply have members of management develop tactical plans misunderstands the whole purpose of marketing planning. Without the frame of reference provided by marketing objectives and strategies, tactical plans will have no focus and little credibility.

Any business, whether professional or commercial, has to operate in a market for its services or products. Every market segments according to the priority of needs of the various groups of clients. These needs are dynamic, and must constantly be reassessed by the supplier. Thus, the firm can make optional use of its resources of time and money in its selection of the segments of the available market on which it intends to concentrate. In allocating these resources, the firm must define the appropriate framework for communicating, providing and charging for its selected range of services, and cope with the pressures of demand, competition, legal restriction and change, and the consequent availability of staff and of capital.

If a business, then, wishes to be more than a victim of history or circumstance, it must plan, organise and control its activities specifically, and, wherever possible, quantitatively. Precise marketing planning is the only meaningful way to define how a firm wishes to relate to and influence its business environment. Form 1 shows the stages through which the plan must pass.

The purpose of a formal plan

The marketing plan has three main aims. First, to be certain that all the objectives set by the firm are clearly related to specific actions (and by corollary that large amounts of expensive time are not taken up by activities which have little or no effect on the achievement of objectives).

Secondly, that the individual efforts of all staff are concentrated on the actions specified. In particular, all staff should be aware of the key priority actions which keep the firm in business today and tomorrow. At its simplest, this could be ensuring that every account is examined to identify additional business potential, or perhaps that invoices are submitted immediately they are due.

Thirdly, that all the activities specified in the plan can be measured, assessed and improved, as the planned year progresses.

Setting marketing objectives

Naturally, writing a plan presumes that senior managers know the markets in which they operate, have clear marketing objectives, and have the power to authorise or recommend action to agreed cost levels.

All firms have financial goals expressed in budgets of fee revenue and expenditure (see Form 2). However, since sales and profits can only be made by working with clients in the markets we select, the first task must be to translate the financial objectives into market objectives; they must answer the question 'what results must be achieved in the marketplace to produce the financial objective we wish to see?'.

Meaningful answers can only be produced by considering two inter-related analyses.

- What opportunities and threats will be present?
- What are the strengths and weaknesses of the firm?

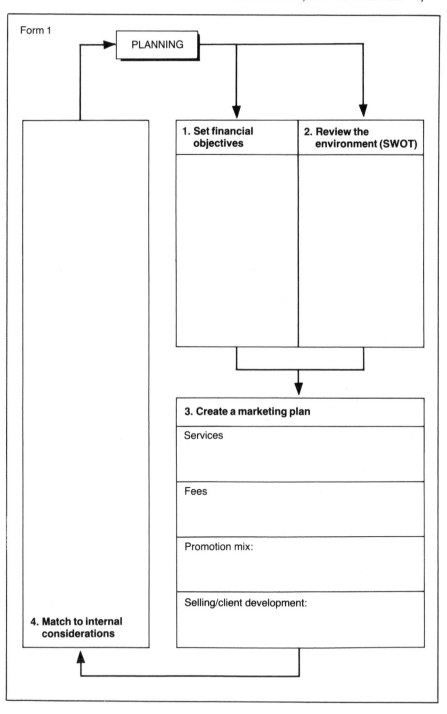

Form 1

PLANNING

1. **Set financial objectives**

2. **Review the environment (SWOT)**

3. **Create a marketing plan**

Services

Fees

Promotion mix:

Selling/client development:

4. **Match to internal considerations**

Form 2

Financial objectives

	Last year's actual	*Next year's plan*
Fees other		
Total		
Costs		
Profit		

Market opportunities and threats

The simplest and most unbiased way is to carry out a basic analysis of the
quantitative and qualitative structure of the markets in which we operate
and the current trends we can perceive. A format for such an analysis is
seen in the example below and is recorded on Form 3. (This kind of
format will help keep the process manageable.)

EXAMPLE   Market opportunities and threats

1) **How is the market structured quantitatively?**

1.1)   How many people/organisations of what type are there in our
market who have a need for our kind of services (e.g. corporate/
private/large/small/geographic location)?
1.2)   What services do they currently use?
1.3)   How much of the services do they use (e.g. annual spend)?
1.4)   How often do they use the services (e.g. annually/monthly)?
1.5)   Who do they use?
1.6)   What services do they not use?
1.7)   How do existing and potential users gain access to services like ours
(e.g. personal recommendation/directories)?

2) **How is the market structured qualitatively?**

2.1)   Why do existing and potential customers buy/not buy?
2.2)   What do they think of the services they buy (e.g. good value/
overpriced)?
2.3)   What do they think of the firms who supply the services (e.g. too
big/too small/helpful/unhelpful)?

3) **How is the market served competitively?**

3.1)   Who are our direct competitors (i.e. other similar firms)?
3.2)   Who are our indirect competitors (i.e. 'overlapping' firms)?
3.3)   What are their strengths and weaknesses (e.g. services/size/staff/
image/fees/marketing skills/geographic coverage)?

4) **What are the quantitative and qualitative trends?**

- market/segment size;
- market/segment requirements;
- market/segment structure;
- market/segment location;
- competition.

Firm's strengths and weaknesses

We can then assess the strengths and weaknesses of the firm against the requirements of our current and our potential markets, and compared

---

Form 3

Market

Opportunities   *Threats*

Action   *Action*

---

with the abilities and services of our competitors (see Form 4). We must consider objectively and dispassionately our standing in seven key areas:

- client base;
- range of services;
- fees structure;

Form 4	
Firm	
Strengths	*Weaknesses*
Action	*Action*

- promotional and selling activities;
- planning systems;
- organisational structure;
- controls and measurement procedures.

A format for such an analysis can be seen in the example below.

EXAMPLE   Firm's strengths and weaknesses

---

1)   Client base

1.1)   What is our current client base, by size, by location, by industry?
1.2)   How does our disposition of clients (client mix) compare with the market mix?
1.3)   Are our clients in growth sectors of the market?
1.4)   How dependent are we on our largest clients?

---

2)   Range of services

2.1)   How closely does our range of services reflect the market's needs?
2.2)   How does our range compare with competitors?
2.3)   Are the majority of our services in growth or decline?
2.4)   Is our range of services too narrow to satisfy our markets?
2.5)   Is our range too broad to allow satisfactory management of performance?

---

3)   Fee structure

3.1)   What is the basis of our fee structure?
3.2)   Do our direct and indirect competitors structure in the same way?
3.3)   Are our fees competitive?
3.4)   Do our clients perceive fees as 'value for money'?

---

4)   Promotional and selling activities

4.1)   With which clients/recommenders/influencers are we communicating?
4.2)   What do they know and feel about the firm?
4.3)   Are we communicating with enough of the 'right' people?
4.4)   What means of communication are we using?
4.5)   What attitudes exist in the firm towards 'selling' services?
4.6)   Is each person in contact with clients capable of selling the full range of services?
4.7)   Do they possess the necessary knowledge and skill in selling?

5)   Planning marketing activity

5.1)   Do we have agreed plans for the marketing and selling activity?

5.2)   Do the plans state activities as well as objectives and budgets?

5.3)   Do we have individual as well as corporate plans?

6)   Organising for marketing

6.1)   How is the firm's marketing activity organised and co-ordinated?

6.2)   Are authority and responsibility for each person clearly defined?

6.3)   Are our people committed to marketing the firm and its services?

7)   Control and measurement of marketing

7.1)   Have we defined 'success' for ourselves and our staff?

7.2)   Have we established key result areas to measure that success?

7.3)   Do these standards examine marketing as well as professional standards?

7.4)   Do we measure performance against desired standards and take corrective action?

Clearly, this is only a skeleton and many supplementary questions may be necessary to get specific and objective answers. What is essential is that honest examination establishes definitely the firm's standing in its markets.

EXAMPLE

One particular kind of research being used more and more in professional services, to provide a clear picture of image and positioning in the market, is that of 'Perception Surveys'. These can have very practical results, leading to information and hence changes which are a real spur to business development.

Take the example of an established firm of chartered surveyors. Traditionally a firm concentrating on estate management and development, it had grown its residential and commercial property business in the 1980s and had set up a specialist division to handle leisure and tourism developments.

The firm had not adopted any formal roles and marketing plan, but had depended on the property portfolio advertising in the key journals such as *Country Life*, and PR aimed at the property journalists and leisure writers.

As the boom in the property sector dwindled away the company came under increasing competitive pressure. For the first time it appointed a marketing director as it realised it required a central co-ordinating function to develop the appropriate marketing methods for each of the divisions. This new specialist adopted a planning procedure and took the opportunity of using specialist marketing consultants to set up a strategic marketing plan. In addition he immediately initiated a review of the corporate image of the company, as development in this area had fallen behind that of competition.

The consultancy obtained immediate agreement that any planning should be based on the attitudes of clients (and non-clients) and an assessment of the services of the chartered surveyors in relation to its main competitors. Therefore, a perception survey was set up among a series of target groups for each of the various divisions, including recent clients, lapsed clients, non-clients, intermediaries, financial journalists and even competitors. However, before these audiences were interviewed, the consultancy also interviewed a cross-section of management to ascertain what they felt about their positioning in the market and how marketing would assist them.

The management felt that the company had a strong image in the market, that they would be viewed as a 'traditional' company and that clients would rate them well as most would have had a long relationship with the firm. The management also found it difficult to take on board how the marketing plan would assist them as they said 'they were busy enough'.

Following this analysis in-depth semi-structured qualitative interviews with 22 clients were carried out. In addition, structured qualitative research was also carried out by sending 30 self-completion questionnaires to 30 property media journalists. Following these initial evaluations quantitative research was also undertaken among the main client base, consisting of 1,000 self-completion questionnaires – 255 of these were returned.

In the qualitative phase of the project the clients regarded the professional expertise of the firm as high. The quality of the work was good and there was little criticism of standards. The firm's level of services was considered to be on a par with that of other major competitors. The firm was considered to have a high profile in leisure (the newest division), landed estates and up-market residential, with a low profile in the commercial sector. The firm was seen as trustworthy, reliable, honest and staffed 'by decent types'. It was also seen to be poor in communicating with its client base, with one-third of the informants saying that they were not even aware that the firm had other divisions, apart from the one which they used. The majority of the clients wanted a more proactive approach to their business by the firm.

In contrast the survey among the journalists showed that the firm had the lowest profile in the Press, indicating that they had not appreciated the extent of the firm and its operations.

In the quantitative phase of the project the clients were asked to rate the services of the firm, using 'attitude statements' which were drawn up to help the informant in the survey discriminate between the firm and its competitor.

The firm's strength was seen to be 'helpful staff', 'professionalism', 'personal service', 'confidentiality' and 'quality of work'.

As a result of this perception survey the firm realised that it was required to improve:

- its image in the marketplace, as being a more proactive firm;
- its sales ability by providing clients with a more 'creative' approach to their requirements, full of ideas and developments;
- the ability of the professional staff. A training programme was initiated to increase their awareness towards marketing, and to improve their own sales skills;
- its overall marketing approach. Its emphasis on PR had not been proved effective and it was clear that the firm urgently needed to become more aggressive with its sales and marketing, improve its communications and become more 'competitive'.

Perceptions surveys are therefore beneficial as they help a firm to see itself as the clients see it and to thus focus and target its sales and marketing more effectively.

Using this comparative analysis between the market and the firm, the partners or managers are in a much stronger position to translate financial goals into true marketing objectives, which are achievable in the marketplace, but within the firm's scope.

Without such objectives, it is impossible to focus and to place any tactical activities in order of priority. Yet the main options available to us in marketing objectives are limited – perhaps sixfold.

- **To increase market share**   In a static market this can be done by 'conquest selling', or winning business from other firms.
- **To expand existing markets**   This objective will focus on selling the fullest range of services to existing clients and market. It also presumes

very close co-operation between audit and activities, and other services.

- **To develop new services for existing markets**   This can involve simply the revision of existing services or the introduction of radical new services, as some of the larger firms have done with computer systems.
- **To develop new markets for existing services**   This is attractive, and lower risk than some options, but is finite, especially so in some service areas (e.g. the accountants' market for statutory audit, since there are only so many to be done).
- **To develop new services in new markets**   This is an example of true diversification. This usually carries the highest risk of all marketing objectives. Many firms do not even consider such objectives. Future pressures, however, for the growth necessary to keep good staff, may force a reassessment.
- **To improve the profitability of existing operations**   When growth opportunities are limited, many firms must in the short term seek higher returns from higher productivity and greater cost-effectiveness of their operations.

From the analysis of market opportunities and threats, and the internal assessment of strengths and weaknesses, the firm will select the marketing objective(s) which will best achieve its financial goals for the planning period (see Form 5).

Developing marketing strategies

The next stage in planning is probably both the most important and the most neglected by the majority of firms – the identification of all the potential strategies which could be followed to achieve a particular marketing objective. The two are often confused:

- the objective is **a desired result** in the marketplace;
- the strategy is **a course of action** to achieve that result.

The purpose of the strategy is to focus effort, co-ordinate action and exploit identified strengths of the firm. By corollary, the purpose is to avoid waste of resources on peripheral and non-productive activities (see Form 5).

Clearly, different objectives will require very different strategies. For example, some of the main courses of action open to an accountancy firm may be as follows.

Form 5

Marketing objectives

Marketing strategies

Marketing objectives	*Some possible strategy alternatives*
To increase share of the existing market	Marketing segmentation and concentration of resources on selected segments Developing service applications and range extension Range of registered firm names for different segments
To expand existing markets	Increasing the frequency of client purchase Increasing service usage (in other applications) Opening new branches
To develop new markets for existing services	Expanding the range of segments currently dealt with Overseas expansion
To develop new services in new markets	Diversification by purchase/takeover Technological extension, e.g. financial systems into software services Exploitation of corporate resources and skills
To increase profitability of existing business	Improving the total service package offered to each client account Marketing audit and productivity analysis Systems selling: 'turnkey offerings' Reduction of service range

The selection of strategies need not be mutually exclusive. Often a combination can provide even stronger effect in marketing plans. However, the greatest danger for a firm, at the point of selecting appropriate strategies, is that it may be tempted to adopt too many courses of action. Such a mistake spreads management too thinly and prevents commitment of maximum effort to the prime and most important courses of action.

Marketing planning, then, must begin with a thorough and creative attempt to choose the most appropriate focus for the entire firm's marketing effort. The determination to concentrate simplifies the tactical marketing plans which must then follow for the range of services to be offered, the fees to be charged, and the promotional and selling actions to communicate with the chosen markets.

Tactical marketing planning

Establishing the range of services to be offered

The actions taken thus far have established what we wish to achieve in the market, and the main lines of action most likely to achieve those objectives. Much marketing planning breaks down because these strategic aims are not pursued with resolution into the detailed tactical planning. Throughout the marketing planning process, constant reference back must be made, to ensure that all decisions reflect our strategic aim and that we are not dissipating our efforts by continuing habitual activities.

The range of services offered by the firm is the basic unit of exchange between the firm and its clients. However, clients are becoming more perceptive and demanding, facing the current severe commercial pressures. Only if our service range continues to offer perceived satisfaction to clients' needs and problems will they continue to purchase from us.

The 'captive' market of the past begins to look less secure as fee levels are questioned, business is competitively 'tendered', new types of service are marketed and some clients, alas, may cease trading altogether.

An additional problem faced by most firms arises from the simple fact that in the majority of firms the 'production' and 'sales' resources are one and the same. Thus, at times when there is a heavy workload, all staff and management spend all their time doing the work, and when the workload slackens, all hands are needed for selling. This 'feast and famine' cycle, well known to many firms, and referred to earlier, leaves no time for new service development or modification. And, sadly, experience shows that new services do not simply evolve from the market demand. They require a conscious exercise of will.

For survival and growth depend in part on a regular review and development of the range, and of individual services within the range. The fundamental objective of the review is to ensure that the services offered satisfy client needs in the growth sectors of the market.

In taking decisions on range, some firms have found it useful to examine their current position using a format like that shown in Form 6, a modified version of the more complex Boston Consulting Group Matrix, which essentially serves the same purpose.

Next, taking into account the firm's marketing strategies, decisions can be made on new service development or range reduction. With new service development, either existing staff must be developed in the necessary skills or new staff possessing the necessary skills must be recruited.

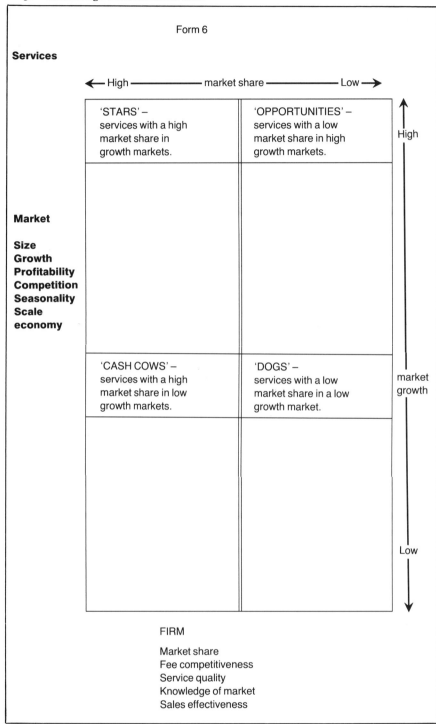

Form 6

Services

←— High ——————— market share ——————— Low —→

'STARS' –
services with a high
market share in
growth markets.

'OPPORTUNITIES' –
services with a low
market share in high
growth markets.

High

Market

Size
Growth
Profitability
Competition
Seasonality
Scale
economy

'CASH COWS' –
services with a high
market share in low
growth markets.

'DOGS' –
services with a low
market share in a low
growth market.

market
growth

Low

FIRM

Market share
Fee competitiveness
Service quality
Knowledge of market
Sales effectiveness

Individual service development

Having decided on the range, firms must consider the individual services within the range, because client needs and competitive offerings change over time.

As a result, individual services tend to exhibit life-cycles, passing through the four stages of introduction, growth, maturity and decline.

- The introductory phase is normally one of heavy investment in researching, creating, developing and testing the service on the one hand; and creating client awareness and acceptance on the other.
- The growth stage involves promotion and 'distribution', during which a level of high quality must be maintained and a reputation established.
- The maturity stage is potentially the most rewarding as revenues and profits reach their peak. Growth slows down as market demand is saturated and competitors enter the arena. It can also be the most dangerous phase as complacency sets in and conscious observation of market trends subsides.
- If nothing is done, the service goes into decline as demand decreases and competitors introduce more effective offerings. In extreme cases, the firm can come under severe pressure as it attempts to revamp the service or develop replacements.

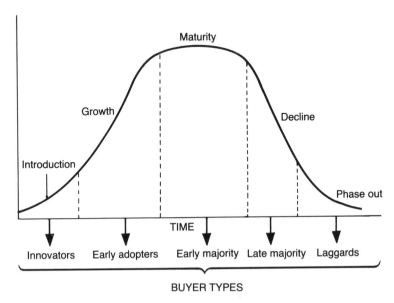

Figure 2.3   Product life-cycle

While the life-cycle concept (shown in Figure 2.3) clearly applies to professional services, it is probably too general to be of practical day-to-day value. What is important is that firms recognise its implications:

- long-established, mature services may remain the same in principle as they were years ago, but they will have to change in detail to meet changing client needs;
- new services may have to be developed, both to meet new clients' needs and to keep out competitors who see them as a means of ultimately acquiring more major business;
- there may well be opportunities to offer a range of differently priced variants for different clients and different problems;
- as a harsh economic climate forces corporate clients to seek productivity improvements in all functions of the business, so they become more demanding, but the same pressures may also produce new opportunities.

If a systematic approach is to be taken to service development, the firm must set aside time to permit thorough assessment annually as part of the planning process (see Form 6A).

ACTION

Consider running *separate* service review and development meetings, rather than adding this as an item on the agenda of managers' meetings reviewing many things. This can focus attention and prompt action with more certainty (this technique can work for other topics in the marketing area: the marketing plan, fees, major client review).

Establishing the firm's fee policy

Many firms know very little of the market view of fees. For example, ask yourself these questions.

- How aware are clients of the levels of fees – the actual levels and the hourly rates?
- How do clients perceive fees? Does, for example, a higher fee imply in their minds higher quality, or do they view fees as a commodity price with no differentiation between firms?
- Are there 'fee barriers' in a client's mind which we must avoid in any quotation for business?

Form 6A

Services plan

Unchanged services

Modifications to existing services	
Service	Action and timing

New services	
Service	Action and timing

Deletions from the range	
Service	Action and timing

- How far can we price differentially because of the perceived and accepted reputation of the firm?
- What differentials should be used on 'assignment pricing' between different levels of staff?
- Is 'investment pricing' of use for major new clients where extra time is invested in the first assignment, to ensure thorough examination of the company and first-class quality, so that further repeat work is more easily identified and sold?
- How far can our fees be made more economic to the client by range selling? Can additional services be dovetailed with existing work, both to increase revenue and eliminate future selling time?

ACTION

Consider whether the basis for setting fee levels on every job in prospect is clear. It must be a blend of maximising profitability and the likelihood of getting the work; of giving value for money and relating sensibly to competition. Certainly accountants will need no prompting to appreciate the benefits of marginal increases of fee levels on margins. Just reviewing the whole process more regularly may be enough to effect changes.

Fees are a critical area of the firm's marketing mix and one that tends to receive too little analytical attention. Far too often the decision is simply to keep in line with the competition, or to work essentially on a cost plus basis. In fact, fees should reflect the firm's overall policy at the strategic level and show creative flexibility at the tactical level, up or down depending on the threat or opportunity.

EXAMPLE

A large consultancy firm operated by having an essentially hierarchial fee structure, that is the most senior people cost most and vice versa.

They had recruited a number of people who, in addition to their other skills, had very good computer skills. These people were encouraged to sell those skills to clients. They did so with some success. The firm then found it had developed a whole new area of business in the computer field. The skills of the new people were in constant demand (so much so that they had no time to fulfil their original brief), and clients reported very favourably on the quality and creativity of the work.

But, all this work was being charged out automatically at the lowest rate because of the system of pricing. This reflected not the nature of the work,

but the newness of the professional staff and their position in the firm. Yet the work was in an area where competitors charged much more. Changes were made, which improved profitability, but not before precedents were set and many existing clients were difficult to persuade of the change.

In spite of the current pressures on fees, many firms can ease the situation by concentrating more on providing clients with the satisfactions they want, communicating the fact that it is being done, and proving that the financial value of the service is greater than its cost.

Determining fees and pricing structures

Any company or firm setting its fee levels or pricing structure must take account of its costs, the likely demand, the competitive response and the attitude of its market.

In professional service firms, fee levels may be less sensitive to these factors than would be the case with, for example, a food distributor.

ACTION
Special treatment for the small, that is the small job and the small client. Which person reading this can honestly put their hand on their heart and say that they do not have any client who they would in fact be better off without? Honestly? The time spent without them could perhaps be better spent finding more profitable replacements. It is a sad fact that many acorns never grow into giant oaks. Realistically there are some jobs and clients you should refer elsewhere (perhaps to where they can dilute your competitors' profitability!).

The concerns for professional service firms

The primary task of the firm in setting fee levels is not so much to be accurate within a few pounds, but more to ensure that the client gets value for money. Thus, the emphasis is on setting the fee in advance, justifying it during the conduct of the assignment, and confirming its value through the quality of recommendations, and reports leading to action.

In searching for profit improvement through better pricing, the firm should also consider where it can offer enhanced value without significantly increasing its own costs.

For example, would a few more days' investigation of a client problem produce recommendations worth considerably more to the client, thereby justifying a fee which reflects not the cost of the time but the worth to the client business?

At a strategic level, the firm needs to set its fee levels in line with its overall marketing policy. For example, if its intention is to increase the number of large assignments and reduce its reliance on small ones, it may want to set a minimum fee level for small jobs which both accelerates the process and ensures that those small jobs which are undertaken produce an acceptable return.

At a tactical level the firm will also want to consider some of the pure 'marketing' approaches to fees (see Form 7).

Planning public relations, advertising and promotion

Having decided on the markets to be served, the services to be offered and the fees to be charged, the firm must consider how it will communicate them to actual and potential clients (see Form 8).

The major non-personal means of communication are public relations (PR), advertising and sales promotion. Linked to these are other aspects of the firm's operation that enhance or detract from its total offering. Some are expensive, like the firm's premises, some inexpensive but vital such as the telephonist.

Since a service is being offered, communication and distribution become almost synonymous. For example, a communications target (e.g. local chamber of commerce) can also be a 'channel of distribution' to a large number of potential clients – an intermediary. A brief comment is now made about the techniques in context of planning them; Chapters 3 and 4 investigate them further.

Public relations

The aim of PR is to create and maintain a favourable climate of opinion in which the firm can operate. Every firm will have an image whether it likes it or not. It is therefore important that the actual image reflects what the firm intends in its marketing strategy.

The first task is to define those sectors where the firm wants to have a favourable reputation. Typical groups might be financial institutions (banks, insurance companies etc.); other professional firms (solicitors);

Form 7	
Fees plan	
Overall fee strategy	Action and timing
Specific tactics	

Form 8

PR/Advertising/Sales promotion plan

Target groups	Awareness and attitude	Action and timing

trade bodies (trade associations, chambers of trade); government bodies (local, national); social groups (Rotary); the media (press, local radio); potential clients, or whatever a specific service makes relevant.

Having identified these target groups, the next step is to find out what image they currently have of the firm.

- Do they know the firm and its services?
- What is their perception of the firm and its services?

Some of this information can be obtained by 'keeping one's ear to the ground'. If this is insufficient, formal market research may have to be undertaken. There is no need for great expense, since a small sample in a telephoned survey may well be adequate.

Then, once the present awareness and image have been identified, the firm can set its PR targets. For example, does it need to reinforce or change its present image?

At this stage the firm can decide which PR activities will be most cost-effective in achieving the desired image goals. Typical methods will include:

- press publicity and developing good relationships with writers and editors;
- membership of influential bodies, both professional and social;
- use of a 'house style', which is consistent in all written material;
- public speaking engagements.

Remember that there are specific ethical guidelines covering some of these areas, for instance a precise methodology regarding articles.

Advertising and sales promotion

Advertising as a part of PR can be defined as communication through bought time or space. As such, it can provide information to existing and potential clients, attempt to persuade, create dissatisfaction with competitive offerings or reinforce existing purchasing habits.

However, the nature of professional services and the manner in which they are bought means that the use of advertising will always have to be severely limited. For example, it is exceptionally difficult to assess the best time for advertising to coincide with potential client needs. Additionally, some ethical restrictions make substantial expenditure on advertising an innocuous activity of questionable value.

More specific plans, however, can be made for sales promotional activities. Sales promotion is primarily a tactical activity designed to advance services towards clients. Typical objectives may be:

- to introduce a new service and encourage its trial;
- to display existing services to potential clients;
- to increase clients' usage of the range of services.

Opportunities for sales promotion are limited, compared with fast-moving consumer goods, for example, and would probably remain so even if the guidelines were modified. Nevertheless, there are numerous related activities which can promote or 'push' the services towards potential clients.

One clear and positive promotional tactic lies with the use of seminars. They provide a vehicle to introduce new services and to establish the professionalism and credibility of the firm. They can ensure awareness of the full range of services available, and develop existing clients' personnel to make certain that they receive full value from systems that firms may install.

Of lesser complexity, but still of importance in the area of promotion, is the planning and structuring of the company's literature. In many firms, a great deal can be done to increase the clarity and promotional impact of brochures describing the firm's range of services.

The manner and quality of the presentation of reports and proposals, even of correspondence, has promotional impact, and great care must be taken to establish a conformity of house style with the requirements of the chosen marketing strategy.

Some of the apparently minor details are of great significance in the promotion of the firm's image and services. For example, since many firms have to be largely reactive to clients, their reaction and response must be swift and positive.

Some professional service companies set specific response times within which all enquiries must be actioned. The quality of both personal and telephone reception has both an immediate and a lasting effect on the clients' total perception of the firm.

Thus, the nature of how professional services are bought, and existing professional ethics, limits the use of the non-personal tools of communication. None the less, in today's competitive conditions, even small promotional actions can be very effective. Certainly PR has a definite role to play in creating a favourable environment in which the firm can operate.

Specific PR activities can put the firm's name to the forefront of the minds of influencers and recommenders. This systematises an area where many firms already spend time, for example in regular liaison with intermediaries and which can expose the firm to actual and potential clients.

PR with existing clients should not be neglected either; for example, do they know that recommendations are welcome?

Advertising has a limited role to play, but specific limited sales promotion can have a marked effect on specific activities. Both PR and promotion should therefore be included in the marketing plan (see Form 8).

Planning and sales activity

The prime focus of all promotional activity is face-to-face selling, which is the most relevant and effective form of communication for any firm offering professional services. For, by definition, professional services are people-intensive: the people are the product.

The greatest opportunities both for extending existing client work and for generating new clients arise in personal interviews with client decision-makers. Some firms still have a distaste for looking at this process as 'selling'. However, if a client has a particular need or problem and the firm is able to provide a relevant service which will offer a cost-effective solution, it is the firm's duty to communicate the service as persuasively as possible. For the firm which recognises and accepts this fact, two further stages are necessary:

- the firm as a whole should have a specific sales plan; and
- individual managers or partners must be skilful in persuasive communication.

The latter is dealt with in Chapter 6. The sales plan is, however, part of the firm's marketing planning process and we should consider it here (see Form 9).

The firm will have a quantified and timed statement of its total required level of fees for the planning period, usually the fiscal year. It must also assess what proportion of total fees can be expected to come in automatically and therefore the balance which will require positive selling.

This balance must then be examined against marketing strategies and broken down by service type, by marketing or industry sector, and by existing or new clients to give purpose and focus to selling.

The greatest opportunity for increased fees normally lies in selling

Form 9

Sales plan

New business to be obtained

Individual targets	
Name	Target

Actions and timing		
Name	Action	Timing

more of the range of the firm's services to existing clients. With current clients, the true needs are more obvious, the firm's credibility is higher, so the amount of time needed to sell the ideas will thus be smaller, as will the selling cost.

A C T I O N

Consider, as some firms now do, setting sales targets for individuals. As all work has to originate with successful sales meetings, it is actually a small step to specifying where this will be. It does not mean sharing equally, of course, but is a question of matching amounts to be sold to expertise and time to be made available.

The targets, of course, represent only the forecast, or the objective to be achieved. To complete the sales plan, the activities to achieve targets must be specified also. Thus we must find out the following.

- How many proposals need to be accepted (whether formal or informal)? In other words:

$$\frac{\text{Total new business fees required}}{\text{Average new business order size}}$$

- How many proposals need to be submitted? In other words:

$$\text{No. of proposals accepted} \times \text{Average conversion rate}$$

- How many enquiries must be received?
- How many new clients must be secured?
  In which markets?
  With which services?

The intention of such precise specification is twofold. The first is that tactical activity should be positive and not simply responsive. Thus, we ensure that tactics reflect the strategic aims of the firm. The second is that by timing the activities, the 'feast and famine' cycle of work is avoided, a feature which is so characteristic of many service companies.

A C T I O N

Consider whether you currently have all the necessary data to make such an approach work; if not start it soon and in as little as six months you can be basing action plans on some hard facts which will make everything that follows more focused.

Organising and controlling marketing activities within the firm

If results are to be achieved from all the firm's marketing work, then consideration must be given to organisation of, and responsibility for, the various activities. The nature of partnerships as opposed to limited liability companies raises very special difficulties here, and nowhere more than in the responsibility for, and control of, marketing activities. All the partners must be agreed on the critical importance of these actions. They must also agree on precise responsibility for the particular actions which are necessary (see Form 10).

There are clearly two distinct types of work in what has been discussed in this chapter. First, there is the planning work such as data collection on markets, analysis and decision on objectives and strategies, and construction and communication of plans and systems. Thus, in some firms, the responsibility for undertaking this is given to a 'practice development' person.

Secondly, there follows the implementation work – the contact by promotion and selling of existing and new clients which must be carried out by the whole firm. Because of the range of services, some firms have set up 'project teams' for the largest clients to supply the full range of skills and experience required to satisfy client needs.

Any organisational weaknesses become apparent when examining the links between planning and implementation. In most firms, the success of marketing planning is dependent upon the goodwill and the frequency of communications between senior members of the firm, particularly if the firm, and its services, are divisionalised.

Two factors seem to aid success here. First, that responsibility should be concentrated rather than spread. Thus, if a new service, or new market, is to be developed, it is more effective in the early stages to commit a single person or small group totally to that action. Secondly, that the activities are precisely defined, quantified and timed at the planning stage. However, the definition must specify the links between the results desired and the activities necessary. Without such quantification, self-delusion is all too easy and the effort expended will rapidly be deflected elsewhere.

The control process

The second factor, the importance of precisely defining, quantifying and timing the activities at the planning stage, underlines the essential nature

Form 10

Organisation

Activities   Responsibility of:

of the controls which need to be exercised. Any marketing control will measure actual performance against pre-set standards to decide when and where corrective action may be necessary.

The firm must decide first what kinds of standard are necessary. Of course we commence with results. Decisions must be made on what the firm sees as constituting success.

- What level of what profit at what time intervals?
- What level of contribution per man, group or department?
- What level of man-hours worked by whom, by when?
- What level of chargeable hours?
- What number of assignments/contracts booked?

These questions and others provide the results standards, and these are measured by most firms.

Controlling causes

In marketing control, however, we must also set standards for the marketing activities; standards which will measure the causes of the results noted previously. For example, do we set standards for the following?

- The numbers of enquiries/contacts to be generated?
- The type and profile of contact needed?
- The numbers of proposals for which type of service to be submitted?
- The conversion rate to booked work to be achieved?
- The sequence of actions with major clients, particularly for extension of work and increase of business?

These standards are the crux of effective marketing in the firm. We must have the tools to assess and measure causes, to identify quickly which activities require change or greater support, so that results may be effected fast (see Form 11).

Collection of information

Sometimes this type of control will require different information from that commonly examined in a professional firm. Do we, for example, need information on the following?

- Each enquiry/contact and its source?
- Each proposal/its nature and value?

Form 11

Controls

Activities	Standard	Information tools	Responsibility of

Action and timing

- Each proposal refused and the reasons for refusal?
- Levels and timing of work booked?

We need a simple recording system to yield us this key information, especially in the 'selling' activity. It is only by collecting this information that we will refine and improve our marketing activity in the current competitive conditions.

Our quantitative analysis will define such areas as the average assignment size, average proposal size and the new/existing client ratios. This is critical in setting realistic targets.

Causal analysis will define what cause/effect relationship exists between promotional effort, contacts gained and contracts booked. This helps us decide on the most cost-effective use of promotional time and money. Our lead-time analysis – analysing the lead times between contact and proposal, and proposal and booking – is critical in deciding *when* sales effort must be stepped up, or when recruitment will be needed. It also has tactical use in signalling possible cash-flow problems several months ahead.

Analysis of reasons for booking or refusal of work – particularly strength in, or lack of expertise in, or lack of knowledge of, a prospective industry, high fee levels – all signal to the marketing controller possible changes necessary in the service range, the fee policy or the training of personnel. It also provides interesting sidelights on the current activity of the competition.

Taking corrective action

Once we have identified these types of relationships, it becomes much easier to set diagnostic standards working backwards from the required fee revenue target.

Here is an example.

Work required next year	£350,000	
Average assignment size	7,000	50 clients
Historic existing:new client ratio	46:4	4 new clients
Booked:proposed ratio	1:2	8 new proposals or £56,000 proposed to 8 prospective clients
Enquiry: proposed ratio	3:2	12 new contacts (NB: Not one per month. Most must be made early in the year)

Our lead-time analysis may tell us that these must be generated in the first six months, at which stage we are seeking five new contacts per month for January to June.

Given such a concept, with the analysis to support it, control will then monitor monthly against the standards set. Corrective action will be of two kinds.

- What actions will sell more?
  — More contacts?
  — More proposals?
  — Larger proposals?
  — Better conversion/selling?
- Where do we find more staff? And how do we ensure existing staff have appropriate skills? (See Form 12.)

Control approached in this way keeps attention focused on causes rather than effects. It is only by changing causes that one can hope to change results. In reality, of course, averages and ratios vary, and sometimes causes are difficult to identify. Often, random events seem to play a major part. However, one must avoid making perfection the enemy of the good, and at least control what does yield to analysis.

Planning is essentially only the thinking that proceeds action. But it needs formalising. The plan should be in writing. The entire planning process discussed here can be documented very simply, the 12 forms shown can be used or adapted, and will become the basic process to control marketing action.

But it must be your plan. A system, however good, cannot do the work for you. The process must be tailored. This is for three main reasons. First, what you and your firm want to do is essentially different from other firms. Secondly, planning must take account of ever-changing circumstances in the market, among clients and others who may use your firm's services. And, thirdly, both these factors demand a creative approach that finds and presents attractively the things that make your firm able to meet needs a little differently, and a little better, than your competitors; not in every respect, of course, but certainly in some. (If you do not do this, then you are, in the longer term, likely to be in trouble.)

What has been presented in this chapter is an approach to planning; guidelines that are intended to assist both the thinking and the action involved in making all the necessary actions and activity more certain, and, in turn, more effective.

Form 12
Training required

What	Who	Action and timing

The example which concludes this chapter, reflects elements of the whole planning process.

EXAMPLE
The following example points up the logic and practicality of the planning process, even for the smaller firm. The marketing plan uses information about the present to shape the future. Let us now examine each of these stages in sequence.

The company mission
The most successful entrepreneurs have a clear concept of the firm they are trying to build. For this vision to become a reality and the planning to start, you need to spell out both what you are trying to do and the constraints within which you wish to work. So, while the term 'mission statement' may seem like just more imported American jargon, it does have practical implications.

Mission statement
This is how a professional woman expressed her business idea in a recent seminar:

'I worked for several years in the City of London as an accountant specialising in taxation. I have interrupted my career to start a family and have now moved to Hertfordshire, where I would like to set up my own practice.

'I would like to become a respected member of my profession and of my community. At present, I cannot work for more than five half-days per week but I hope, within five years, to have built up a client base of firms who are well respected in the community. From this base, I can start my own practice employing others at some future date.

'I do not wish to join another practice. I want to keep this business under my control and, if possible, have something to hand on to my children.'

A frank statement of this kind is invaluable for planning the market position of her business since it defines:

- the personal satisfactions she is seeking from the business;
- the geographical market in which she will operate (Hertfordshire);
- the type of client she is seeking and, by implication, the type she is not desirous of being associated with;
- the type of service she can offer (and is unable to offer);
- how fast she wishes the business to grow;
- by implication, what profits she will need to make to remain viable and independent.

During the next stage, she will explore whether this concept of the business will be realiseable in the area she has designated. In this analysis, she may identify better opportunities. On the other hand, she may find that she needs to think through what she has to offer and, in the worst case, drop her plan altogether.

The analysis of the market for accountancy services in Hertfordshire.

● **Demography**   As living in London becomes even more costly, young professional couples are settling in Hertfordshire and the other population is moving out.

Opportunities   The newcomers may be seeking tax advice. As they are new to the area, they will not already be committed to an accountancy firm for this advice.

Problems/threats   Some of the newcomers may themselves be accountants and so compete directly.

● **Government decision**   Stansted Airport is to be developed on the Hertfordshire/Essex border.

Opportunities   New firms will be attracted to the area who may require accountancy services.

Problems/threats   Larger accountancy firms may well set up branches near Stansted.

● **Economic environment**   The economy is showing distinct signs of improvement.

Opportunities   The first firms to benefit are likely to be small building contractors.

Problems/threats   Once she gets involved in this business, the down-market image may not be good for her firm. How can she turn them down without discouraging those she does want?

● **Social values**   There is a greater tendency towards self-employment by those who live in the area.

Opportunities   There will be a sizeable proportion of people requiring basic tax advice. Some may represent good, long-term prospects.

Problems/threats   How can she find them? How can they be provided with low-cost, standardised advice?

● **Legislation**   Accountants are now permitted most forms of advertising.

Opportunities   For the first time in the history of the profession a newcomer can actively seek to attract clients and grow quickly.

Problems/threats   The big partnership will already be using this facility and will have more funds that she has access to.

● **Distribution** Banks and building societies, the traditional sources by which clients are referred to an accountant, are more active in helping the smaller business.

Opportunities Bank managers may be grateful for a wider choice of firms to which they can refer clients, especially if these firms have relevant, specialised expertise.

Problems/threats Banks are offering their own tax and financial consultancy services and could become her competitors.

● **Technological breakthrough** With the widespread adoption of microcomputers by business, accountants can offer their clients systems that are easier to use.

Opportunities Not all accountants are conversant with the software and she will have a distinct advantage with her recent experience in the City.

Problems/threats How will she convey her advantage over the competition without infringing the Accountants' Code of Practice?

The factual basis

The second stage of the analysis involves the gathering of the information that needs to be quantified in order to segment the market.

The factual basis for accountancy services in Hertfordshire

An analytical sequence suitable for the accountant in Hertfordshire is as follows.

THE STRUCTURE OF THE MARKET
● Which type of organisation needs accountancy services (by segment)?
● How many of them are there in each segment?
● Which types of service do they use?
● How much do they spend per year?
(Answers to these questions denote the 'relative size' of different segments.)

THE ATTITUDES IN THE MARKET
● What do different market segments consider value?
● What do they think of the services they are using at present?
● What do they think of the accountancy firms they use?
● What makes them change their accountant?
● How often does it happen?
(Answers to these questions denote the vulnerability of segments to your marketing efforts.)

THE COMPETITION
- Who are the competitors (direct/indirect)?
- Where are they?
- What fees do they charge?
- In which segments are they most strongly entrenched?
- How complacent are they?
- What range of services do they offer?
- How will they respond to competition?

(Answers to these questions show how you need to modify your assessment of the best market segments for you.)

- In which way is the market changing?

(This gives you a further chance to modify your choice of segment.)

SWOT chart for accountancy services in Hertfordshire

STRENGTHS
Unique tax advice competence. Good knowledge of software available for tax work makes her independent of requirement for large staff. Good references from previous clients. Price not difficult to justify in terms of savings in tax using computer modelling.

WEAKNESSES
Growth must be controlled so that business is not created which goes to a competitor. Needs to canvass new service organisations before they move, but not able to travel far with present family commitments.

OPPORTUNITIES
Service organisations moving to area will not take to sleepy local accountants. The firms in this market have complicated tax problems which require a sophisticated approach.

THREATS
Service organisations less dependent on locally based firms. Direct competition may move in at any time. Indirect competition from software houses. Two such firms are already exploring the possibilities.

From this, it will be seen that the accountant has a number of strengths which line up with at least one type of opportunity, but on the threats side several factors need careful monitoring. Several opportunities, on the other hand, have been rejected and one main one selected.

Before moving away from planning we should mention the far-reaching implications all the factors mentioned have within the firm, which are not so directly related to marketing, but which are affected by marketing.

For instance, the choice of direction on market service development will have an effect on the following.

Recruitment	Do new people coming into the firm need different skills from those already in place?
Training	Are new skills required by any existing staff, technically or on selling skills for instance?
Motivation	Doing the same kind of work again for other clients may be good for productivity and profitability, but can be tedious. How assignments are staffed will have a bearing both on how a first job is conducted and on what the prospects are for the future.
Administration systems	These take time, but if they are worth while then time will pay dividends. A new system may mean briefing, and an element of control and feedback, to make it work.

Any of these aspects may deserve their own format in the system, as was illustrated in Form 12 (Training).

(This example is reproduced from the book *Making Marketing Work* by Gerald Earls and Patrick Forsyth, 1989 (Kogan Page), which is a guide for small businesses.)

Now, we will move on to things persuasive.

√3 A BASIS FOR PERSUASIVE COMMUNICATION
Planning promotional activity

'Even emperors can't do it
all by themselves.'

Bertolt Brecht

If marketing is not a euphemism for advertising, then neither is promotion. Promotion describes a number of different techniques and
implies a plethora of combinations and ways of using them.

As Figure 3.1 below shows, while the various techniques of promotion
act to put professionals in front of prospective clients, or generate
enquiries, they cannot, by their nature, produce actual fee-paying clients.
Only the process of sale can convert initial interest generated by promotion into actual business.

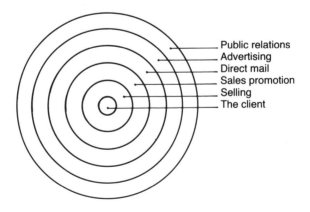

Figure 3.1   Communication mix

A brief comment about each of the ingredients of the communications mix will serve to put them into context: the aim of **public relations** is to create or maintain a favourable climate of opinion in which the firm can operate. Every firm will have an image, the question is whether it projects the right image and how strongly. It is therefore important that the actual image reflects what the firm wants. This applies equally for individual offices as for the whole firm.

The first task is to define those 'publics' among whom the firm wants to have a favourable reputation. Having identified the target groups, the next step is to find out what image they currently have of the firm.

- Do they know the firm and its services?
- What is their perception of the firm and its services?

Some information can be obtained by 'keeping one's ear to the ground'. If this is not sufficient, more formal market research may have to be undertaken.

In cases where perception surveys have been done, and an increasing number are being conducted, the results often provide the firms involved with some sobering food for thought. For example, one firm found they were falling between two stools, being perceived as neither local, with the special knowledge that implied, nor as part of a major group with its attendant advantages. Another regular source of concern from such surveys is the ignorance of the full range of services available from a firm, even among existing clients.

Once the present awareness and image have been identified, PR targets can be set, i.e. who should know and perceive what about the firm? The firm can then decide which PR and promotional techniques will be most cost-effective in achieving the desired image goals. Typical methods include the following.

- **Press publicity and developing good relationships with writers and editors** This does not just happen, it means taking the initiative, following up, and delivering – sticking to deadlines and so on (for example does your local radio station know if you have someone prepared to comment where appropriate?).
- **Membership of influential bodies** This does not just happen. Some- one (the right person) actually has to belong and take part. It takes time, but can lead to good contacts, and such bodies as trade associa- tions in industries where the firm works or wants to work should not be neglected. Contacts, once obtained, should be followed systematically,

and this may be as simple as arranging to call them rather than waiting for a call that never comes.

- **Use of 'house style' for brochures and written material**   Again it does not just happen, someone has to decide what is needed and to maintain the image. Brochures are a case in point; for many firms the brochures are the same as everyone else's, out of date, introspective, boring and – most often – banal. A vital point to remember is that it is not just a case of making them look better (though this is important), getting the message right comes first and a graphic designer may not be the best person to do this. This may be better done by working *with* a copywriter or consultant; though you cannot escape the responsibility of deciding *what* is said.

- **Public-speaking engagements**   These have to be sought out and you have to field the right person, i.e. someone who can make a presentation of a quality that will get them asked back (not whoever is most senior or happens to be available). If done well presentations can certainly produce enquiries.

Advertising can be defined as communication in bought space, the intention being to attract existing and potential customers to the firm and its services. It can:

- provide information;
- attempt to persuade;
- create dissatisfaction with competitive offerings;
- reinforce existing purchasing habits

Limited budgets may preclude mass action here, although some activity may be important and some may be done collaboratively on behalf of particular professions.

Therefore, while advertising may be used beneficially, especially by the larger firms, the 'best buy' in terms of promotional mix for the medium-sized firms will perhaps continue to be public relations and promotion, planned and followed through as well as reactive; coupled with an increasingly planned, organised and professional sales effort.

Direct mail, or promotion through the post, is another matter; essentially only a specialist form of advertising, it has considerable relevance for most firms and warrants a chapter of its own (see Chapter 5).

Sales promotion encompasses a number of elements, often used together as a 'campaign' around one particular service or at one time. The use of newsletters, events, briefings etc. provide good examples.

More strident techniques than these may never pay dividends for professionals, who, as with any other business, must select what is appropriate and, of course, work only with what is ethical.

Perhaps the area of greatest change is that of **selling**. Nice guys do in fact sell in some firms and certainly in many comparable fields. Nice guys who don't sell go bankrupt, or at least – in an area where some business continues to beat a path to the door – they fail to meet their growth or profitability targets (and that is bad enough).

Selling will not just happen either. To be professional and acceptable, selling needs to be planned. The client contact run must increase the chances of business resulting from it. Yet it remains an area of weakness. Promotional activity is geared primarily to producing enquiries; consider what happens when an enquiry is received. Someone is referred, perhaps by an intermediary, and telephones the firm. What happens? Is the response specifically designed to give the best impression? Who speaks to the enquirer? Who goes to visit them if appropriate? Is the action specified to increase the chances of business resulting or is it dealt with by whoever is in the office that day, has time or is most senior?

To ensure success responsibilities, even targets, must be laid against individuals. Sales activity must then be deployed acceptably so that the techniques are made full use of but clients remain content; so that we run the kind of client contact we want and that clients find they like.

Certain firms already gear up their sales activity and use techniques, routine in other business, to bring a sales edge to their contacts.

Overall, the relaxation of the rules on advertising has probably benefited the big firms and fostered the current trend towards polarisation of the larger firms and the others, though the big firms may not benefit as much as they think, and the market as a whole for professional advice may expand to the benefit of all. Advertising may allow the medium-sized firm to develop small, well-defined market segments, but major expenditure is unlikely to be cost-effective for what can only ever produce prospects rather than actual clients.

To date, the pace of change has not been such that the most marketing-oriented firms have left the others behind, but action is necessary to close the gap. If it is delayed simply because of a distaste for change, it will be found more difficult to take later rather than sooner. When it does take place, the promotional activity that follows must be persuasive. That is the nature of promotion; money spent, for example, on a brochure that is not persuasive is wasted.

Having advocated a planned approach to promotional activity, let us turn to the kind of planning involved.

The planning process

From the client's viewpoint, professional service firms appear numerous, similar, and by no means the only source of some of their services.

There are few professionals today, like the man who did not believe in promotion until he found he had to put a 'For Sale' notice outside his premises, who feel business will just arrive. Most accept that the world is unlikely to beat a path to their door and that some form of promotion is necessary. It attracts business, preferably of specific sorts and in the required quantity, and helps make your firm distinctive from the competition.

Successful promotional activity needs to be based on a continuous process of review and action, and preparing and implementing a comprehensive promotional strategy demands time, skill and a systematic approach.

Perhaps the first thing to consider is who does this. The laying of responsibility is crucial. In a business where client pressure, and perhaps where the democratic partnership process can make a focusing of attention more difficult, someone has to wear the 'marketing hat'. That person does not have to do everything, in fact, perhaps the reverse is true. What is needed is a co-ordinator and, above all, an initiator of activity.

Many firms are beginning to alter their attitude to promotion. One firm has removed marketing, that is sales and promotional matters, from the agenda for regular partners' meetings (often one suspects at the end of a busy day), and now organises separate sales promotion meetings to ensure that attention is focused on these important topics. Unless this line is pursued there is a real danger that promotion matters will drift.

The checklist (shown in Figure 3.2) makes clear 12 key points which will then be examined in more detail below. They can be considered under five main sequential stage headings.

 Analyse the firm's needs

The prime difficulty in the analytical stage is not so much the identification of the need, but ensuring that the need is real and not imaginary.

N.B.

1. Analyse market and clearly identify the exact need.
2. Ensure the need is real and not imaginary, and that support is necessary.
3. Establish that the tactics you intend adopting are likely to be the most cost-effective.
4. Define clear and precise objectives. *+ Budget*
5. Analyse the tactics available, taking into consideration the key factors regarding:
   —the market;
   —the target audience;
   —the product/services offered;
   —the firm's organisation/resources.
6. Select the mix of tactics to use.
7. Check budget to ensure funds are available.
8. Prepare a written operation plan.
9. Discuss and agree operation plan with all concerned and obtain management decision to proceed.
10. Communicate the details of the campaign to those involved in implementing it and ensure that they fully understand what they must do and when.
11. Implement campaign ensuring continuous feedback of necessary information for monitoring performance.
12. Analyse the results, showing exactly what has happened, what factors affected the results (if any) and how much it cost.

Figure 3.2   Promotion plan checklist

Identification of a need can come from:

- formal research;
- own company investigation;
- professional staff;
- specific market demands; and
- our own observations.

Such analysis is part of the total marketing review (see Chapter 2). Promotionally we are primarily concerned to show clearly the interrelationship of client categories (i.e. the kind of firm/organisation they are), products (i.e. the kind of work categories involved) and business (i.e. new business – a new client, extension – an existing client buying more etc.). We may well have to plan different strategies to impact specific areas, for example to increase work done for a specific kind of business with whom we have not had prior contact.

Once a need has been clearly identified, it must be established that the kind of support you intend using is likely to be the most cost-effective method of fulfilling that need. Then the planning stage can commence.

Preparing the operation plan for the practice

The first stage of any plan must be the quantification of the objectives. A clear statement of exactly what you want to achieve stated as specifically as possible is needed. An objective which says 'to improve business' is just not precise enough, whereas an objective which states 'to improve the number of new clients buying services by 50 per cent this year' makes it clear to everyone exactly what needs to be done and above all how success will be measured.

Once the objective is finalised the selection of tactics can take place. This will depend on a number of factors:

The market available to the firm
- What is its nature?
- Is it buoyant or is it in a low period?
- Is it price-conscious? If so, how?
- What is the competition doing?
- What is the client profile?

The target audience
- Types of people/organisation?
- What are their buying habits?
- What motivates buyers?
- What are their current attitudes to promotion?

The services (standard or tailored) offered by the firm
- What is its current performance?
- What are its strengths and weaknesses?
- What promotional support has it received in the past?
- Capacity available?
- Market profile/image?
- Position in life-cycle (see page 31, i.e. is it seen as new and interesting or old and dull?

Organisation of the firm
- What are our current sales and promotional methods?
- Would some tactics cause internal difficulties, e.g. in terms of administration?
- Is the firm involved in any other activity which might affect what we want to do or detract from it?

Having answered these questions there may still be a number of alternative tactics, all of which could be suitable for achieving the objective. Which one to use will depend on which is the most cost-effective.

Once the decision on tactics has been made, the details should be formalised into a written operation plan. It is always worth writing this down, even if yours is a small firm. This should not be a one-off exercise, but will eventually provide a reference which can be updated regularly so that it always sets out the plan for the next period. Planning of this nature is a 'rolling' process. It should include:

- background information as to why the promotional support is necessary;
- the objectives;
- a profile of the target audience(s);
- reference to service details;
- details of additional support other than that which you are actually planning, perhaps that being done by associated offices;
- budget details – how much the action is estimated to cost;
- details showing exactly how the plan will be implemented;
- controls, standards and methods of obtaining results;
- an action plan, or timetable, showing what actions are required, when they should be carried out and by whom.

There are a variety of ways of making the decision on the budget more logical, for example using comparisons with competitors, standard percentages of revenue and so on. (This concept is developed in Figure 3.3.)

Implementation preparation

As long as the operation plan has been correctly prepared, the pre-implementation preparation should be a formality.

This can only be achieved if the operation plan has been discussed and agreed with everyone concerned with the support activity, well before any action is required. This can ensure you pick up ideas (or identify snags) from everyone in the firm – some of whom may surprise you with their constructive comments.

Do not forget either that if everybody feels involved they will more easily commit themselves to the next stage. In a business where your 'production', 'sales' and 'promotional' resources in terms of people are the same individuals, the way in which the tasks are shared out and the certainty of getting things done is very important.

There are several approaches to the complex issue of setting the promotional budget.

1. Percentage of sales

To take a fixed percentage based, usually, on forecast sales relies on the questionable assumption that there is always a direct relationship between promotional expenditure and sales.

It assumes, for example, that if increased sales of 10 per cent are forecast, a 10 per cent increase in promotional effort will also be required. This may or may not be realistic and depends on many external factors. The most traditional and easiest approach, it is also probably the least effective.

2. Competitive parity approach

This involves spending the same amount on promotion as competitive firms or maintaining a proportional expenditure of total 'industry' appropriation or an identical percentage of gross sales revenue compared with competitive firms. The assumption is that in this way market share will be maintained. However, the competition may be aiming at a slightly different sector and including competition in the broadest sense is no help. If you can form a view of competitive/industry activity it may be useful, but the danger of this approach is that competitors' spending represents the 'collective wisdom' of the 'industry', and the blind may end up leading the blind!

It is important to remember that competitive expenditure cannot be more than an indication of the budget that should be established. In terms of strategy it is entirely possible that expenditure should be considerably greater than a competitor's – to drive him out – or perhaps for other reasons, a lot less.

Remember that no two firms pursue identical objectives from an identical base line of resources, market standing etc., and that it is fallacious to assume that all competitors will spend equal or proportional amounts of money with exactly the same level of efficiency.

3. Combining percentage of sales and competitive advertising expenditure

This is a slightly more comprehensive approach to setting the budget,

Figure 3.3   Setting the promotional budget

but still does not overcome the problems inherent in each individual method. It does, however, recognise the need for maintaining profitability and takes into account the likely impact of competitive expenditure.

4. What can we afford?

This method appears to be based on the premise that if spending something is right, but the optimum amount cannot objectively be decided upon, the money that is available will do.

Look at:

● what is available after all the other costs have been accounted for, i.e. premises, staff, selling expenses etc.;
● the cash situation in the business as a whole;
● the revenue forecast.

In many companies advertising and promotion are left to share out the tail-end of the budget; more expenditure being considered to be analogous with lower profits. In others, more expenditure on promotion could lead to more sales at marginal cost which in turn would lead to higher overall profits.

Again this is not the best method, demonstrating an ad hoc approach that leaves out assessment of opportunities in both the long and short term.

5. Fixed sum per sales unit X

This method is similar to the percentage-of-sales approach, except that a specific amount per unit (e.g. per man-day sold) is used rather than a percentage of pound sales value. In this way, money for promotional purposes is not affected by changes in price. This takes an enlightened view that promotional expenditure is an investment, not merely a cost.

6. What has been learned from previous years?

The best predictor for next year's budget is this year's. Are results as predicted? What has been the relationship of spending to competition? What is happening in the market? What effect is it having and what effect is it likely to have in the future?

● Experiment in a controlled area to see whether the firm is

Figure 3.3 continued

underspending or overspending. As the chairman of a major company once said, 'I know that 50 per cent of our advertising expenditure is wasted, the trouble is I don't know which 50 per cent'.

- Monitor results which is relatively easy, and the results of experiments with different budget levels can then be used in planning the next step (although you must always bear in mind that all other things do not remain equal).

7. Task method approach

Recognising the weaknesses in other approaches, a more comprehensive four-step procedure is possible. Emphasis here is on the tasks involved in the process of constructing a promotional strategy as already described. The four steps of this method are as follows.

- **Analysis** Make an analysis of the marketing situation to uncover the factual basis for promotional approach. Marketing opportunities and specific marketing targets for strategic development should also be identified.

- **Determine objectives** From the analysis, set clear short- and long-term promotional objectives for continuity and 'build up' of promotional impact and effect.

- **Identify the promotional tasks** Determine the promotional activities required to achieve the marketing and promotional objectives.

- **'Cost out' the promotional tasks** What is the likely cost of each element in the communications mix and the cost-effectiveness of each element?

What media is likely to be chosen and what is the target (i.e., number of advertisements, leaflets etc.)? For example, in advertising, the media schedule can easily be converted into an advertising budget by adding space or time costs to the cost of preparing advertising material. The promotional budget is usually determined by costing out the expenses of preparing and distributing promotional material etc.

The great advantage of this budgetary approach compared with others is that it is comprehensive, systematic and likely to be more

Figure 3.3 continued

realistic. However, other methods can still be used to provide 'ball-park' estimates, although such methods can produce disparate answers. For example:

- we can afford £10,000;
- the task requires £15,00;
- to match competition £17,500;
- last year's spending £8,500.

The decision then becomes a matter of judgement, making allowances for your overall philosophy and objectives.

There is no widely accurate mathematical or automatic method of determining the promotional budget. The task method (number 7) does, however, provide, if not the easiest, then probably the most accurate method of determining the promotional budget.

Figure 3.3 continued

Implementation

The success or failure of any promotional activity, providing it has been thoroughly planned, then rests on how well it is implemented. The effectiveness of the implementation will depend on how well the details are communicated around the practice and then controlled. Therefore, the details of what is to be done must be communicated in such a way that they are clearly understood by everyone.

ACTION
Consider putting the action plan elements of what will be done, when and by whom (particularly the promotion plan) on a visible wall chart and running it as a rolling plan. This method really can be easier to action than a document.

Effective methods of controlling the implementation must be set up to obtain maximum feedback while promotional activity is running. This will permit any necessary changes to be made at the earliest opportunity.

The post analysis of results

Any promotional campaign can involve a great deal of personnel time and is often expensive in terms of opportunity cost, that is time which could be spent earning fees, supervising projects or both. This is true regardless of what is spent on the other aspects.

You therefore want to know how money is being spent, and what achievements are obtained from that expenditure. Examining the detailed results of every form of promotional activity will show clearly:

- what the situation was prior to the activity;
- what we aimed to achieve (the objective);
- what the situation is after the promotional activity has ended (and what we have achieved);
- whether we met our objectives entirely and if not, why not;
- whether there are any factors outside our control which might have influenced the result, what they were (e.g. competitive activity, legislation changes) and their effect;
- what has happened to the rest of the market or at least our near competitors;
- what the effect might have been had we not carried out the promotion;
- what the budget was and how it was spent.

Careful analysis of what has been achieved is important, not least as part of the planning and consideration of what to do next, which should be occurring in a continuing cycle.

No promotional activity plan can be carried out in isolation. Promotion, in a service business, involves all aspects of that business. A service business must be just that; professionals must be truly client oriented. Only if the service elements are, together, of the right level, will final conversion to purchase occur. The best promotional plan we can conceive will still fail if any other factors let us down. For example, a client may attend a luncheon put on by the firm and be persuaded to take an interest in services beyond those he currently uses. If, when he phones the office later to get more details, the switchboard handles the call badly or his contact does not have the right details to hand, the chances of his being persuaded decline.

The two key links here are people and administrative systems. Both need to be checked and maintained at an appropriate level, someone must ask, 'Do our people – all of them – really complete that link correctly? Are they really selling, not just providing information? What is the quality of the letters they send? Are clients impressed with the response when they telephone us?' And how do you know these things? (When did you last telephone your own office incognito to see how clients are really dealt with?)

Similarly, the systems and procedures we use also need to be geared to what is right for the client. Are procedures simple, straightforward and easily understood by the client? Are any necessary details of procedure explained to them? Or is there a danger that methods and practices are not tailored to helping the client, but have grown up haphazardly over the years for no good reason?

Once promotional activity has brought prospective clients to our door, all the other resources we have must be actively geared towards converting them into actual purchasers. Sometimes things seem designed to prevent or ignore the final step rather than to increase the danger of making a sale!

Finally, bear in mind just exactly what it is the firm is promoting – not just various services, but other reasons why clients use a professional firm (remember there are alternatives) and why they should use your firm in particular.

The client demands expertise, knowledge of the, perhaps complex, technicalities of your specialist field. He demands objectivity, impartial advice that appears to be telling him what is best for him (not what will make the firm the most money), and he demands efficiency, the time and hassle taken out of what the layman finds a complicated and perhaps uncertain process. He will use your services only if he feels they will provide these things. He will use your firm only if he feels, or rather if you persuade him, that you will provide them more effectively than will the alternatives.

Planning and implementing a soundly based systematic promotional plan is not easy. Nor is ensuring that all the back-up resources, people, skills and systems are geared to converting the initial enthusiasm created in potential clients into actual business. But it is certainly necessary, and done successfully provides a sound basis for securing and, more importantly, enlarging, your business.

The link with sales activity

As has already been seen, promotional activity is not only designed to produce 'leads', the raw material of sales activity, it can only produce leads. With experience you will be able to monitor the level of promotion necessary to produce the required number of leads, relating this in turn to the kind of formulae that can be used to provide an indication of what the required number should be in a particular period.

This is not difficult, though data has to be recorded in a suitable manner for sufficient time to provide relevant historic data. Using our fee targets for the future period and historic information relating to average assignment size, the ratio of new clients needed to augment continuing work with regular clients, and the ratios between work proposed and booked, and the number of enquiries that do result in work being proposed, you can estimate how many enquiries you are seeking.

Regular monitoring of these latter ratios, and a watch on the trends, will often provide useful information as to how well enquiries are being handled and on the quality of proposal writing.

This example, which the reader will remember from Chapter 2, makes the point.

Work required next year	£350,000	
Average assignment size	7,000	50 clients
Historic existing:new client ratio	46:4	4 new clients
Booked:proposed ratio	1:2	8 new proposals or £56,000 proposed to 8 prospective clients
Enquiry: proposed ratio	3:2	12 new contacts (NB: Not one per month. Most must be made early in the year)

Having generated the right number of leads it is crucial to respond to them in a way that makes the best use of them and that increases the likelihood of them progressing to actual business. In addition, realistically, some screening must go on, since not all leads are equally valuable, some are time wasters, some of low potential, some seek expertise the firm does not have, or want work done in areas the firm does not wish to pursue. Until it is clearly known what priority is involved, all leads should be responded to with the same degree of consideration.

Everyone in the firm must be briefed as to how to respond to enquiries.

It may be useful to have an enquiry form. This can act as a checklist, making sure the right information is collected; as a record and as a prompt to ensure that progressing action is taken (see Chapter 7).

The rules regarding what action is taken are simple. It must be 'customer oriented', designed to give the right impression and progress matters appropriately. Whoever handles it must be dependent on sales skill as well as technical competence, and not simply a factor of who is in the office on a particular morning.

The first objective is to make sure you meet the client, giving yourself an opportunity to discover exactly what he needs and to structure the whole on-going sequence of customer contact with him in the way you want and in a manner he will find persuasive but, of course, acceptable.

This whole sequence, including the written proposal stage, is the subject of a later chapter. It is worth stating here, however, that is a continuous process. First in the sense that the conversion of enquiries takes time, numbers of meetings, visits and letters over a period of perhaps weeks or months. Many an enquiry has been jeopardised and many a job lost because of poor follow up. This process must be handled systematically and, if necessary, persistently and time found for it to fit in with 'production' responsibilities. Furthermore, once the business is booked, the process does not stop, but involves a continuous process of review and action. With existing clients every meeting should be regarded as a potential opportunity to identify new work possibilities, sow the seeds for new projects or propose new work.

- **Sell on**   Offering new, different services to those already handled.
- **Sell up**   Increase the value of existing work and extend the scale of involvement.
- **Sell across**   To other parts of the client company (subsidiary locations, etc.).

Seek references to other sources of work and, of course, simply repeat the kind of work you have done in the past.

'Time is money' may be an an old cliché, but sales effort and client contact of the sort described takes time. And the more certainly it is carried out, the better the conversion from opportunity or prospect to firm business and the greater will be the impact on profitability.

A final point that should be mentioned in this area brings us back to people and responsibility. The firm must have some sort of 'account manager' system so that someone accepts responsibility for the process of review and continuous selling to clients, and for the progressing of each and every enquiry. In this way things will not go by default. Indeed, it follows that failure to meet this responsibility once it has been laid down is just as unacceptable as a failure in technical competence. This topic will be explored in Chapter 7, which reviews the various techniques and tactics that will make up the activity specified in the plan to enable this sort of link with sales activity.

4 THE PROMOTIONAL MIX
Tested techniques and how to use them

'It is only shallow people who
do not judge by appearances.'

Oscar Wilde

The 'target' chart shown in Figure 3.1 of Chapter 3 set out the essence of
the various techniques at the professional's command and showed their
differing roles. Now we investigate these more closely to see how they
work, how they can be used and what impact they will have. Consider first
the firm's overall image.

Image

Image is always important to any organisation. It can be powerfully
descriptive. Think for example what a clear, detailed picture comes to
mind of some companies just on a mention of their name – Marks and
Spencer, Habitat – yet, exactly what does come to mind is, on analysis,
often subjective. It is image, rather than detailed factual knowledge.

It is even more important for a service which is inherently intangible
and which may have a limited amount of permissible promotional techniques with which to work. Imagine Mr Smith needs an accountant, but
he does not know one. He can look one up in a directory, but then what –
is one whose name begins with 'A' better than any other? So he checks
around, he asks people and finally his bank manager recommends one or,
more likely, two names. He picks one and phones them. At this stage he
still knows virtually nothing about them, but at every stage he builds an
initial impression in his mind. It is cumulative, and such initial impressions may be difficult to shift.

He observes the way the phone is answered, how his call is handled,
what action is suggested, what questions asked; he visits one of the

partners, he notes the plate on the door, the reception, the welcome, whether he is expected or kept waiting, what is provided for him to read, whether he gets a cup of coffee. Certainly he may be impressed by the meeting, but he continues mentally to file and assimilate the other details, the brochure he was given, the follow-up letter he receives. And so on and so on, and, if the cumulative impression of all these details is poor, he may question the firm's competence, question the ability to relate to his needs, his problems. Every detail counts; if he finds only a three-day-old newspaper in reception he is entitled to question the efficiency of the firm. Even one detail that gives the wrong impression is too many.

The importance of all this is compounded by the fact that he may well be going through the same process with two or more firms and making comparisons. Things are getting more competitive and it is a pity if the wrong impression is given by default.

What, therefore, are the key issues in this area and how can you make sure they are working for you? It is as much a question of attitude as organisation. To illustrate this, take, for example, two positions that are key to the firm's image, the telephone switchboard and the receptionist.

The telephone switchboard

> **ACTION**
> Consider telephoning your own office occasionally (or asking someone to do it for you), to get some objective feedback about just how clients, and prospective clients, are received.

For every incoming call, the telephonist is the first person to whom a client or prospective client speaks. The impression given then is vitally important, and deserves far more attention than many give it.

A desultory mumbling of the telephone number (eventually) by way of a greeting, and then an excellent chance of being misrouted or left in a silent telephone limbo, are telephone techniques that we have all come across. Given the choice, we try, as customers, never to suffer such treatment twice. We take our business elsewhere.

A good telephonist answers promptly and politely – an overworked switchboard is no excuse for delay or rudeness and more money will go on lost business than on recruiting another telephonist. Greetings should be short, friendly, informative; '5493' is not suitable even if said with a question mark. 'Hello' is equally useless and impolite, for it invariably puts the onus on the caller to ask, 'Is that Countryside Consultants?'.

'Good morning, Countryside Consultants, may I help you?' said with a reasonable degree of enthusiasm, is well worth the trouble. Telephonists who do this, and their other tasks properly are valuable members of their firm and should be paid accordingly.

If the telephonist is required to ask the caller's name, he should be sure to use it when he puts the call through, e.g. 'Mr Smith, I am putting you through to Mr Brown now'.

However, it is pointless to do that if what happens next is that a phone rings on Mr Brown's desk, and Brown has to establish for himself who is calling. If the telephonist has discovered the name, he should phone Brown and say, 'Mr Smith is on the line for you, Mr Brown', before connecting him.

The good telephonist does not keep callers waiting, especially in silence. Some callers cannot hear if the phone extensions are ringing; for all they know they have been forgotten and Mr Brown has not been called yet. Calls are expensive. If the person being called does not answer or cannot take the call, the message should be, 'I am sorry Mr Smith, but Mr Brown is not available – may I take a message?'.

If Brown is being called to the phone, the telephonist should speak to the caller frequently to reassure him, to apologise for his wait and give him the opportunity to leave a message and ring off. Messages must be taken down carefully and accurately.

A message pad tailored for your particular firm, printed (with, if necessary, carbon copies) and on a standard size paper, preferably A4, not only ensures messages are taken clearly, it gives them an added importance and often removes the necessity for transcribing, as the resulting sheet can be neatly added to correspondence, a client file and so on. Very few client requests or enquiries have to go astray for the extra trouble of preparing such a form to be shown to be worth while. A formal enquiry form appears in our discussion of client development in Chapter 7.

The good telephonist treats the caller with consideration. If the caller asks for a person by name, he should be put straight through unless specific instructions have been left for certain calls to be re-routed. The telephonist should know all names and functions of staff (the internal directory should be sufficiently detailed) and know enough about the firm's affairs to avoid the retransferring of calls.

Impressions about the firm are formed in numerous ways, and many people gain their first impression over the telephone. Everyone who uses it, and the switchboard operator most of all, should therefore appreciate that courtesy and consideration cost nothing.

Reception

Just as important for its 'first image' responsibility is the role of reception. As obvious as this may seem, many firms still greet clients and visitors with a cold, bare room, one stained table and a broken ashtray for furniture, yesterday's newspaper or an out-of-date professional journal for reading, and a frosted glass panel with a bell push and 'ring for attention' sign by way of a greeting. Only slightly better than the unfriendly sliding panel is the presence of a totally bored school leaver, who takes an age to look up from a magazine, to mutter 'Yes?'.

The reception area and the receptionist, the switchboard operator, the letterhead and other printed material – these all provide opportunities to advertise your firm. The image they portray is the image people have of the whole firm.

The receptionist should greet callers in the same manner as the telephonist, adding a personable, cheerful countenance. He should have an up-to-date list of everyone in the firm, know where to direct callers, who to contact by telephone and how to handle impatient people.

A very common fault is to give the receptionist nothing else to do but receive, which means that often he has nothing else to do at all. A caller who finds a receptionist reading or gazing blankly into space, or sees him doing this while the caller waits for an appointment, can hardly think of the firm as being dynamic and thriving.

Appearance is as important as attitude, which means that the receptionist should be smartly dressed and the whole reception area should have a clean, pleasant look. It should never be used as a 'goods inwards' department, and other staff should only be in the area if they are meeting a visitor, not conducting an internal argument about client problems or management attitudes.

The reception area should also be a 'silent salesman'. In addition to the firm's printed brochures other items, a series of visually appealing photographs relating to the firm could perhaps be on display. The reception area is also an ideal place to exhibit awards, certificates, letters of commendation etc.

Unexpected visitors should always be seen by someone from the department concerned, if not by the very person the visitor came to see – even if it is only to explain to the visitor that an appointment is essential, and to agree a time for one. If an enquiry cannot be dealt with fully, a member of staff should explain why, help the visitor as much as possible and provide him with all available literature, and ensure that an appointment is made when he will be able to get what he requires.

If a visitor has to be kept waiting for any length of time, it may create a far better impression if someone from the office, rather than the receptionist, comes to tell the visitor that he will have to wait, offers a cup of tea or coffee, something to read and perhaps explores his needs in order to help brief whoever will subsequently see him. Be honest about time. Do not say there will only be 10 minutes' wait when you know full well it will be half an hour. This only guarantees 20 minutes of annoyance.

Anyone calling on a firm begins forming an impression the moment the building is seen. A potential client, even if only subconsciously, will be wondering 'Will this firm satisfy my needs?'. Since no one likes to be kept waiting, the reception area can become a most critical place for lost opportunities. Everything the firm does in its contacts with callers should be done to ensure that the client answers his unspoken query with 'Yes, this firm is likely to satisfy my needs'.

Every member of the staff must recognise that the first essential in making the right impression is to gain the confidence of the buyer. A positive attitude helps here and should show itself in numerous ways.

Interest
It is hard for anyone to maintain interest in the face of indifference. Enthusiasm is infectious. People should gain the impression that the firm is glad to be in contact with them – helping clients is the reason for the firm being in business, and they should not be seen as the tiresome interruptions which some seem to think they are.

Staff should listen to problems, ask questions and be concerned to provide satisfaction with service. A client who feels that a company is not solely interested in his money will always come back, and even higher prices are unlikely to shift his allegiance.

Courtesy
In all circumstances, staff should try to stay polite and calm, however severe the aggravation. If someone complains, apologise sincerely and do not attach qualifications or excuses to the apology. The normal reaction is to 'fight back', but the person who keeps cool invariably emerges the winner. An unreserved apology costs nothing, and is the best way to deflate an irate complainer: besides there is often more to the matter than is assumed at initial contact. Turning away those who arrive just at closing time, or putting on an act of devastating self-

sacrifice to postpone lunch by two minutes, does nothing to enhance the firm's image.

Efficiency

Enquiries and queries should be dealt with quickly and effectively, even if the client is simply to be contacted in order to be informed of a delay. No one should ever be committed to a particular course of action without first checking that it can be fulfilled. Never make promises unless they can be kept! Personal promises, however lightly given and seemingly unimportant, must always be honoured: a promise to phone back with some information should be kept even if the information cannot be obtained as quickly as expected. It is another case of the need to put ourselves in the other person's shoes, and imagine what he expects us to do – and then do it.

Loyalty

However tempting it may be to blame another person or another department of the firm when faced with the consequences of your own inefficiency or mistakes, you should always try to back the firm.

Telling people that not everyone in the firm/company is efficient, saying something like, 'Oh, I agree with you – you've no idea what it is like working in this madhouse', does nothing for the image everyone should be working so hard to create.

Attitudes of this kind do not just happen; staff must be briefed, trained and motivated. It is a continuous process, and one which, obvious though much of the foregoing may seem, is not made full use of by many firms. As such, this represents a significant opportunity to stand out from the crowd.

The client's viewpoint

There is a tendency for those in professional services to be rather introspective in describing what they do. They catalogue their services by saying 'we are . . .', 'we have . . .', 'we do . . .', when they should be stating what is in it for the client. Clients buy to meet their needs, they buy, and consider buying, by looking at things from their viewpoint. Any promotional message needs to reflect this. It is too easy for a message to become full of jargon and concerned entirely with features (what the service or part of it is), rather than with benefits (what the service or some aspect of it will do for the client).

This concept is described in more detail in Chapter 6 which deals with personal persuasive techniques.

Written promotion

Not only is there a continuous projection of image through what exists in print about the firm – from business card to brochure – but there is also a range of much more specific promotional and sales objectives implied by many printed items.

Design, preparation and particularly the writing of these items is crucial, well worth some time and money, and possibly some professional assistance. One firm who my own company recently assisted with the rewriting and design of their corporate brochure felt it worth while to add half as much again to a print bill of between £3–4,000. This does not mean that small inputs from outside, at less cost, are impossible, they are not, and they can help.

The total process is, perhaps surprisingly, complex. The chart in Figure 4.1 makes this clear; it shows the sequence of events involved in producing a brochure intended for recruitment purposes. Every product is different but this flow chart acts as a rule of thumb for planning a job-specific schedule. The complexity and importance of detail is immediately apparent. Only by handling such a project systematically will the end result stand a chance of achieving its objectives.

Getting things into printed form

You may well wish to do all this yourself, liaising direct with a printer. On the other hand you may need professional assistance with copy (the words used in the material), with design and graphics (how the material will look); artwork must be prepared for a printer to work from; a printer and printing process must be selected and proofs checked, colours matched etc.

In either case the process of choosing the right assistance is crucial. In selecting a printer, describe the job you want done, look at work he has done before, ask how long it will take. As much of the print business works on a jobbing basis it may be useful to know how much of the work he will do himself.

With an agency or freelancer on the 'creative' side, who will be concerned with design, graphics, copy etc., you are really seeking a partner in the implementation of a part of your marketing strategy. Again, look at what they have done in the past and for whom. Ask how well it worked,

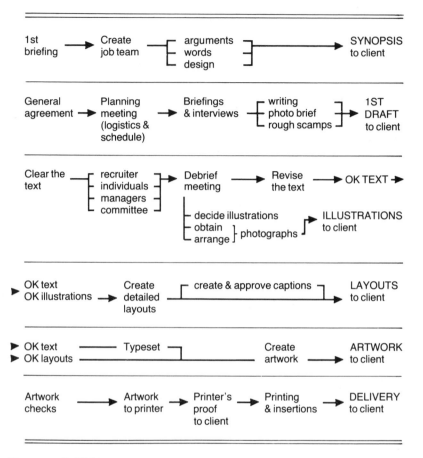

Figure 4.1   Publishing process

has that client come back to them for more, can you check personally with a satisfied client? Making the right choice is an important decision, and it may well be worth selecting from a number of people. Your final judgement may well be influenced by those elements of the job with which you need most help; for example the fact that it is easier to find someone who will make a brochure look nice than someone who will ensure its overall message, the words and way it is presented meets your objectives, and is therefore able to do a really persuasive job on those who see it.

Brochures

Brochures are designed to act in your absence, perhaps as a reminder of a meeting, perhaps to show to those with no other knowledge of the firm.

Some have a specific purpose, perhaps to support a graduate recruitment programme or to introduce a new service. Others are more general and intended only to tell any prospective client 'all about the firm'.

Sometimes these two uses of brochures overlap and a smaller firm may have only one brochure intended to do all these jobs from recruiting staff, persuading clients and so on.

This is an area of increasing professionalism, and great care is needed in defining the objective, creating the right message and making sure the brochure looks good and reflects the image the firm intends to project. The days of the bland, general brochure, very similar to those of other firms, describing the chronological history of the firm and everything it does, and intended to be used for everything, is rapidly passing. What is needed is the ability to support contact in each particular area with something specifically designed for the particular job. This may mean separate brochures for recruitment and client usage, it may mean the 'corporate' brochure is a folder with separate inserts aimed at different target groups or different types of client, or it may mean a revised brochure every year. It may even mean a difference between the sort of brochure that it is right to give a prospective client after a preliminary meeting and the sort suitable to present to an intermediary, e.g. another provider of professional services, who can act to recommend you.

Overall what must be created is something accurately directed at a specific group, with a clear objective in mind, and – above all – it must be persuasive. This may seem basic, promotional material is there to inform, but it must do so persuasively, that is its prime purpose. Many professionals have tended in the past to produce material that, while no doubt ethical, is so circumspect as to be largely ineffective. This does not mean moving to something that is inappropriately strident, (which might in any case be self-defeating), but it does mean a greater emphasis should be placed on client needs and benefits (what services do for people, rather than what they are).

Essentially, a less introspective approach, better designed to its purpose, is the rule. What does this mean?

- A front cover that has the name of the firm clearly shown and/or that makes some offer of benefit. The reader must be clear, at a glance, why he should read on.
- Leaflets are expensive, so you cannot afford to waste space.
  There is, or should be, lots to say about the services you provide.
- It should make clear how a reader makes contact with the firm, since

this is, after all, the whole purpose of the communication.
- Photographs, or any illustrations, should be clear, captioned if appropriate, and have some bearing on the content.
- Above all, the text must be truly oriented to the client, their view and their needs, and persuasively and attractively written.

There are a few rules to be observed about brochures, and any rules one might define are made to be broken, because they must be creatively constructed to reflect the image of the firm graphically, and aim their chosen message directly at the group involved.

Letters

The volume of paper produced in business is incalculable – memos in triplicate, invoices in quadruplicate, letters, confirmations, orders, reports, tenders, complaints, and forms, forms and more forms.

No wonder then, that individual letters become diluted by the sea of paper around them and command little attention. The major consideration is to move paperwork on as fast as possible before the next lot arrives: to deal with it, to file it (though 90 per cent of it will then never be referred to again) or preferably destroy it quickly.

Therefore it is well worth considering how to attract the best attention from what you write. Unless awareness is maintained there is a danger that writing becomes routine, letters and documents being compiled on 'automatic pilot', and without any consideration of how they can be made persuasive. Many kinds of letter need to have a persuasive element:

- letters accompanying brochures;
- letters accompanying proposals;
- letters answering or following up complaints;
- post-audit management letters etc.

and even more simple letters, perhaps confirming an appointment.
No matter what the subject of the letter is, it must:

- command attention;
- be understood; and
- be acted upon.

The last point is the crucial one in differentiating sales or persuasive communication from simple factual communication.

If your letters are to do this, you have to take some care in preparing them; in this age of dictating machines, rush and pressure, it is all too easy to just 'dash them off'.

Preparing persuasive 'sales' letters
Before a letter is drafted, remember the principles of selling, and in particular remember to see things through the client's eyes. Then ask yourself five questions.

- For whom is the letter and its message intended? (This is not always only the person to whom it is addressed.)
- What are their particular needs?
- How does our service or proposition satisfy those needs – what benefits does it give?
- What do you want the client to do when he receives the letter? Each letter must have a clear objective, and these objectives must be:

  — commercially worth while, within the firm's overall strategy;
  — stated in terms of client needs;
  — realistic and achievable with available resources;
  — specific, clear and time bounded; and
  — capable of evaluation with a Yes/No answer.
- How does the client take this action?

The last two questions are frequently forgotten, but they are very important. It should be perfectly clear in your own mind what you want the recipient to do and this must then be put equally clearly to the client. But even having achieved this, you can lose the advantage if lack of information makes it difficult for the client to understand exactly how he takes the action.

The principal object of writing a 'sales' letter is to draw the reader's attention to the reasons why he should take action and explaining what benefits he will gain is of paramount importance. It is therefore essential that you know for whom the letter and its message are intended.

The client's reasons for buying the benefits he will gain must be related to his position in the client organisation and what the service does for him, rather than what the service itself is. Description of the service and what are its features is one of the functions of the leaflets, or brochures, which often accompany letters to new contacts.

Criteria for successful persuasive letters
Perhaps before anything else, a persuasive letter must be attractively laid out, grammatically correct and well typed. That will at least give the

impression it has originated in an efficient and reputable firm. Any company selling a service must try particularly to convey neatness and efficiency as a cornerstone of its image, and will inevitably be let down by sloppy letters.

The most important part of a letter is its first sentence. It will determine whether or not the rest of the letter is read. People seldom read a letter in the same sequence in which it was written. Their eyes flick from the sender's address to the ending, then to the greeting and the first sentence, skim to the last – and then, if the sender is lucky, back to the first sentence for a more careful reading of the whole letter. So the first sentence is about the only chance we have of 'holding' the reader, and it should arouse immediate interest.

But gimmicks should be avoided. They invariably give the reader the impression of being talked down to. So what makes for the best opening?

THE OPENING
Write out the name of the person you are writing to. Seeing it written down will help you visualise his point of view. Always address the letter to a person rather than to 'Dear Sir'. It is much less formal, everyone likes hearing their own name, and unless we write 'personal' on the envelope, there is no fear that the letter will lie unanswered in his absence.

Keep references short and subject headings to the point – his point. Do not use 'Re'.

Make sure the start of the letter will:

- command attention;
- gain interest; and
- lead easily into the main text.

For example ask a 'Yes' question; tell him why you are writing to him particularly; tell him why he should read the letter; flatter him (carefully); tell him what he might lose if he ignores the message; give him some 'mind-bending' news (if you have any).

THE BODY OF THE LETTER
The body of the letter runs straight on from the opening. It must consider the reader's needs or problems from his point of view. It must interest him. It must get the reader nodding in agreement – 'Yes, I wish you could help me on that'.

Of course, you are able to help him. In drafting, write down what you intend for him and of course list the benefits, not features, and in particular benefits which will help solve that problem and satisfy that need.

You have to anticipate his possible objections to your proposition by selecting your strongest benefits and most convincing answers. If there is a need to counter objections, then you may need to make your letter longer and give proof, e.g. comment from a third party, that your benefits are genuine. However, remember to keep the letter as short as possible.

It is easy to find yourself quoting technicalities to the client, rather than selecting just one or two benefits which will be of particular use to him in his situation, and which support the literature.

The aims are as follows.

- To keep the reader's immediate interest.
- To keep that interest with the best benefit.
- To win him over with second and subsequent benefits.
- To obtain action by a firm close.

THE LETTER ENDING

In drafting your letter you can make a (short) summary of the benefits to him of your proposition. Having decided what action you are wanting the reader to take, you must be positive about getting it.

It is necessary to nudge the reader into action with a decisive close. Do not use:

'We look forward to hearing';
'I trust you have given . . .';
'. . . favour of your instructions';
'. . . doing business with you';
'I hope I can be of further assistance';

which are just phrases added as padding between the last point and 'Yours sincerely'. Where you want to prompt action you must finish in a specific manner, for example:

- ask him to telephone or write (or say what you will do);
- give him some sort of prompt to action now rather than later (perhaps while a member of staff suggested for the project is available).

Finally, sign the letter yourself whenever possible, and consider letting your secretary use their own name rather than 'pp' if you are not able to sign.

If you use a postscript make sure it is a final benefit – an extra help to closing. Remember a PS gets read, so do not regard it as just for omissions, but consider how you can use it for emphasis. Like footnotes, people really do read them!

Many people have acquired a habit of artificiality in writing, approaching it quite differently from their way of talking to a client, and in a way that lessens the chances of obtaining the commitment they want.

Language is important too, to the tone, feeling and acceptance of the message. This topic will be commented on in the next section as part of a consideration of those crucial documents, proposals.

We return to the question of letters in Chapter 5; and proposals, another key element of written persuasion, are examined in Chapter 6.

Advertising

Advertising has been an area of very different practice around the professions. Some have always been allowed to do it, others only more recently or in a restricted way (only recruitment advertising, for example, or advertising an event, publication or seminar), and for some it is still not allowed under ethical rules. For most it is unlikely to be a major part of the communications mix. Anything that is done, however, must be done in the context of how the whole process works.

The role of advertising is still sometimes misunderstood in the professions. Leaving the ethical debate on one side for the moment, we will now review some of the essentials of advertising and put them into context among the whole range of techniques.

First a definition. Advertising is 'any paid form of non-personal communication directed at target audiences through various media in order to present and promote products, services and ideas'. More simply, it can be called 'salesmanship in print or film'.

The role of advertising, as one of a number of variable elements in the communication mix, is 'to sell or assist the sale of the maximum amount of, in this case the service, for the minimum cost outlay'.

There are a variety of forms of advertising, depending upon the role it is called upon to play among the other marketing techniques employed, in terms of both types of advertising and the target to which it is directed. These include by way of example:

- national advertising;
- retail or local advertising;

- direct mail advertising;
- advertising to obtain leads for salespeople;
- trade advertising;
- industrial advertising.

A more specific way of understanding what advertising can do is to summarise some of the major purposes of advertising generally or objectives that can be achieved through using advertising in particular ways. A representative list, though by no means a comprehensive one, is as follows:

- to inform potential customers of a new product or service;*
- to increase the frequency of use;*
- to increase the use of a product/service;*
- to increase the quantity purchased;*
- to increase the frequency of replacement;*
- to increase the length of the buying season;*
- to present a promotional programme;*
- to bring a family of products together;*
- to turn a disadvantage into an advantage;*
- to attract a new generation of customers;*
- to support or influence a franchise dealer, agent or intermediary;*
- to reduce brand substitution by maintaining brand loyalty;*
- to make known the organisation behind the product/service (corporate image advertising);*
- to increase the strength of the entire industry;*
- to stimulate enquiries;*
- to give reasons why wholesalers and retailers should stock/promote a product;
- to provide technical information about a product/service.*

There are clearly many reasons behind the advertising that we see around us. They are not mutually exclusive of course and many of those listed apply – or could apply – to professional services, particularly those marked *. Whatever specific objectives the use of advertising seeks to achieve, the main purpose is usually to:

- gain the customer's attention;
- attract customer interest;
- create desire for the product or service; and
- prompt the customer to buy.

Advertising is, therefore, primarily concerned with attitudes and attitude change; creating favourable attitudes towards a product or service should be an important part of the advertising effort. Fundamentally, however, advertising also aims to sell, usually with the minimum of delay, but perhaps over a longer period, in the case of informative or corporate (image-building) advertising.

Any advertisement should relate to the product or service, its market and potential market: and, as a communicator, it can perform a variety of tasks. It can do the following.

Provide information
This information can act as a reminder to current users, or it can inform non-users of the product's existence.

Attempt to persuade
It can attempt to persuade current users to purchase again, non-users to try the product for the first time and new users to change brands or suppliers.

Create cognitive dissonance
This means advertising can help create undertainty about the ability of current suppliers to best satisfy a need. In this way, advertising can effectively persuade customers to try an alternative product or brand. (In terms of some ethical rules, this technique would appear to come under the heading 'knocking copy' – which is specifically prohibited.)

Create reinforcement
Advertising can compete with competitors' advertising (which itself aims to create dissonance) to reinforce the idea that current purchases best satisfy the customer's needs.

Moreover, advertising aims to reduce the uncertainty felt by customers immediately following an important and valuable purchase, when they are debating whether or not they have made the correct choice.

Types of advertising

There are several basic types of advertising and these can be distinguished as follows.

Primary

This aims to stimulate basic demand for a particular product type, for example, insurance, tea or wool. This has already been the subject of some experiment in accountancy and other professions.

Selective

This aims to promote an individual brand name, such as a brand of toilet soap or washing powder which is promoted without particular reference to the manufacturer's identity.

Product

This aims to promote a 'family' branded product or range of related brands where some account must be taken of the image and interrelationship of all products in the mix.

Institutional

This covers PR-type advertising which, in very general terms, aims to promote the company name, corporate image and the company services.

Advertising media and methods

There is a bewildering array of advertising media available. Here are some of the most popular methods of advertising, with a guide as to how they are used.

- **Daily newspapers** often enjoy reader loyalty and, hence, high credibility. Consequently, they are particularly useful for prestige and reminder advertising. As they are read hurriedly by many people, lengthy copy may be wasted.
- **Sunday newspapers** are read at a more leisurely pace and consequently greater detail can be included.
- **Colour supplements** are ideal for advertising, but appeal to a relatively limited audience.
- **Magazines** vary from quarterlies to weeklies and from very general, wide-coverage journals to very specialised interests. Similarly, different magazines of the same type (e.g. fashion) appeal to different age and socio-economic groups. Magazines are normally colourful and often read on a regular basis.
- **Local newspapers** are particularly useful for anything local, but are

relatively expensive if used for a national campaign. They are some-times used for test market area advertising support.

- **Television** is regarded as the best overall medium for achieving mass impact and creating an immediate or quick sales response. It is arguable whether or not the audience is captive or receptive; but the fact that TV is being used is often sufficient in itself to generate trade support. Television allows the product to be demonstrated, is useful in test marketing new products because of its regional nature, but is very expensive.

- **Outdoor advertising** lacks many of the attributes of press and tele-vision, but it is useful for reminder copy and a support role in a campaign. Strategically placed posters near to busy thoroughfares or at commuter stations can offer very effective, long-life support advertising.

- **Exhibitions** generate high impact at the time of the exhibition but, except for very specialised ones, their coverage of the potential market is low. They can, however, perform a useful long-term 'prestige' role.

- **Cinema**, with its escapist atmosphere, can have an enormous impact on its audience of predominantly young people; but without repetition (i.e. people visiting the cinema once every week) it has little lasting effect. It is again useful for backing press and television, but for certain products only, bearing in mind the audience and the atmosphere.

- **Commercial radio**, playing popular music for young people, offers repetition and has proved an excellent outlet for certain products. It is becoming apparent that the new local radio stations appeal to a wide cross-section of people and thus offer 'support' potential to a wide range of products.

- **Direct mail** offers great flexibility for the advertiser. It is particularly useful for assisting special promotions in certain regions (national coverage of the consumer market being very expensive), and in the industrial and service field where it can be tailored to suit a very specialised audience. Direct mail is so popular in industrial marketing that the major emphasis is on producing a mail shot that is sufficiently different to be noticed and read. The other fundamental problem is the wastage caused by inaccurate and out-of-date mailing lists.

Not all media outlets will be appropriate to the nature of the services offered by a professional firm; indeed, some are still specifically excluded from use by some areas of the professions.

Before finalising any advertising plans it may be useful to check to see what media decision will be best. You can run such a check by listing the alternative media options, and putting down the advantages and disadvantages of each alongside.

This not only acts as a prompt but also gives you, on one sheet of paper, a summary document which will assist in making the final decision on a logical basis. This concept can be employed whatever advertisement(s) you consider placing.

Figure 4.2 shows one example (relating to recruitment advertising). The blank format can be used for a specific situation of your own. Media selection is a complex technical business where professional advice is probably essential, however this chart is intended to provide a basis for some decision.

Advertising professional services

In many ways this sort of advertising is no different from any other, but there are certainly key factors that have been found important, and will apply to the advertising now taking place in the professions. The following are the key factors.

- Unlike consumer advertising, much advertising of professional services will play a secondary role to that of personnel selling. Such advertising aims to create awareness, stimulate interest and generate enquiries for further information or personal contact. It is in fact true to say that in professional services advertising will never actually sell anything. It only makes the later stages easier and more cost-effective; it provides the raw material for selling by producing leads or enquiries. Direct mail, one of the most effective techniques in other fields for providing this effect, is covered in Chapter 5.
- Less money is likely to be spent on advertising professional services than many mass appeal consumer goods because most accountancy services can be advertised more selectively to more defined markets. There are in fact, not surprisingly, fewer potential buyers for accountancy than toothpaste.
- The buying decision and communications problem is different from consumer advertising. Consider the constraints which face the buyers of professional services. They need to achieve cost targets, they need to justify the purchase to others such as colleagues, the board and shareholders, for example.

Clearly, several people within one organisation may be involved in the

Media	Advantages	Disadvantages
1. National dailies and weeklies	—large circulation —minimum delay before advertisement is published —proofs supplied to enable final advertisement to be changed or mistakes corrected —specialist staff frequently available to give advice	—typesetting variable in paper-set advertisements —expensive —your advertisement competing with large number of others
2. Local daily, evening and weekly newspapers	—attracts local people and so avoids waste —costs lower than nationals —minimum delay before publication —acts as a guarantee back-up to a national advertisement at little cost	—would not be seen by good candidates outside circulation area —specialist jobs unlikely to draw sufficient number of applications —may not be seen by senior people
3. Trade specialist magazines	—usually inexpensive compared with national newspapers —seen by specialist readership if you are only intending to address this group, e.g. those in specialist industry	—long delays between each issue, frequently one month —advertisements often not seen by target audience for weeks after publication —job advertisements rarely featured prominently —not usually regarded by senior people as a primary source of jobs
4. Specialist selection agency publications of candidate lists (recruitment only)	—very cheap or free —large number of specialist categories to choose from —quantity available useful guideline to whether spending money on advertising will be worth while	—lists usually made up of professional job hunters/job hoppers —facts often suspect or, like estate agents' house descriptions, the truth is embroidered
5. Commercial radio and television	—very wide coverage especially at peak listening hours —speeds of acceptance of advertisement and broadcast —impact —more people listen to radio and watch television than read newspapers —gain attention of those not necessarily thinking of using/ changing accountants therefore less likely to notice advertisements in newspapers	—usually very expensive —cost usually means insufficient information can be provided —risk of not being seen or heard by those available during evening or at weekends

Figure 4.2   Choosing the most appropriate media for your advertisement

decision to purchase professional services and thus the advertising message may have to compromise between detailed information for one and a more general statement of facts which clearly relate to the company's problems and how they can be solved.

The potential market for professional services can be smaller and more specialised than for consumer markets and, therefore, media must be chosen very carefully and selectively if advertising is to communicate effectively to a good percentage of prospect companies, and a large number of buying influencers, without undue waste.

Remember that mass circulation newspapers and magazines can be used again on a selective basis. Such journals can help create and maintain a required image, and also create the opportunity of communicating to 'unknown' or less definable members of a potential market, and to intermediaries. No matter how skilled and expert the analysis and interpretation of background information has been, the stage will always arrive at which the advertisement must be appraised by a combination of logic, the known background data and sheer judgement.

We must pre-suppose that the analysis of the market has led to a sensible choice of media and advertising strategies, and that these have been communicated to whoever is going to produce the advertisement.

At its best the advertisement strategy statement should be brief and economical, and should do its job in three paragraphs.

- The basic proposition – the promise to the client – statement of benefit, to whom.
- The 'reason why' or support proof justifying the proposition, the main purpose of which is to render the proposition as convincing as possible.
- The 'tone of voice' in which the message should be delivered – the image to be projected, and not infrequently the picture the client has of himself which it could be unwise to disturb, or indeed wise to capitalise on.

N.B.

In other fields some of the finest and most effective advertising has sometimes been produced without reference to an 'advertising strategy', or for that matter without knowledge of market facts. However, although research cannot always give all the details, or for that matter always be infallibly interpreted, it can give strong indications and reduce the chances of failure.

Most executives, when faced with a rough or initial visual and copy layout, have an automatic subjective response, 'I like it/I don't like it', and while the creator may attempt to explain that the appraiser is not a member of the target audience, it is obviously difficult to be objective.

Nevertheless, while an attempt must be made to be objective, there are few experienced advertising or marketing executives who can say that their 'judgement' has never let them down. Advertising remains as much art as science and this is no doubt as true for professional services as it is for other products.

Trade advertising

It is often not sufficient to advertise to consumers alone, particularly as it is important that distributors are willing to stock and promote a product.

Certainly the sales force has a prime role to play in ensuring that stocking and promotion objectives are achieved. However, trade advertising also has an important role to play in this respect:

- it can remind distributors about the product in between selling calls;
- it can keep distributors fully informed and updated on developments and changes of policy;
- it can also alleviate problems associated with the 'cold-call' selling of less well-known products.

Trade advertising is usually confined to specialist trade publications and the use of direct mail communications from the company to its distributors.

Most trade advertising occurs prior to major consumer advertising campaigns to help ensure the buying-in of stock in anticipation of future demands to be created by future consumer advertising.

Thus, when new products are launched, or special promotions introduced, trade support is often achieved through special offers ('13 for the price of 12') or increased (introductory) discounts, all of which trade advertising can effectively emphasise.

This type of advertising can also communicate to the trade the advantage of new products as well as the timing and 'weight' of advertising support which is to come.

There is a distinct parallel here with intermediaries who are of course important to the professions and to whom messages can be directed specifically and separately, in order to influence them.

It will be interesting to see whether, now advertising is increasingly permitted, some of it is directed towards closely targeted groups such as banks and other key intermediaries.

Having reviewed something of the general principles of advertising, we must now turn to its application for professional services. The questions which you must ask are as follows.

- Does the advertisement match the strategy laid down?
- Does the advertisement gain attention and create awareness?
- Is it likely to create interest and understanding of the advantages of a particular service?
- Does it create a desire for the benefits and conviction of the need to buy?
- Is it likely to prompt potential clients to action?

In other words, does the advertising communicate? Will people notice it, understand it, believe it, remember it and buy it?

EXAMPLE
With regard to press advertising, a good advertisement is brief and economical – it should do the job in three stages:

- **the basic proposition, or 'promise' to the client, is a statement of what the benefit is for him;**
- **this is followed by a justification of the proposition, which renders it as convincing as possible;**
- **finally there is the 'tone of voice' in which the message is delivered, or the image to be projected.**
This will reflect the image the client has about himself in a positive way. This is expanded in Figure 4.3 which lists the sequence necessary to achieve this, and suggests some examples of methodology.

The pre-test of advertisements, even on a comparatively informal scale, can often pay dividends.

Corporate image or identity development

An important area where professionals can now use advertising is in the building and clarifying of the firm's corporate image. This process begins with a name, but extends to other visual features, e.g. typography (and logo design), colour, design, slogans. These provide a foundation from which other advertising can work and thus assist in creating, stimulating and maintaining demand.

Among the arguments in favour of a clear corporate image (what would be called branding in product marketing) are the following:

- memory recall is facilitated, leading to more rapid initial buying action or greater frequency of buying, thus creating deeper loyalty;
- advertising can be directed more effectively and linked with a 'common vein' to other company communications programmes;
- a clear image leads to a more ready acceptance of a firm by intermediaries;
- the importance of price differentials, particularly vis-á-vis competition, may be diminished;
- additional services may be introduced more readily;
- the amount of required personal persuasive selling effort may be reduced;
- a clear image makes market segmentation easier, i.e. different approaches may be developed to meet specific categories of client.

Because of the need to clarify the range of tasks and techniques involved

Objectives	Methods
Gain attention	**1.** Select right media **2.** Buy enough space **3.** Impact headlines
Interest reader	**4.** Involve client **5.** Make big promise **6.** Solve problems **7.** Present facts **8.** Communicate quality
Make reader desire benefits of your services	**9.** Show benefits for him **10.** Don't bore – romance **11.** Testimonials **12.** Message clear – simple **13.** Be honest

Get action from reader and make a sale	**14.** Summarise benefits
	15. Ask reader to buy:
	    • call
	    • telephone
	    • attend reception
	    • put in coupon
	    • make a choice
	    • save time – money
	    • buy now
	16. Ask for commitment clearly

Figure 4.3   Ingredients of a good advertisement

in advertising, and because the present rule relaxations are in a major part concerned with it, advertising has taken perhaps more than its fair share of space in this section. It should be remembered that what is necessary to ensure a successful promotion campaign is the right mix of different promotional techniques. Some techniques, like direct mail which has proved very effective in marketing some professional services, have only recently been permitted. While others, for example the simple technique of producing an effective brochure, may be a better option, especially for the smaller firm. The effect on the market of campaigns by the larger firms, and what responsive action this may necessitate, remains to be seen. Certainly, the ability to indulge in advertising should not negate action in the other areas; ultimately, what will need to be discovered is the mix which, for any individual practice, has the most cost-effective impact on the process of securing new business.

Progress reports (management letters)/Newsletters

These two categories of communication are worth separate comment. The first, including letters and documentation sent at any key stage of a project, and normally making specific suggestions for the future, are often lost opportunities. Of course the formal summary and the checklist of actions for the future is important, especially at the last stage of a project. In promotional terms it is also the first stage of what we intend to do next, thus there are three elements: summary; checklist for future action; and proposal (or even hint of proposal) for future involvement. These do not necessarily need to go in one document; it could be in various forms, a letter and attachments for example. Certainly, the third element needs to be there, written persuasively and then followed through in subsequent meetings and contacts. All the principles of making written communications persuasive which we mentioned earlier then apply.

Similarly, for newsletters or the kind of document that goes out either regularly or occasionally, or sometimes even to celebrate events such as the opening of a new branch office; these should also be promotional documents. They do not only exist as a service to inform clients, though this is important, but also to assist particular promotional objectives such as the selling of the range of services.

> ACTION
> Consider producing two versions of any newsletter, or even three,
> one for clients, one for prospects, one for 'influencers' – the extra
> cost may well be worth while, as each feels they are receiving
> something specific to them and may respond accordingly
> (alternatively, different covering letters may be used).

In both cases a clear identification of the objective before the message is
finalised is important, and because like so many of the promotional tactics
available they will not individually do a complete job, the link to follow-
up action is crucial.

Public relations activity

Public relations can provide a planned, deliberate and sustained attempt
to achieve understanding between you and your public. You should be
aiming at the kind of understanding that whets the appetite for more
information, that in fact prompts enquiries, re-establishes dormant contracts and reinforces your image with existing clients.

Not only is PR activity potentially a powerful ally in your promotional
armoury, it is also free. Well, it is often compared with advertising –
which is communication in bought space – but, of course, there is a catch.
PR takes time, and in professional services time is certainly money; ask
any client! Therefore in too many organisations PR is neglected; staff are
busy, even overstretched, and opportunities are missed. Yet if the power
of PR is consistently ignored, then at worst not only are opportunities
missed, but the image that occurs by default may actually damage your
business prospects.

In many ways, therefore, time spent on PR is time well spent and often
more a case of relationships rather than resources.

Press relations
This very specific form of PR can pay dividends, though you must bear in
mind that, unlike with an advertisement, you cannot guarantee what is
going to be said. Having said that, there is no reason, of course, to feel
that the press will always be critical.

So where do you start? There are routine mentions and more particular
stories, and in part much of the impact of both sorts of material is
cumulative. Clients will sometimes comment 'we seem to see mentions of

the firm pretty regularly', but have difficulty remembering the exact context of what was said or written. To achieve this cumulative impact you need to be constantly on the lookout for opportunities of getting a mention in the press and by the media.

Even routine matters, perhaps the appointment of a new staff member or a move of office, can be written up. All that is necessary is first to remember to make these announcements, and then to take a disproportionate amount of care and attention about the way they are made. For instance, the announcement of an appointment is much more likely to be printed if there is a photograph with it. This takes a little more organising but is well worth the trouble. So the first necessity is to be able to issue an appropriate, acceptable press release. The ACTION section below sets out the key principles and an **EXAMPLE** is also given.

Beyond the routine announcement, things get a little more difficult. News means exactly that, and, while it may be of interest to you that the firm has 25 partners, inhabits an 18th-century mansion, or specialises in tax problems for rich landowners, a journalist will tend to find it difficult to imagine readers starry-eyed with excitement as they read of it in his newspaper or journal. You will have to find something with more of an element of news to it; it may be genuinely different, it may be a first comment on something but it must have something of real interest about it.

If you begin to gain a reputation as a source of good comment, stories and articles, then your press contacts will start to come to you and the whole process may gain continuity and momentum.

A C T I O N   *Composing a press release*
There are two, perhaps conflicting, aspects to putting together a press release that will stand a good chance of publication. The first is to comply with the 'form' demanded by the newspapers, magazines and journals to whom you send your release; the second is to stand out as being of genuine interest from the very large number of releases received by the Press.

Take the 'form' first.

- It should carry the words 'Press [or News] Release' at the top, together with the date, preferably at the top left-hand side of the first page.
- If an embargo is necessary, (i.e. a request not to publish before a certain date, to ensure news appears as near as possible

simultaneously – once an item has been in print others will consider it of less interest), it should be clearly stated 'EMBARGO: not to be published before [time] on [date]'. Underline or use capitals for emphasis.

- At the top you should insert a heading, not too long but long enough to indicate clearly the contents of the release or to generate interest in it.
- Space it out well, with wide margins, reasonable gaps between paragraphs and so on. This allows sub-editors to make notes on it.
- If it runs to more than one page make sure it says 'continued' or similar at the foot of the page, even break a sentence at the end of the page.
- Similarly, to make it absolutely clear that there is no more, you can put 'end' at the foot of the last page.
- Use newspaper style. Short paragraphs. Short sentences. Two short words rather than one long one.
- Keep it brief, long enough to put over the message and on to a second page if necessary, but no more.
- The first sentences are crucial and need to summarise the total message as far as possible.
- Avoid overt 'plugging' (although that may well be what you are actually doing). Do not mention names etc. right at the beginning, for example.
- Try to stick to facts rather than opinions: '. . . this event is being arranged for all those interested in minimising their tax liability' is better than '. . . this event will be of great interest to all those wanting to minimise their tax liability'.
- Opinions can be given, in quotes, and ascribed as such to an individual. This works well and can be linked to the attachment of a photograph (which should be a black and white print and clearly labelled in case it gets separated from the release).
- Do not overdo the use of adjectives, as this can jeopardise credibility.
- Avoid underlining things in the text (this is used as an instruction in printing to put words underlined in italics).
- Separate notes to the journal from the text as footnotes, for example, 'photographers will be welcome'; they could get printed as part of the story.
- Never omit from a release, at the end, a clear indication of the

person from whom further information can be sought and their telephone number (even if this is also on the heading of the first page).
● Finally, make sure that it is neat, well typed and presentable and that it lists enclosures. Obvious perhaps, but important none the less.

And now, how can you make sure your press release stands out? Fewer rules exist here, but there are perhaps two important ones.

● Do not 'cry wolf'. Save releases for when you really have a story. If you send a series of contrived press releases, there is a danger that a good one will be ignored among them.
● Make sure the story sounds interesting and, without overdoing things, be enthusiastic about it. If you are not enthusiastic, why should they be? Perhaps the only good thing in the world that is contagious is enthusiasm.

Finally, on the following page is an example, included with some caution because a good press release thrives on an element of individuality. While it may illustrate some of the points mentioned above it should not be copied slavishly.

Speaking assignments

'By their deeds ye shall know them' may be true for some, but with any service it is not that simple. The client must take your competence to carry out any particular project on trust, or rather he will make inferences, looking at something he can see or measure and likes, and literally say to himself 'that means they should be able to perform what I want well'.

Formal presentations, whether at functions you have convened or events at which you have been invited to speak, provide a dramatic example of this principle. They can be a way both of developing the overall image of the firm and prompting specific enquiries. Taking advantage of this potential opportunity area is dependent on cultivating opportunities to speak and on the firm being able to field people who can do a good job on such an occasion.

There is all the difference in the world between being willing to speak and being invited. There are countless opportunities at conferences, seminars, association meetings and so on. All of these events have

EXAMPLE

FINANCIAL TIMES
PITMAN PUBLISHING

Practical guidance for those in
professional services on the
gentle art of persuasion – a new
publication from Pitman Publishing/
Financial Times   April 1992

As competitive pressures in the world of professional services continue,
Pitman Publishing today published *Marketing Professional Services – a
handbook*, a comprehensive review which describes a practical,
systematic approach to the promotion of professional firms.

It reviews both the process of putting together a promotional plan and
comments on its implementation. It has sections covering the various
techniques involved including advertising, public relations and
presentation skills. The book has been written by marketing and training
consultant, Patrick Forsyth, who is principal of Touchstone Training and
Consultancy, and conducts seminars on this topic for a number of
professional bodies.

The author commented:

Promotional, presentational and sales techniques have not traditionally been
regarded as the professional's stock-in-trade. But, in areas where many have felt
that 'nice guys don't sell', competitive pressures are changing the situation and
many are having to get to grips with all the 'business-getting' techniques reviewed
here. The book is designed specifically to help this process.

The book shows how a firm can be persuasively presented, yet in a way that
maintains the professionalism of the business and is acceptable, indeed
useful, to clients.

The book is available now, price £30.00.

ENCLOSED – photograph of the author
                    – leaflet about the book

For further information please contact: Pitman Publishing,
128 Long Acre, London WC2E 9AN.

hard-pressed organisers who often find it difficult to find the right people to speak. Keep in touch with them. They look in turn to others, for example the secretary of a trade association, to recommend speakers to them. Keep in touch with these people too.

Local radio too, with an ever-expanding network of both commercial and BBC stations, presents regular opportunities for interviews or presentations, though it is wise to brief yourself on how an interview is carried out before appearing for the first time.

The important point to remember is that if you, or one of your colleagues, does undertake a speaking assignment, you (or he) must do it well enough. How well is that? In promotional terms, this means well enough to make an impact that will affect image and prompt enquiries, ultimately well enough to be asked back. That way the process becomes less time-consuming and more effective. What is more, as some speaking engagements pay a fee, you can even be provided with promotion and be paid for it.

Finally, do not neglect the audience you have among your own clients. The kind of function you may organise at Christmas, which is primarily social, may benefit from a short, but more formal, presentation. This, and other occasions certainly all demand a crisp, competent presentation.

Before turning to how to make the presentational element effective, however, we will digress a little to review the kind of promotional event (which many call client seminars) at which some of your presentations may take place.

Client seminars

These are, in themselves, an excellent form of promotion for many, though they require other means of promotion to assemble the participants so that such an event can be conducted.

But first let us clarify what we mean by 'client seminar'. The term describes an event, one at which a number of clients or non-clients (or prospects), or indeed both, are present. The event has, first, the objective of providing information to those present in a manner they will find appropriate and useful. Secondly, this information must be presented so that some members of the group will do business with the firm now or in the future, or, if they are existing clients, go on doing business with the firm and do more in the future.

The scale of such events varies. It can be:

- an hour's briefing, say on new tax legislation, by one partner in the

firm's offices, concluding with coffee and an informal chat;
- a half-day session, with several partners speaking, arranged in a local hotel and with a morning break and lunch, and might look in more detail at one issue or at several, perhaps linked, issues; or
- a full day's seminar or even a training course (some of which charge a fee) – perhaps conference-style – with several speakers, or a tutorial with one speaker.

In every case, other elements may be involved, for example, showing a video, and the audience may be of any size from ten or a dozen to a hundred or more. Both clients and prospects may attend. Whatever their format, whatever the information content, these events are, from the firm's viewpoint, 'promotional', and must be organised as such.

Client seminars can be a disproportionately important part of the communications mix. They can be:

- cost-effective;
- manageable;
- directed precisely at specific groups of potential clients;
- focused on individual aspects of the service.

They can have:

- an immediate effect;
- a longer-term effect.

They can:

- reinforce relationships with existing clients;
- secure new clients;
- promote the range of services;
- introduce new services;

and, very important, they can do so in a way which – by providing a first opportunity to demonstrate professional competence – goes some way to overcoming the problem of selling an intangible service.

Professionally run, as part of the on-going promotional activity, client seminars can pay dividends. But, and it is a big but, if they are not, then the damage they can do is also considerable. This may range from simply tying up time and resources to no good effect (though that is bad enough), to actively reducing the image presented to client and prospective client alike. The dangers mostly have their roots in the thinking, planning and preparation that precede such an event.

EXAMPLE

Here are three instances which warn of the range of things that can go wrong, and the inherent fragility of what is involved.

CASE I

Three partners in an accounting firm are involved in a client seminar presentation linked to recent tax changes. The first is a poor speaker, ill-prepared, with few visual aids and even less ability to use them. After ten minutes the audience is nodding off and, despite the best efforts of the other speakers, the event never really recovers.

Why? The first speaker, a senior partner and head of his section, was assumed to be the best person to speak, by virtue of his seniority, not by his ability to do so.

CASE 2

In a meeting room in a local hotel, a video is being shown during an afternoon event. It is a good, dramatic statement about the topic. As it runs, the evening begins to draw in; at the conclusion, when the TV monitor is switched off, the room is quite dark. At this point, the organisers realise no one knows where the light switch is. A hiatus ensues, during which it takes five minutes to summon the banqueting staff of the hotel to rectify the situation (the light switches are in an adjacent passage). With the lights back on, the partners have to work doubly hard to overcome the aura of inefficiency that has descended on the group.

Why? Nobody thought to check, or even to ask what should be checked. Perhaps everyone involved thought someone else was attending to the details.

CASE 3

A group are meeting to review past promotional activity. A client seminar is being criticised for having cost much and produced little. Yet, they recall, at the time it seemed to go well. Indeed one client has been signed up – a useful project that is proceeding well.

Why no more of a response? An assumption was made, perhaps, that organising a good event is enough. No follow-up action was planned, no link made to other promotional activity, and the impact remained stillborn.

And so it goes on. The list of possible hazards is long and varied:

- slides that cannot be seen at the back of the room;
- speakers who cannot be heard;
- materials, for distribution, of poor quality or out of order;
- a venue that proves inadequate in some vital respect.

But the potential rewards are considerable. They include the ability to communicate persuasively and cost-effectively with a group of people, to prompt individual meetings in order to follow up and put forward proposals, and to tie down work fast with people who already feel they know something of the firm's expertise.

All that is necessary is that setting up and running such an event is approached systematically, implemented efficiently and followed up professionally. The aim is to run the kind of event we know will act persuasively and which attendees will find appropriate and useful (preferably more appropriate and useful than other firms' events they may attend).

Because the cumulative detail of planning and organising such events is so important to their success, some checking before embarking on the process is to be recommended. The previous paragraphs about client seminars are adapted from an audio/manual package produced for the Institute of Chartered Accountants entitled *How to make Client Seminars Successful.* While prejudiced – I wrote it – I would recommend it to anyone planning such an event. It sets out guidelines to ensuring planned, professional and persuasive events.

How to make an effective presentation

'The human brain', as a wise man once said 'is a wonderful thing. It starts working the day you are born, goes on and on and only stops the day you get up to speak in public.' In fact, even an inexperienced speaker can give a clear, interesting presentation and hold an audience's attention, it is only a question of learning the necessary skills.

Overall there are three key factors involved if a presentation is to be well received. First, it must be audible. This may seem obvious, but if people have difficulty hearing they will not take in even the best-turned phrase or way of putting things. Secondly, it must be understandable. If people have trouble following the sense they will not keep up or find the presentation easy. Thirdly, it should be enjoyable to listen to. This is perhaps the most important factor of all and one that is dependent very largely on the confidence of the speaker. So, what creates confidence? Well, for one thing, the security of preparation.

Preparation

This is quite simply the key to success. Carefully selected and prepared material will be more likely to come across well, and familiarity with the material gives a sound foundation to your confidence. When making your preparations you should consider the following.

- **The kind of audience to whom you must speak**   Consider carefully who they are, how much they already know about your topic, their attitude to it and how fast they can take in more information. Clearly, if you anticipate hostility or great interest, you can pitch your presentation accordingly. Unless the presentation is directed accurately at the audience there is a danger that they will quickly feel bored.
- **The purpose of your talk**   The objective will condition the whole nature of the talk, for example is it intended to give a broad overview or detailed information? Do you want the audience to do anything as a result of what you say? Whatever the objective, the talk must reflect it in its nature and form. With the audience and objective clearly in mind you can proceed to the next stage.
- **Writing down what you will say**   Remember that all good presentations must have a beginning, a middle and an end, so it is a good idea to jot ideas down under these headings. Often you will have more material available than you need for the time allotted, so ideas have to be pruned, put into the most logical sequence and key points, or even sentences, noted. Most effective speakers do not read their notes (it is in fact very difficult to produce a fluent talk that way), indeed a full text may often be avoided so that this cannot happen. Notes should therefore highlight key points, headings, examples and so on, with only perhaps the first and last sentence written out in full. Cards may be better than sheets, but whichever method you use they should be numbered – if you drop a sheaf of unnumbered pages just before a talk, this is guaranteed not to be good for your confidence! A good tip is to number them in reverse, i.e. the last page is 1, so that you can always see clearly how much more you have to cover, which is useful in judging when you will finish.

Format of speaking notes

The format of any notes from which you speak is important. Their form may well have a bearing on how well the presentation goes. Some speakers (but relatively few) can manage without notes; others use a few headings and still others need something more elaborate.

By way of example, consider something down the middle. In the **EXAMPLE** below, you will find set out the opening of a talk on marketing accountancy (a conference paper I presented, reported, as near as I can recall, verbatim). Then, Figure 4.4 shows the kind of note that might well be suitable as 'speaker's notes' for this talk. Two colours used on this note would give added guidance.

It is very much a matter of personal preference and experience how you do this, but it is worth a conscious effort to find the format that suits you best. The overall presentation planning chart shown in Figure 4.5 will help you plan the structure and content of any talk.

With practice you will get to know how many minutes your chosen style of notes represents.

EXAMPLE

Ladies and Gentlemen, Good Morning . . .

I am very conscious of being the only non-accountant here. Your conference programme is full of important topics, concerned mainly with the constant updating that must go on continuously in a profession that is, I know, so dependent on being able to guide its clients through a jungle of constantly changing technicalities.

My talk appears under the title 'Indecent Exposure? A promotional plan for the practice'. This too is an important topic, but one that many in the profession view with mixed feelings. I will try to bear this attitude in mind as I speak.

Though it is an attitude which reminds me of the story of the businessman who didn't believe in promotion or advertising and didn't do any – until he had to put a 'For Sale' notice outside his premises!

So it is with accountancy and promotion; something has to generate sufficient business and the question is therefore not so much whether you need promotion, but how much is needed. Given that you want to run a profitable practice, to receive more in fees than you incur in costs, and to increase business – then the need for a process that ensures a sufficient flow of work is not in doubt. Promotion is concerned with producing that flow of business, how much is necessary is dependent on the market; so is what manner of promotion is best, though this is influenced also by the ethical rules of the profession.

Some of these ethical rules, like the precise circumstances in which you can distribute a brochure, and which seem to an outsider a little bit like 'Alice in Wonderland', are under review. More of that later.

It is certain that competitive pressures have increased and that in a profession convinced that 'nice guys don't sell' there has nevertheless been a gradual acceptance of the need for marketing – this process continues steadily if suspiciously.

And what about this word 'marketing'? It is in no sense a magic formula. Currently perhaps there is still a situation where too many accountants don't even understand the word. Not surprisingly perhaps as it is confusingly used.

Marketing is not advertising (the focus of much, perhaps too much, of the ethical debate), nor is marketing a euphemism for selling. The word is used in three main ways. Let me try to make these clear. First, it is a *concept*, that of seeing our business through the eyes of the customer or client and ensuring profitability through providing value satisfaction to him. Secondly, it is a *function*, the total management process that co-ordinates this approach, anticipating the demands of clients, identifying and satisfying those needs by providing the right service at the right price and time, and in the right place and manner. Thirdly, it describes a series of *techniques* that make the process possible. These include research, advertising, selling and other promotional factors, and involve many other considerations from how we set prices to the image we want to project.

Everything implied by all three is important to accountancy and can play a part in developing the practice.

The other factor to have clear in our minds is the way in which the pressures of competition are increasing. Not so much business just walks in the door these days, and the role competition plays in this trend can, I think, be divided into three areas of influence.

These are professional competition, particularly the activity of the larger firms, 'unprofessional' competition, that of banks and others, and the clients themselves, ever demanding greater value for money.

Let's look at these in turn . . .'
(And so on – this represents the first few minutes of an hour's talk – given in the days when the ethical restrictions in this profession were first being lifted.)

Giving the presentation
A number of points should be borne in mind once you get to your feet.

WORDS
Some people have a natural feel for language, others must work at it;

Conference notes

Ladies and gentlemen

only non-accountant – other topics
                              ↓
                    constant updating process

(title **Indecent Exposure** – a promotional plan for practice
                              ↓
                    also important topic, viewed with mixed feelings

                    story of man who did not believe in ad (For Sale)

So it is with accountancy – not whether promotion is necessary but how much

Promotion → profit growth

                    influenced by market and ethics

competitive pressures (nice guys don't sell) →

acceptance of marketing – confusing
                              ↓
                    definition (not advertising)

used in 3 ways – concept
                – function
                – techniques – all apply

(Next) competitive pressures – (not so much walks in the door)

    again 3 elements
        ↓
                professional

                unprofessional

                client pressure

Figure 4.4   Speaker's notes

observation and practice can help. Other factors, for example, repetition, can add to what you say; as can comparisons, contrasts, aliteration, and anything that adds a descriptive element to what is said. But it is the way you use the words that is even more important.

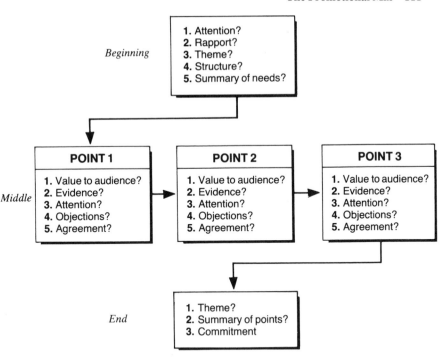

Figure 4.5   Presentation planning chart

VOICE

Whether or not you have a naturally attractive voice you can add to its effectiveness by the way you use it. Start with an appreciation of how you come across now. This is easily done with a small tape recorder. Then you can work on the following.

- Speed – not so fast that your speech is garbled or glib, and not so slow that it is boring.
- Pace – the ebb and flow of talk adds variety and spontaneity.
- Pitch – this can change the feeling; for example, adding a question mark into a phrase. Some women may need to pitch their voices down a little to avoid sounding 'squeaky'.
- Pauses – these can change the sense of what is said and add impact. A pause can be very effective – even dramatic – if used in the right place.
- Emphasis – this probably needs to be given more exaggeration than normal speech and is important not only to sense, but can add interest, enthusiasm or urgency to a message.

All of these together, with the overall tone of authority or friendliness for instance, can be used to add to the delivery.

Precision is also important, as you can see in the example below.

EXAMPLE
The following examples, culled from observation of actual events or role-playing training sessions, make the point about the importance of precision.

- **In talking about 'our fragmented range of services' (when trying to describe a divisionalised company structure) one professional surveyor found he inadvertently put a negative feeling in the mind of his listeners.**
- **An architect, rehearsing a talk to be given at a conference in Hong Kong, spent some time (of an all-too brief spot) describing to his audience the characteristics of high buildings when the venue overlooked Hong Kong's harbour skyline – a gesture would have sufficed.**
- **An accountant was asked what he meant by 'personal service', pondered a moment and then said 'I suppose I mean we do it with people' – a blinding glimpse of the obvious, though he in fact had interesting things to say about exactly how his firm operated, to the benefit of its clients.**
- **And, on many occasions, remarks prefaced by 'I think', 'Possibly' or 'It seems that' when, without circumspection, what should be said is positive (e.g. 'These are the key issues').**

VISUAL AIDS
These can add to any presentation and perhaps the most important visual aid is yourself. Stand up, match your expression to your words, use your hands to emphasise points and avoid visual factors that distract, such as mannerisms (tapping your pen, rattling the loose change in your pocket, shuffling notes, looking at your watch). If you want to keep an eye on the time, put your watch flat on the table or lectern in front of you where your audience cannot see you glancing at it.

Other visual aids should be used as appropriate, but bear in mind that too many can become confusing and they must be allowed to speak for themselves. If, for example, you put a graph of some sort on an overhead projector slide, then pause for a moment so that people can take it in – they will not read and listen at the same time. Finally, once you have used a visual aid and passed on, remove it, switch off the projector or remove or cover a flipchart so that it does not distract. Remember 'a picture is worth a thousand words' – checklists are useful, but a sufficient proportion of your visual aids should actually be visual.

TIMEKEEPING

This is an important discipline. The audience should know how long you will speak (this means that you tell them if the chairman does not) and then stick to what you have said. If you overrun, acknowledge the fact, saying perhaps that you must close in a couple of minutes but would like to add a couple of points first. Not only is all this a courtesy to your audience, but it prevents the group having a part of their minds busy wondering when you are going to stop!

A good structure to your talk is essential. This will include an attention-getting start and clear instructions, a logically organised main theme developed in the middle of the presentation, and an ending that wraps up the topic and, if possible, finishes with a flourish. Figure 4.5 illustrated this shape in more detail.

Putting a point over with confidence and enthusiasm can give you the impact you want. Approached in this way, while you may still be nervous (even the best, most experienced speakers are), there will be no need to be worried. This is certainly a skill which more and more professionals must be comfortable with; in many larger firms it is a subject of priority in training. It is an ability that clients respect and may increasingly demand; a topic that is revisited in Chapter 6.

Centres of influence

This phrase is used to describe a group that perhaps consists of a number of different kinds of organisation, having in common their ability to recommend, introduce or even just produce opportunities for meeting people. They range from national bodies, for example, associations, to social groups, trade bodies, individuals such as the local bank manager or solicitor, and even charities. Some imply only the need to keep in touch, though this must be done systematically; that is, regularly and acceptably. The latter implies a maximum frequency of contact which must be judged in each case, but acceptability is also conditioned by manner and the reason a contact is made. It will make a greater impact if there is a particular reason, even a superficial one for the contact. Others need a more active involvement, like being on the committee or even chairman of a relevant association or similar body.

In either case, time is spent and there is the danger both that, because it is time-consuming, nothing happens; and at the other extreme that some-one gets so sucked into committee work that other priorities suffer. Yet such activity is clearly a cost-effective way of producing leads.

> ACTION
> Consider reviewing, at least annually, on what bodies, committees
> etc., the firm should be represented specifically allocating who will
> do what. This will spread the load, allow more to be done, make
> representation appropriate, and should include decisions on who
> will not do things as well as who will, on the basis of picking those
> most able to make the necessary input rather than those who simply
> like a particular involvement.

If, in addition, a regular reporting back occurs and this is in turn linked to
a record noting where new business emanates from, then it is comparatively easy to make sure such effort is cost-effective and that a real return
is in evidence.

In many a practice this is an area where prevailing wisdom is often
misinformed or out of date. For example, an intermediary whom one
partner regularly lunches every few months may produce nothing, while
another who is beginning to pass on prospective clients is neglected.

This is another area that should not be allowed to go by default and it
pays to ascertain all the 'centres' worth dealing with, list the most important in order of priority, spread the responsibility around, and monitor
the results. This may mean leaving some 'centres' out. So be it. Priorities
can always be changed and there is no reason for the list to remain static.

Articles/Papers

Even a simple press release is dependent on having something to say, but
this is even more true of articles. Their promotional power is often
considerable and they can sometimes earn a small fee. More importantly,
they provide an opportunity to demonstrate your approach, expertise,
competence and professionalism; in a service business where the 'product' cannot be tried and tested, therefore, as a form of exposure to the
public they are especially valuable. (Why else would I agree to write this
book!)

Investigation will often reveal a much greater list of potential places of
publication than first thought might suggest. Many periodicals find it
quite difficult to find people to contribute articles – or at least to do so
reliably. Editors of journals like to work with people who 'deliver'; that is
who present a manuscript on time, tied to whatever layout and form the
magazine specifies. Those who do this and write something worth

publishing can expect to be asked to contribute again or may make further suggestions themselves.

It is important that opportunities in this area are taken up. If the senior partner cannot string two words together, then someone else can do it. One person may brief another to do the writing (joint authorship is quite acceptable). It is worth organising, planning and thinking about articles in these ways so that something happens – the daunting thought of a blank sheet of paper and 2,000 words to write on it will otherwise tend to ensure that nothing does happen.

ACTION
Consider linking some of these activities to maximise impact – an article written up from a conference session, for instance, or vice versa.

Conclusion

A number of times in this chapter I have used the words 'it does not just happen', and certainly at this stage of summing up, I make no apology for using them again – planning promotional activity is the key to success in this whole area and it does not just happen. Chapter 3 set out the sequence and thinking process involved. There is a danger that this seems such a daunting process that it gets left undone, with any promotional tasks being handled on an *ad hoc* basis. Although an element of promotion can usefully become responsive, for instance a request for a specific article which is then written, unless the firm is to be at the mercy of events there is no escape from the need to plan.

In fact, the planning process need not be onerous, certainly not once the first plan, which may be a more complicated process, has been set out. This is because planning is a 'rolling' process, the plan only needing updating and extending once it exists rather than starting again from scratch. As long as it exists in writing, this updating need not be elaborate. The key element is probably best kept in diary form, translating overall intentions to timed action and this can be run forward literally month by month.

Another crucial factor in the whole process is responsibility. It is in many ways not easy for a firm, geared to directing the professional work, to ensure that other tasks, however important, get the necessary commitment; especially one that may in the early stages be considered peripheral. Responsibility means just that; it does not imply doing all the work, but making sure it does get done. Someone has to take on this role. In the larger firms this is easier, perhaps; at least the sole practitioner knows unequivocally who must do it, but someone must.

A further key to success in promotion is co-ordination, and with that, timing. Whether it is making sure the graduate recruitment brochure is ready before the recruitment campaign starts, or that sales activity is implemented at the right stage of the financial year, both are critical. It is in this respect that the laying of responsibility is so important, as someone must set the timing and pull the strings together – something which is difficult to achieve through a committee.

EXAMPLE

Take a classic promotion: the newsletter that so many accountancy firms circulate after a Budget. The very way this is instigated sometimes categorises how it will be regarded and progressed. It is an awkward job – important, but requiring a lot of work in a short time to get it out and not much thanks for whoever takes it on. 'John did it last year, perhaps you, Mike, can do it this time', says the senior partner. Sighs of relief from everyone else; on to the next item on the agenda.

In fact, if we think about what we want from any promotion, the task quickly becomes clearer, and it is not just printing and circulating a newsletter. Of course there are other factors, greater visibility and better image for the firm, but what we really want is meetings – to engender enough interest to get people to sit down individually and talk to us. From such meetings come new business.

So if we plan back from new business (a new project or client), we can see a number of stages that, appropriately arranged, are most likely to produce what we want. This will take the form of a main sequence with other activities producing an overlapping and enhanced effect. For example:

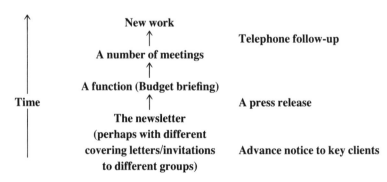

With clear objectives (a specific number of meetings, with specified types of people) the amount and detail of activity necessary to initiate this becomes clearer. Then we can ask questions, the answers to which will prompt a series of planned actions, taken in a way designed to be most likely to produce the results we want.

Here are some examples.

- What kind of newsletter (ours/bought in/a combination)?
- What covering letter? And how many different ones?
- A function? If so what type, when, with what brief, speakers, etc.?
- What supporting activity is necessary? Press release etc?
- What administrative action is necessary to set all this up?
- Who should be involved?
- What lead times are involved (almost certainly longer than you think)?

Beyond this we need to be sure the basic, creative questions are asked.

- Is a standard newsletter (like last year) enough?
- What alternatives are there etc.?

It is very easy to perpetuate the same approaches.

Clearly, what is described here involves more than simply a decision as to who will 'get the newsletter out'. But the alternatives may well be poles apart. On the one hand, we may look back and are able to say it went well – meaning only that it was produced, looked attractive, went out on time, and a few people mentioned receiving it or expressed their thanks. On the other hand, we may find ourselves scheduling genuinely useful, additive meetings, working towards specific objectives, and in due course signing up new projects or clients as a result: with peripheral activity, a press comment, for instance, adding to the impact. In other words the additional trouble, largely more thought, further ahead, can pay dividends.

If one accepts that the process discussed here is necessary and even assuming the process is well co-ordinated, then the detailed skills involved may still be, to one degree or another, alien. This in turn may imply the necessity for either external support, or training or both. Courses tailored to the professions, which are offered on marketing topics, go some way towards providing help, but with some large firms spending considerable resources on training, more than this may be helpful. Certainly, in circumstances where, for instance, a new brochure is being put together, it is a pity to 'spoil the ship for a ha'p'orth of tar'. A graphically superb treatment of a poor message in a brochure may do just that and might have benefited from a bit more professional assistance to make sure it was right.

The last point which should be made in summary concerns commitment and persistence; this applies both overall and to the finer details. It is often that extra call, sometimes not made, to an editor about a possible article, to an intermediary about a possible collaboration, that pays dividends. It is easy to rationalise, usually with reference to the pressures (and fees) of client work, about why there is never time to follow up opportunities. On the other hand, it is galling to follow one up only to find that you have been pipped at the post by a competitor.

Of course it is easier to read about the promotional ideas and planned approaches presented here than it is to implement them, and just saying 'Yes, we should do that' does not take you too far. Therefore, to bridge the gap between the theory and implementation, the need to originate and implement a promotional plan should again be stressed. The approach to planning is essentially practical, and is designed to facilitate implementation and increase the chances of gaining new business.

After that it is up to you. An increasing proportion of the business and profit you want in the future will be dependent on promotion.

Promotion has only one final objective, to produce more business. To do that it must be persuasive; promotion that is so circumspect as to be less than persuasive is not just less effective, but useless. This is as true of direct mail as of anything yet discussed. Direct mail will be the subject of the next chapter.

5 PROMOTION BY POST
Making it appropriate and effective

'What is written without effort is
in general read without pleasure.'

Samuel Johnson

Promotion by post merits its own chapter in this book for several reasons. It is already well proven as an especially useful technique for professional service firms. But it is deceptive, appearing easier to use than it is. In addition, many of the principles explored in detail here have relevance for other forms of promotion, a brochure, for example, may or may not be designed for mailing purposes, but it is always important.

Like all promotional techniques, direct mail cannot be considered in isolation. It is part of the mix, and may most appropriately be used in conjunction with other techniques, all intended to produce enquiries that will then need to be converted by personal persuasive selling skills, to actual signed-up clients.

Somehow, feelings about direct mail seem to run high. Some people regard it as intrusive. Everyone appears to know someone who has been mailed three times in the same week about something entirely inappropriate, and addressed wrongly as 'Dear Madam'. Some people regard it as more than intrusive, ranking it somewhere between picking your teeth in public or being unkind to animals.

In the world of professional services, and elsewhere, existing views may be deeply ingrained. Way back in the days BA (before advertising), whether such views were accurate or not did not matter, no advertising was permitted and there the matter ended. Now, after the changes to the guidelines that permit advertising, direct mail and more, building up an increasing list of permissible techniques which, for many, mean a whole range of elements becomes important.

They must all be viewed dispassionately and the best mix selected and deployed. 'Best' in this context means most cost-effective, and most likely to have the desired, promotional effect. If one element is omitted or underrated simply through prejudice, that is a waste. Business is becoming too precious to allow any of it to go by default.

Direct mail is, in fact, only a form of advertising. No more, no less; albeit a specialised form. It is used very successfully in a wide range of industries and applications, many of them perfectly respectable – charities, banks, building societies and so on. What is more, although of course there is the occasional annoyance, it is used for the most part without upsetting the people to whom it is directed. If they are not interested, they throw it away; a process which is not really so unlike turning over an advertisement page in a magazine in which one is not interested. Of course direct mail is wasteful. It hurts to think of so many of your carefully penned words ending up in the bin. But it is no more wasteful than other forms of advertising. All advertising is in a sense wasteful – what matters is whether it produces a cost-effective response, whether it pays for itself long term.

Contrary to popular belief, direct mail is read. The post office, who spend a great deal of time and money studying the effectiveness of direct mail, recently demonstrated through research that more than 90 per cent of it is opened and more than 75 per cent of it is read. The trick is less to achieve this, therefore, than to ensure your offering will stand out from others, will generate interest and will be seen as persuasive.

So direct mail does not replace anything, rather it adds to the range of techniques available. It is no more a magic formula than any other individual technique. But it is likely to suit professional services well. It is flexible; certainly more flexible than advertising. Direct mail may mean either four letters, or 40, 400, 4,000 or 40,000. It does not have to be done on the grand scale, it can be targeted at small specific groups; it can be undertaken progressively with so many shots per week or month being sent. It is personal and can be directed at the decision-makers, their advisers or both. It is controllable, it can be tested, implemented progressively and results can be monitored to ensure it provides a cost-effective element in the total promotional mix. As it is likely to be low cost per contract, and campaigns can be varied so much in size, there are likely to be very few firms which could not experiment with the technique. It is specific and may be directed broadly, selling the firm, or be part of the promotion of particular services.

So, direct mail has a lot going for it. It is a proven technique in other fields, it can be used on a small scale, it can be targeted on specific market segments, and it can be tested and monitored much more easily than many other forms of promotion. It may well prove even more important to the development of professional firms than other forms of advertising. Time will tell.

So, if you have read this far, I hope you continue with an open mind to read this review of exactly what direct mail is and how it can contribute to your overall promotional activity.

We will consider first some of the background factors and the basics of the component parts of a direct mail campaign before looking at how, creatively, the response to it can be ensured.

Who to mail

Who, rather than what, because it is very much better to mail individuals by name rather than organisations. It is, of course, possible to address 'The Finance Director, XYZ Limited', but if you know the name of the appropriate contact this will always produce better results.

The intention is to communicate with decision-makers and, to a lesser extent, with influencers. However, the people a particular firm needs to approach are not an easy group to define. It will vary depending on the size of the firm, where it is located and what mixture of services it offers. It will include individuals, those in whatever position who are regarded as decision-makers and others who can in any way act as recommenders.

Often, in fact, professionals do not have a clear idea of who is most important. A firm may think they are in touch with all local recommenders, say, while having no system to check that contact is occurring regularly, nor to link results to the contacts which do occur. No system may exist either to hold names and addresses in comprehensive form so that they can be mailed conveniently. As a result, contact may be diluted with an important influencer. There may be similar uncertainty regarding client contacting, and certainly with prospective clients.

An interesting area of research, and one that is being used by some professionals is into exactly how, by whom and in what circumstances particular services are purchased.

The effectiveness of any mailing is clearly dependent on mailing the right people, i.e. on the quality of the mailing list. There are two separate approaches to the question of lists, either build your own or use other people's (or a combination of both, as they are not mutually exclusive).

Outside sources of lists abound, available most often for rent, sometimes for outright purchase. Rented lists are well guarded and will always include 'seeded' names so that the owner of the list can monitor their use. This prevents lists hired for one-time use being copied and used again. Using outside lists can be very useful, not least because it avoids the problem of holding them, printing off labels and much of the administrative detail involved. Sources of lists are well documented (the regularly updated *Direct Mail Databook* published by Gower Publishing is a good reference, for example).

At the same time, informal sources, ranging from companies you know to chambers of trade or commerce, may also be useful. In addition, you can cull names from a wealth of directories (those that do not make their entries available in list form), not simply to mail once, but to record and use again.

Holding and maintaining the list

Mailing lists are a perishable commodity. They have to be maintained and updated. The latter is important; people move jobs, positions, addresses and like to be addressed correctly.

The simplest form of list maintenance is a card index and for some small lists this may be quite adequate. Beyond this some settle for lists on A4 sheets that can be photocopied direct on to A4 labelled sheets, but, further than this, the computer revolution has made many a labelling system obsolete. Although some firms still use metal plate systems, for example, for all practical purposes list-holding now necessitates a computer. As a result most, even quite small, systems are able to hold lists and can be programmed with additional facilities (for instance, mail-merging systems which allow letters to be produced with the name on the label used in the letter).

Computer companies, and their distributors, will be only too willing to offer help and advice. If you have an existing system, the new element must be compatible with it and while there is a profusion of good standard software available, it is important that this will give you the exact operation you want.

For example, you may wish to:

- print out by company/organisation as well as individual names;
- rebate-sort, i.e. to deliver post to the post office pre-sorted in a way that qualifies for lower rates (though note that it also takes longer to deliver);
- link into other record systems, client, debtors etc.;

- print quietly or at a certain speed;

or simply avoid your labels looking as if they have come off a computer system.

All the caveats of purchasing this sort of equipment apply. Like all such systems, exactly what will suit you needs some investigation if you are to end up with something truly suitable. Even when you do, then as the saying has it 'when your system works well, it's obsolete'. I make no attempt here to itemise specific equipment or software as what is available changes while you watch. But this is no excuse not to make decisions to buy. However long you wait, there will always be a better system available tomorrow.

Deciding the message

Before any sort of mailshot or campaign can be put together, you must decide the objectives; what are you selling and what response are you looking to prompt? You may say that the answer to this is obvious. You want to sell the firm and its services, and you want people to buy them, but this may prove too simplistic a view to enable the construction of an effective mailshot.

Like all promotion, direct mail can only produce enquiries. It may do so in specific ways:

- requests for information;
- agreement to a meeting;
- acceptance of an invitation to a function;

for example, but recipients are unlikely to come, cheque in hand, to the door saying 'Please take this, and start Monday'. So you will have to sell them on a route to a purchase decision as well as on the service you offer.

To do this, you must be clear what the service is. If you ask (as I do on courses), say, an accountant to describe his firm and the services it provides, he will usually do so by saying they offer such things as 'personal service', 'a comprehensive range of accounting services', or 'partner supervision of every client's work'. This sounds fine until you ponder, or ask, what exactly is 'personal service', for instance, – service by people? So? It is not exactly a full description. This problem is compounded by the fact that if you ask another accountant the same question he says such things as 'We offer personal service . . . a comprehensive range of services . . . partner supervision of every client's work'. Very much the same occurs if the professional is a surveyor, architect or consultant.

The rather introspective attitude that will often produce this line is unlikely to excite the prospective client; it will now even make it easy for him to differentiate one firm from another. In circumstances where so many different professionals report that it is now the norm for a prospective client to talk to more than one firm, it is clearly important that some differentiation should be built into the message.

Until this area is sorted out you stand little chance of putting together an effective direct mail campaign. Two approaches will clarify the situation. The first relates to the business plan for the firm. Is it here that the base message as to what kind of firm you are, and want to be, is forged. It may be a long and difficult process, but there needs to be a consensus as to the correct 'positioning' for the firm. Is it really to be all things to all people, or does it specialise in some way, in which case, in what way? This is not to say that such statements are unchangeable and are cast in tablets of stone. The firm is no doubt evolving, the market is certainly dynamic, so what is right for today will have to include a direction for tomorrow. Usually, much of the thinking has been going on, much of the information is there; you have only to make yourself put into words, what – in detail – you really mean by saying 'personal service' in your firm to see how much more there is to say.

The same applies to individual services as has been stated for the firm. An architect designs buildings. An accountant conducts audits. A designer designs . . . what? In each case, what exactly do these statements mean? Each implies a range of different things. Larger, smaller; more or less complex. For each, it is necessary to state more specifically what is involved.

Secondly, you must be able to take the clients' view in the way you put over the message. It is empathy with the client that removes the introspection referred to earlier, and which will need to be reflected throughout the task of putting together any sort of direct mail promotion. Knowing how and why clients view your services as they do is a prerequisite to putting any promotional material together, especially material for direct mail, which may be distributed widely and contain elements that are retained by recipients or used regularly for some time as with an accompanying brochure.

The clients' viewpoint

It has been said, in other fields of business, 'Don't sell products – sell benefits'. The same principle applies to professional services. This has been mentioned before and will be discussed in more detail in Chapter 6.

The response

As was mentioned at the beginning of this chapter, having clear objectives for promotion includes having a clear idea what response is looked for as a result of receipt of the 'shot'. Put simply, what do you want people to do if they are interested?

One action, extensively used elsewhere, should be mentioned here first (while making it clear that it is specifically excluded by some professions' current ethical guidelines). That action is telephone follow up. It is often very effective to say in your letter, 'I will telephone you in a few days', and then take the initiative. Otherwise, the need is thus to offer other options of response which will appeal, and do so sufficiently to prompt the recipient to take the initiative.

The temptation is perhaps to go for simplicity – you ring us; or for what we want most – come and see us for a discussion. The more persuasive you feel your message is, the stronger this temptation may be.

Yet the same principle of empathy must be applied. The response, or responses – many direct mailshots provide a choice – must be made attractive in client terms. Will they want to send for more information? If so, how much should we give them (without solving the problem) and in what form? Will they want to meet us? If so, who – senior partner or specialist? Where – our offices, theirs or a neutral venue? Alone or with others – their colleagues, or others interested, i.e. would they expect or like to attend an event? Even minor details are important. For example, they may be more likely to phone us if we pay for the call, or return a card if the postage is paid.

Once a clear view of these areas has been formed, the question of how much direct mail is necessary must be considered, before considering the elements that make up a direct mail promotion.

How much direct mail is necessary?

How long is a piece of string? Unless the question is defined, any answer will do. Assume the firm has a quantified and timed statement of its total required level of fees for the planning period, usually the fiscal year. It must also assess what proportion of total fees can be expected to come in automatically and therefore the balance which will require positive promotion.

This balance must then be examined against marketing strategies and broken down by service type, by marketing or industry sector, and by existing or new clients to give purpose and focus to the promotion.

The greatest opportunity for immediate increased fees normally lies in selling more of the range of your services to existing clients. With current clients, the true needs are more obvious, your credibility is higher, and the amount of time needed to sell the ideas will thus be smaller, as will the selling cost. You can estimate this, and see what more is necessary from new promotion. In both cases this must be linked to your ability to sell.

As far as possible, the balance of business required should also be divided up and assigned to partners and managers as new business sales targets. Because clients naturally prefer professionals who can sell, rather than professional salespeople, all partners and managers responsible for clients should have sales targets agreed, even though they will not necessarily be of equal magnitude.

The targets, of course, represent only the forecast, the objective to be achieved. To complete the sales plan, the activities to achieve targets must also be specified. To recap on a topic referred to in Chapter 2 on marketing planning, we must know the following.

- How many proposals need to be accepted (whether formal or informal)? i.e. Total new business fees required and average new business order size.
- How many proposals need to be submitted? i.e. Number of proposals accepted × Average conversion rate
- How many enquiries must be received?
- How many new clients must be secured? In which markets? With which services?

The intention of such precise specification is twofold. First, so that any tactical activity is positive and not simply responsive. Secondly, so that by timing the activities the 'feast and famine' cycle of work, so characteristic of many service companies, is avoided and promotional activity can be paced so that any positive response can be dealt with. For most firms 10 enquiries a week for a year are more useful than 500 all on one day. Decisions in this area are dependent on the collection of appropriate information and a degree of analysis.

Causal analysis will define what cause/effect relationship exists between promotional effort, contacts gained and contracts booked. This helps in deciding on the most cost-effective use of promotional time and money. Lead-time analysis – analysing the lead times between contact and proposal, and proposal and booking, is critical in deciding when sales effort must be stepped up, or when recruitment will be needed. It also has tactical use in signalling possible cash-flow problems several months ahead. If you can form a view of the number of new contracts necessary, then the size of any necessary promotional campaign is put into perspective. Balanced with a view of budget and an idea of the promotional 'mix', the amount of direct mail necessary through the year can be estimated. This kind of analysis will never be exactly right, but perfection should not be made the enemy of the good – a reasonable estimate, which will no doubt get better over time, can act as a useful signpost. (Here we are recapping on the calculation shown in Chapter 2, you may like to remind yourself of the ratios involved – see page 43).

It is now time to consider what makes up a direct mail campaign.

The elements of the 'shot'

What goes out to the client is put together from essentially four elements, brochures or leaflets, a covering letter, a reply facility and, of course, an envelope. While the envelope is always necessary (I cannot see postcards being used by professionals, though they are, very successfully, by the travel trade), the other components can be varied. A 'shot' might consist only of a letter, or only of a brochure, or of a brochure that incorporates a reply coupon; or it might be more elaborate, a letter plus two or three brochures, and a reply form and a return envelope. Clearly, many permutations are possible. Together the package must carry the total message and that message must be sufficiently persuasive to prompt action from a number of recipients which will make the whole exercise cost-effective.

The word 'mailshot' implies one such mailing, a campaign implies a number over time which may be about different elements of the services, separate except that they are clearly from the same source. Alternatively, shots may be closer and linked, virtually one message stretched across say two separate entities, so that repetition reinforces its impact.

As the way things are done in some cases relates to more than one element or indeed to the package as a whole, in the next sections we look at the basic considerations regarding each element:

- the envelope;
- brochures and leaflets;
- the covering letter;
- the reply device.

The process of creatively putting the promotion together is examined separately later, revisiting some of the elements.

In every case a range of possible approaches, styles and details are identified. Any mailshot using them all would simply submerge under its own gimmicks and become self-defeating. Each does have its place, however, and carefully orchestrated, various combinations can be very effective. It is perhaps important not to take a censorious line in considering them. Of course, there are dangers of inappropriate approaches with professional services, but bear the client in mind and remember that what one man finds pushy, another finds persuasive. What matters ultimately is what causes a satisfactory response, and nothing that does so in a way clients find acceptable should be overlooked. Remember also that the effect of many detailed factors involved throughout the package builds up; a number of points which individually seem of little significance may together increase the response rate noticeably. That said, let us start by taking a look at what the recipient sees first.

The envelope

This must be serviceable. This sounds obvious, but if there are a number of enclosures the envelope must get them to their destination unscathed. Some feel quality directly affects response rates, believing that a white envelope is better than a manilla one. Like many of the possible permutations that are being reviewed, this can be tested (see page 143). An 'If undelivered return to address' message can be included. This may help to avoid waste, or prompt updates to the list by identifying when things are wrongly addressed.

Of course, some recipients will not see envelopes as their secretaries will open the mail. But some will, and some secretaries will clip an informative envelope to the contents before passing it on. So you may consider having the first part of the message printed on the envelope. The purpose of the envelope carrying such a message is not so much to help ensure they are opened (research shows that most are), it is more to influence the frame of mind in which they are opened, aiming to generate some, albeit small, interest even at this early stage. If such a message is appropriate, it may be complete in itself – 'Details enclosed of how to reduce your tax bill', questioning – 'Do you want to pay less tax?', or leave more to be explained by the contents – 'A way to save money . . . details inside'.

Other devices are possible. For example, a window envelope may allow a glimpse of the contents, colour may add to the effect and reflect a corporate colour used inside. Important though the envelope may be, it is what is inside that really generates the response. Post office regulations specify how much and what form of printing is allowed on the envelope.

Brochures and leaflets

These may be items used elsewhere, brochures you give to bank managers, leaflets you display in reception. There is, however, no reason why such material should be suitable and you may need to produce new material, tailored specifically to the job in hand.

In either case, the brochure is unlikely to set out to tell people 'everything there is to know about the firm', rather it must prompt a desire for discussion. Too much information can even have the reverse effect. One hotel, sending direct mail to prompt conference business, found that the numbers of visitors coming to look at the hotel doubled when they replaced a short letter and glossy comprehensive brochure with a longer letter, no brochure and an invitation. This is, of course, a different area but, with a little experience in professional services that can be quoted, this sort of parallel seems worth noting.

The production of brochures generally is an area of increasing professionalism, and great care is needed in defining the objective, creating the right message and making sure the brochure looks good, and reflects the image the firm intends to project. The days of the bland, general brochure, very similar to those of other firms, describing the chronological history of the firm and everything it does, and intended to be used for everything, is rapidly passing. What is needed now is the ability to match each objective in each particular area with something specifically designed for the job. This may mean producing separate brochures for recruitment and client usage. It may mean the 'corporate' brochure is a folder with separate inserts aimed at different target groups or different types of client, or it may mean a revised brochure every year, it may even mean a difference between the sort of brochure that is right to give a prospective client after a preliminary meeting and the sort that is suitable to present to an intermediary.

For direct mail purposes the brochure or leaflet concerned must be specific to the objective set for the particular promotion. Brochures may need to be reasonably self-standing. After all they may get separated from the covering letter, but the total content – letter plus brochure – needs to hang together, to produce a complete and integrated message.

Overall, what must be created is something that is accurately directed at a specific group, with a clear objective in mind and – above all – that is persuasive. This may seem basic; promotional material is there to inform, but it must do so persuasively. That is its prime purpose. The professions have had a tendency in the past to produce material that, while no doubt ethical, is so circumspect as to be largely ineffective. This does not mean moving to something that is inappropriately strident (which might in any case be self-defeating), but it does mean a greater emphasis on client need and benefits (what services do for people, rather than what they are).

Essentially, a less introspective approach, better designed to its purpose, is the rule. What does this mean?

- A front cover that has the name of the firm clearly shown and/or that makes some offer of benefit. The reader must be clear, at a glance, why he should read on.
- Leaflets are expensive, so you cannot afford to waste space. There is, or should be, lots to say about the services you provide.
- It should make clear how a reader makes contact with the firm. This is, after all, the whole purpose of the communication.
- Photographs, or any illustrations, should be clear, captioned if appropriate, and have some bearing on the content.
- Above all the text must be truly oriented to the client, their views, their needs, and persuasively and attractively written.

More than one brochure may be necessary, and these may be different in nature. For example, let us assume a brochure is being sent out about a particular service; if the chosen response is to try to persuade people to attend an informal seminar as a first step to an individual meeting, then two brochures may be necessary. One about the service and another, probably smaller, about the event.

There are few rules to be observed about brochures, and those rules that one might define are made to be broken. This is because they must be *creatively* constructed to reflect the image of the firm graphically, differentiate it from its competitors and aim their chosen message directly at the target group addressed.

> ACTION
> Consider setting a review date for every document printed, not too
> far ahead – brochures can get out of date fast, so that a revised
> reprint can be done if appropriate.

The covering letter

Basics first. It must look right. It must be attractively laid out, grammatically correct and well presented. In selling a professional service this is
especially important since it gives the impression that it has originated in
an efficient and reputable firm.

The letterhead itself is important to the image, up to date yet not 'over
the top' is what should be aimed at, and this is not easy.

Subjective judgements are involved. Ultimately, it is a matter of
opinion and in a partnership this can sometimes mean a safe compromise
which may dilute impact. Consider too whether your standard letterhead
is right for direct mail. Perhaps you should try something different.
Figures 5.1, 5.2 and 5.3, using material from my own company, show how
the impact can be varied by putting information at the top of the page, as
with many standard letterheads, using a different top, or moving all
letterhead information to the bottom of the page so that a headline alone
shows at the top.

The salutation is the next important item to consider. Numbers may
preclude individual salutations. If you are not saying 'Dear Mr Smith', or
'Dear John', what do you say? One answer is nothing. Simply start with a
heading, it does not preclude you finishing with your name. In this case
you should omit 'Yours sincerely' and set the name close enough to the
text so that it does not look as if the signature is forgotten, or matching the
signature (or signatures) in to give a personal touch. If you are only
mailing small quantities you can actually sign them. Figure 5.4 makes this
clear.

On the other occasions a standardised opening may be necessary, for
example: Dear Client (that at least is clear), Dear Sir, Dear Reader, Dear
Colleague, Dear Finance Director (or other appropriate title) etc.

In many ways none of these are taken to be more than a token greeting
and, unless it is something really novel, will have comparatively little
impact. If you can find a form of words you like, perhaps almost anything
is better than 'Dear Sir'!

In selling, face to face, you can adapt your approach to the individual

Figure 5.1 and 5.2 Examples of different letterheads

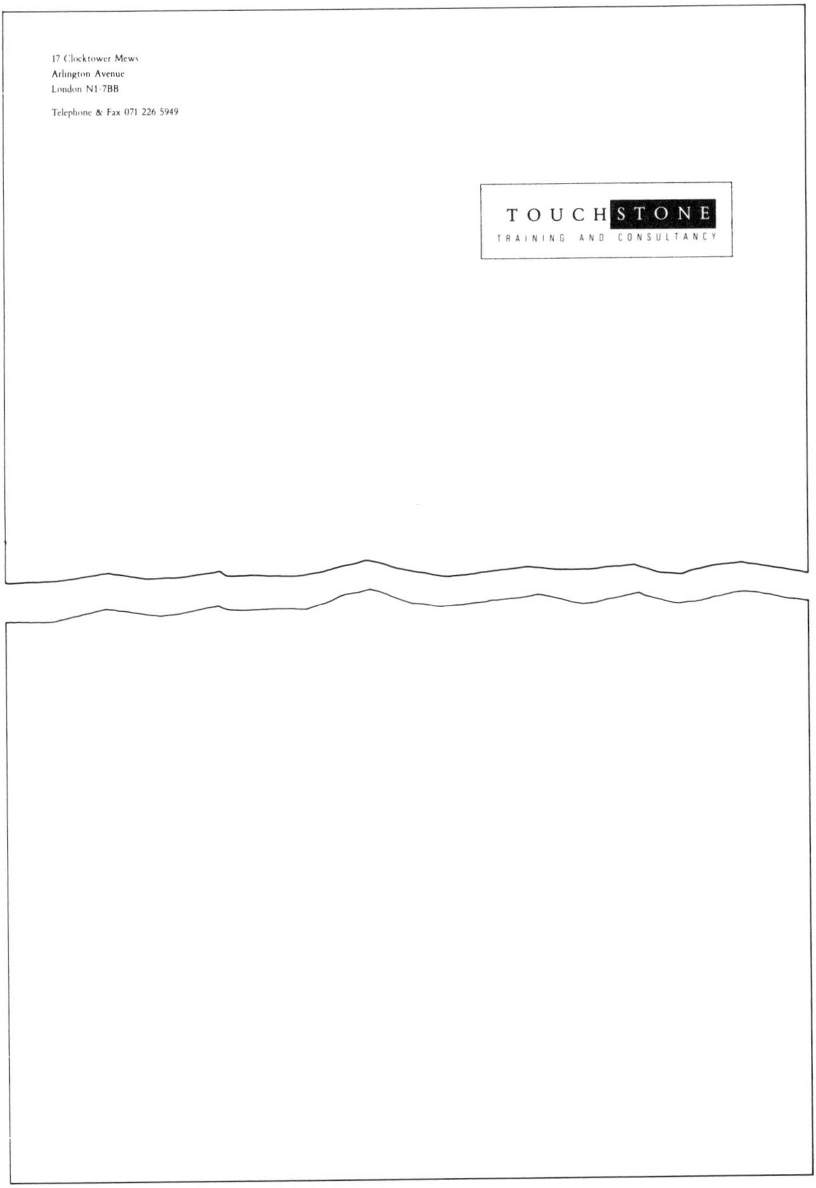

17 Clocktower Mews
Arlington Avenue
London N1 7BB

Telephone & Fax 071 226 5949

TOUCH**STONE**
TRAINING AND CONSULTANCY

Figure 5.2

Marketing
Training Newsletter

17 Clocktower Mews
Arlington Avenue
London N1·7BB

Telephone & Fax 071 226 5949

TOUCHSTONE
TRAINING AND CONSULTANCY

Figure 5.3

'It gave me many
practical ideas I
can use at once'

What one participant said about the seminar which ...

A minimal time spent on such a seminar can begin to give your firm an unfair
competitive advantage - do not hesitate to take it.

PATRICK FORSYTH

[Publication date]

17 Clocktower Mews
Arlington Avenue
London N1 7BB

Telephone & Fax 071 226 5949

Figure 5.4

you are with as the conversation proceeds. In a letter this is not possible, and a formula to structure the approach is useful. The classic sales acronym AIDA (attention/interest/desire/action) works well in providing a structure for letters, and represents accurately the job to be done in prompting a response.

Before looking at how such a structure helps the composition of the letter, consider for a moment what happens when it is received. People seldom read a letter immediately in the same sequence in which it was written. Their eyes flick from the sender's address to the ending, then to the greeting and the first sentence, skim to the last – and then, if the sender is lucky, back to the first sentence for a more careful reading of the whole letter. Research has been done showing a clear sequence (see Figure 5.1), so the first sentence is an important element in 'holding' the reader, and it should arouse immediate interest.

With that in mind consider the sequence of the letter, first as a whole. It will, I hope, be clear by now that the copy for the letter – as for the brochure(s) in fact – is crucial. You are unlikely to be able to dictate it straight away, certainly not to begin with.

A letter will need thinking about, planning, and it will probably go through a number of drafts. Write down the key points, headings, identify the main benefits – create a skeleton. Then with some guidelines in mind you can look at how it all goes together.

Attention – the opening
The most important part of the letter is the start. It will determine whether the rest of the letter is read. The opening may be quite short, a heading perhaps, a couple of sentences, two paragraphs, but it is disproportionately important. A good start will help as you write the letter, as well as ensuring the recipient reads it. Omit or keep references short and make subject headings to the point – the reader's point. Do not use 'Re'. Make sure the start of the letter will command attention, gain interest, and lead easily into the main text. For example:

- ask a 'Yes' question;
- tell the reader why you are writing to him particularly;
- tell him why he should read the letter;
- flatter him (carefully);
- tell him what he might lose if he ignores the message;
- give him some 'mind-bending' news (if you have any).

① (Letterhead) ②

⑥ _____

⑤

③

④ PS _____

_____

①, ②, ③—information, taken in very fast. Who is it from?
④   —if there is one, the PS is the 'most read part of any letter'.
⑤   —an overall scan – do I have to read it all? – use of headings will affect
        this view.
⑥   —from beginning on (provided the opening is effective).

Figure 5.5   Letters: reading sequence

Interest/desire – the body of the letter
The body of the letter runs straight on from the opening. It must consider
the reader's needs or problems from his point of view. It must interest

him. It must get the reader nodding in agreement, 'Yes, I wish you could help me on that'.

Of course you are able to help him. In drafting you must write what you intend for him and of course list the benefits you can offer, not features, and in particular the benefits which will help him solve his problem and satisfy his needs.

You have to anticipate his possible objections to your proposition in order to select your strongest benefits and most convincing answers. If there is a need to counter objections, then you may need to make your letter longer and give proof, for example comment from a third party that the benefits are genuine. However, remember to keep the letter as short as possible – but still as long as necessary to complete the case. If that is two, three or more pages, so be it.

It is easy to find yourself quoting the literature that will accompany the letter to the reader. If you were writing a lecture on the subject, you would probably need all that information. When writing to a prospective client you have to select just the key benefits which will be of particular value to the reader and which support the literature.

The body copy must:

- keep the reader's immediate interest;
- develop that interest with the best benefit;
- win him over with a second and then further benefits.

The next job is to ensure action from the reader by a firm close.

Action – the letter ending
In closing you can make a (short) summary of the benefits of the proposition. Having decided on the action you are wanting the reader to take, you must be positive about getting it.

It is necessary to nudge the reader into action with a decisive close. Do not use phrases like these:

'We look forward to hearing . . .'
'I trust you have given . . .'
'. . . favour of your instructions'
'. . . doing business with you'
'I hope I can be of further assistance',

which are really phrases added as padding between the last point and 'Yours sincerely'. Instead use real closing phrases, for example.

The alternative close:

- ask him to telephone or write;
- telephone or use the reply-paid envelope;
- ask for a meeting or more information.

Immediate gain:

- return the card today and your profitability could be improved.

'Best' solution:

- you want a system that can cope with occasional off-peak demands, that is easy to operate by semi-skilled staff and is presented in a form that will encourage line managers to use it.

   The best fit with all these requirements is our system 'X'.

   Return the card indicating the best time to install it.'

Direct request:

- post the card today;
- telephone us without delay.

In signing off do not automatically use 'Yours faithfully' for 'Dear Sir', and 'Yours sincerely' when the letter is addressed to an individual, but match your phrase to the tone of your general approach. Consider too who will have their name at the bottom of the letter. Replies will tend to come back to them, so should it be the senior partner, marketing partner, a specialist – and how well are they able to cope with any response? Make sure their name is typed as well, as signatures tend to be awkward to read, and that a note of the position they hold in the firm is included. People like to know with whom they are dealing.

   PS Remember the power of the postscript. Secretaries will tell you they are for things inadvertently left out, while direct mailers will tell you they get read. Use them for repetition or to add a final benefit – it can add strength to the message.

   PPS Some people even use two!

   Finally, we should consider the language used in such letters. Many people have acquired a habit of artificiality in writing, approaching it quite differently from their way of talking to a client, and in a way that can reduce your chances of making a sale through over-formality.

The language
Remember, your intention when writing letters is to prompt the reader to action rather than demonstrate your 'Oxford English'. You should write

much as you speak.
  HERE ARE SOME USEFUL RULES.

Be clear	—Make sure that the message is straightforward and uncluttered by 'padding'. Use short words and phrases. Avoid jargon.
Be natural	—Do not project yourself differently just because it is in writing.
Be positive	—In tone and emphasis (be helpful).
Be courteous	—Always
Be efficient	—Project the right image.
Be personal	—Use 'I' – say what *you* will do.
Be appreciative	—Thank you is a good phrase.

The checklist below examines specific aspects of the language used in letters. I hope this is not labouring the point, but professionals, with a strong background in the technicalities of what they do, can have a tendency towards gobbledegook. I recently saw a note tabled at a board meeting on recommendations proposed by a broker about pension schemes. After a long silence someone said 'I don't understand it', immediately joined by a chorus of 'Neither do I'. This must not be the general reaction to the material contained in your direct mail.

PERSUASIVE LANGUAGE CHECKLIST

● *Avoid trite openings*
  We respectfully suggest . . .
  We have pleasure in attaching . . .
  Referring to the attached . . .
  This letter is for the purpose of requesting . . .

● *Avoid pomposity*
  We beg to advise . . .
  The position with regard to . . .
  It will be appreciated that . . .
  It is suggested that the reasons . . .
  The undersigned/writer . . .
  May we take this opportunity of . . .
  Allow me to say in this instance . . .
  Having regard to the fact that . . .
  We should point out that . . .
  Answering in the affirmative/negative . . .

We are not in a position to . . .
The opportunity is taken to mention . . .
Despatched under separate cover . . .

- *Avoid coldness and bad psychology*
Advise/inform
Desire
Learn/note
Obtain
Regret
Trust

- *Avoid cliché endings*
Thanking you in advance
Assuring you of our best attention at all times, we remain . . .
Trusting we may be favoured with . . .
Awaiting a favourable reply . . .
Please do not hesitate to . . .

- *Keep it simple – prefer short words to long*
Approximately **X**   about **✓**
Commencement **X**   start **✓**
Elucidate **X**   explain **✓**
Considerable **X**   great **✓**

- *Prefer one or two words to several*
At this moment in time **X**   now **✓**
Due to the fact that **X**   because **✓**
In the not too distant future **X**   soon **✓**
There can be no doubt about **X**   it is certain **✓**
Should the situation arise that **X**   if **✓**

And aim for short sentences.

And short paragraphs.

Aim for an overall effect that sounds right read out loud. Try it. Get a colleague to read your draft to you. Amend it. Sleep on it. Get it read again. There is no shame in taking a moment to get such an important piece of writing right.

Presentation

Finally, remember that the end product should be neatly presented, in a way that the reader finds convenient.

To ensure the finishing touches and add impact you should think about the following.

- Position the letter on the page according to the amount of the text. It is unattractive if there is a huge expanse of white below a very short letter. Position it lower down, in that case, or consider having two sizes of letterhead paper, and put short letters on the smaller sheets.
- 'Block' paragraphs, with double spacing between each paragraph for greater clarity and smartness.
- Leave at least 1½in at the foot of the page before going on to page two; leave a bigger space to avoid having only one or two lines (plus farewells) for the second page.
- Allow enough space for the signature, name and job title. It is better to carry the letter over on to another page than cram it in at the bottom.
- Note, at the foot of the last page, the enclosures mentioned in the text and sent with the letter.
- Staple the pages together to avoid losses.
- Number the pages.
- Number the paragraphs when a lot of points have to be covered.
- Underline all headings.

Remember layout of this sort of material cannot be simply left to the secretary or typist. The way a letter is to be presented must be specified by the writer to prevent retyping.

Graphic emphasis can be made, in this age of the word processor, in a number of ways, with:

— CAPITALS
— underlining
—   indenting
— **bold type**
— colour
— *italics*

Whilst these should not be overdone they are useful and, in whatever form and combination you select, need specifying.

The reply device
This may be a coupon, a form to be completed or a self-contained reply-paid card. Whatever format you select, its use should be 100 per cent clear. It is fatal to have someone interested to the point of taking action, being put off because how they take action seems unclear or complicated.

So make it clear. Decide what information you want. If you ask for a name and address, adding a request for their job title may make the follow up just that little bit easier. Let them tick boxes rather than write essays. Let them send their business card rather than fill in anything.

Do not forget to include your telephone number, print it clearly and consider the freephone options. It is certainly a courtesy to use reply-paid letters or cards (or freepost). If you opt for reply-paid, do make it first class, since there is something incongruous about asking for an urgent response and then offering a second-class envelope in which to send it back.

Allow enough time, since there are arrangements to be made, and you will need to liaise with the post office. The standard reply-paid format seems straightforward, but requires a licence (thereafter you only pay for those that come back) and must conform to the prescribed format in terms of both size and style of printing.

Think carefully before you omit this element of the total package – an easy means of response can make all the difference to your results. And do not treat it as a simple extra – check it carefully, particularly try asking someone else if the description of *exactly* what you want done is clear, and the method of returning it simple and appropriate.

Here is a final thought, at least for small, specialist shots. Actually putting a postage stamp on the reply envelope, rather than using a printed reply-paid format, can double your responses. Clearly it costs more, you pay for all the reply envelopes you send out rather than only those that come back, but a new client may be worth more in the long run.

Coding, testing and measurement
Having touched on the reply vehicle, as this is primarily what provides feedback, it now seems appropriate to pause and consider the monitoring of direct mail activity. One of the advantages of direct mail is its ability to be tested, and fine-tuned as a result, easily and at low cost.

The reply card can be coded either to the list used, or the mailing material, or both. In other words, different versions of the mailing can be used and a check kept on how responses vary. If different batches of reply cards are produced with variations they can be sorted and checked on receipt. The code may literally be a code, batches A and B (with A or B printed in the corner); or the address may be varied Department X or Y and so on. In this way not only can immediate response be measured but, in the longer term, conversion rates can be checked too. It could be that in monitoring two lists, one produces twice as many initial responses, but the quality of prospect and conversion rate make it less effective.

In terms of the detail of the mailing, if split runs are used a variety of comparisons may be made. This can be well worth checking and you should never underestimate the difference minor changes – which you may even regard as cosmetic – can make.

For example, check factors such as these, one against another:

Copy:	long	*vs*	short
	punchy	*vs*	conversational
Colour	one	*vs*	another
	black/white	*vs*	one colour
Reply vehicle:	card	*vs*	form
	stamp	*vs*	reply-paid
	send business card	*vs*	fill in form
Cost (fees):	reference to fees	*vs*	not
Service	specific service	*vs*	range of services
Illustrations	include	*vs*	not
	photographs	*vs*	line drawings
Offering	further information	*vs*	straight to meeting
	event as first contact	*vs*	one-to-one meeting

In fact, any variable element can be tested in this way continuously over time. Because this process inevitably makes for complications at origination and production stages, it is often neglected. The possible improvement of results that can be created as this kind of database builds up can, however, make the time and effort involved well worth while.

And what sort of results can you expect?

Response rates from direct mail vary enormously. In some fields companies make a good living from response rates of less than 1 per cent, while in others up to 50 per cent may be achieved.

EXAMPLE
It will be useful, and encouraging, therefore, to quote Cheryl Gillan, now marketing director of accountants Kidsons Impey, who remembers one particular campaign:

'In order to pull together a group of prospects for certain aspects of our service, we were running a seminar concerned with the relocation of personnel. We decided to use a specifically tailored list of senior Japanese businessmen, in organisations that would obviously have reasonable movement of personnel on an international basis. We sent them a personalised letter detailing the contents of the conference and it resulted in an acceptance rate of between 30 per cent and 40 per cent of the original list mailed. The total list was not large, probably being about 150 in number. I believe that this shows that if you choose your audience very carefully, and are producing an event in which they are most likely to have an interest, that this is where direct mail is particularly useful.'

Cheryl certainly believes in direct mail, but adds:

'It would appear that some firms when they are sending out direct mail are attempting to be gimmicky so as to appeal to the audience they are addressing. For example I recently saw a letter that was addressed to a target group of physiotherapists which finished up with the line (this is not the exact line but it is very similar) 'Let us take the back ache out of your financial problems'. I do not think this type of wording and this trivial approach really reflects well on the profession. I believe that direct mail should be:

1 targeted specifically;
2 aim to address an issue or problem that that target sector is experiencing;
3 outline the expertise and relevant services that could help with the issue;
4 make it extremely easy for the recipient of the letter to contact the sender.

I would feel very much more comfortable if all marketeers would adopt a business-like approach to this area rather than demeaning it with cheap efforts, e.g. jargon-type messages.'

Costing and timing

Because there are a variety of elements that make up the total it is essential to work out your costs carefully. Prepare a costing sheet, along the lines of the one shown in Figure 5.2, so that you know in advance what will be involved. Do not forget that those costs incurred after the material has been posted, and prompt, efficient and effective action when a reply is received also costs money.

If you are a first-time direct mail user, talk to the post office, who have a number of attractive start-up schemes, including one allowing you to send your first quantity post-free.

As well as keeping a close eye on and a written note of costs, the schedule of timings can also be usefully recorded in calendar style. Copy has to be written, brochures designed and printed, overprinted envelopes need a longer lead time when ordered, and if you are contracting out the collation, insertion and posting this also needs a little time. And so on. If you are working back from a planned arrival date – perhaps you want this to be exactly four weeks before a planned seminar – even the time in the post needs estimating. Always include yourself on the list, maybe sending

Item	£ Cost overall	£ per 000
Brochure—copy 　　　　—design 　　　　—printing		
Letter　—copy/layout 　　　　—printing		
Envelopes		
Reply mechanism—design/print		
Reply-paid (estimate)		
Mailing 　—collating 　—stapling 　—folding 　—inserting into envelopes/sealing etc 　—postage—first class 　　　　　—second class 　—rebate sorting (saving £　　　)		
Split-run, additional cost— 　　　　brochure 　　　　letter 　　　　reply mechanism 　　　　envelopes		
Other enclosures— 　　　　— 　　　　—		
Follow-up costs e.g. brochures publications Event—venue 　　　—catering 　　　—documentation		
Misc.:		
TOTAL		
Never forget the largest cost may well be your time.		

Figure 5.6　Costing sheet

one to your own office, one to your home, and to the homes of one or two colleagues, so that you can monitor exactly when people receive your promotion. And always circulate material internally well ahead of posting, together with any briefing and a special note to those who will be involved in response action once replies start to arrive. It gives quite the wrong impression if recipients telephone saying they want more information about something they have seen in a mailshot and the switchboard (or worse still a senior member of staff) can only say 'What mailshot?' Such 'own goals' must be avoided or the impact is diluted and possible new business may go by default.

Creativity

Creativity to order

Creativity is about making things look different. Perhaps in the context of direct mail and professional services, it is about making things which are essentially similar appear different. As such there can be no magic formula either for 'being creative' or, much less, for creating the 'perfect' direct mail promotion. By definition it involves seeking new approaches, rather than slavishly following a format. This section sets out some principles, and floats some ideas. But it is essentially concerned with prompting an approach that will focus the thinking in the right way, allow you to devise approaches that will create interest and give you an edge on your competition, rather than 'script' things for you. Suggestions are clearly not appropriate for every circumstance and it is certainly not suggested that every factor should be built into every promotion. The trick is in finding a fresh approach and a permutation of techniques that will put over your message in a persuasive manner.

Definition of the brief
First make some notes, and start by reviewing the whole promotional message rather than one component, the letter say, and get absolutely straight in your mind what the overall message is to be. Ask yourself particularly how what you have to say is new, unique or at least different from the way others may present themselves. To whom exactly is it aimed? And is this a sufficiently discrete group? If you try to appeal to too broad a spectrum of recipients at once, you may end up not interesting any of them because your message is not sufficiently specific. Clearly

rather different approaches, even a different tone, will be necessary for existing clients and others.

You must decide whether you are presenting the firm, or particular aspects of it, and if it is the latter what aspects you will pick? Is it of topical relevance? Can you describe it in terms of advantages and benefits and if it includes service can you describe exactly what this means? What are you going to say about costs? What about value for money? What guarantees, proof and testimonials can you offer? And, bearing in mind that the route to action is also important, how can you make the asked-for action attractive?

Put this down on paper in note form, not aiming for final copy, and try to think objectively how it will appeal. Is it the best possible approach? Would it interest *you*? If not you may need to think of additional 'hooks', elements that will generate the interest you want by focusing attention. Here are some examples.

Combinations	— Featuring two things linked together – a Budget analysis and action plan.
Team response	— Something to be responded to by more than one person – a meeting designed for the managing director and his finance director to attend together.
Limited offer	— Only a limited number can attend/of this publication is available.
Status	— Offering people the opportunity to be the first with something, such as meeting at a prestige venue, meeting local opinion leaders.
A competition	— The prize may be the product, for example in promoting personal financial planning a draw for everyone responding might offer a free consultation, or a year's assistance to the winner.
Sponsorship	— Link to an event, perhaps a charitable event, 'meet us on such and such a date, and join us at the local theatre club where we are sponsoring the production of . . . in the evening'.
Highlight the list source	— If you are using someone else's list you can opt to feature the link – 'as a member of . . .', 'as an investor with . . .'
Second chance	— Mail people a second time as a 'reminder' or increasing the appeal.

You can also highlight aspects of the overall message. Here are some examples.

Timing	— An offer that will give benefit 'before the Budget' or 'by the end of the year'.
Exclusivity	— An offer to a select group, e.g. 'only for clients', 'only for local businesspeople', 'only for farmers in Sussex'.
Something free	— Before any commitment, such as a free publication, consultation, or free attendance on a seminar. (These can be linked, i.e. the free publication is only distributed to those who attend the meeting and thus hear more of your proposition.)

Though some admit to doing a good deal more than the above to encourage prospective clients, you may want to consider carefully what you could say promotionally about such practices.

You might consider offering something that must be paid for, such as a publication, consultation or attendance on a seminar.

Even a nominal charge will give a different quality of response and produce fewer time wasters with no real intention of pursuing their interest. Or you can charge, but offer money back if the clients are not satisfied, 'If you do not feel two hours spent at our seminar is worth while we will refund your fee'. Or deduct the costs from money spent by the clients in future.

Or you could try a deluxe version, offering something available with a better, longer, more detailed version only for those replying to the mailing.

Such factors as these are clearly not mutually exclusive. They can be linked, added to, and no doubt bettered. No one knows what degree of gimmick will appeal, be careful of course, but remember that the recipients will probably take a less censorious view than you of such matters. A degree of experiment may well prove worth while and, if you are not prepared to be a pioneer, keep a sharp eye on what is done by others. Finally look carefully at your particular situation – what is there you can offer simply by taking advantage of your circumstances?

EXAMPLE
One branch office of an insurance company sent out a promotion to an explanatory event. With offices in the town centre, they offered coffee and use of their car park on a Saturday, 'spend an hour with us while your wife

goes shopping'. A simple, clever idea – they got through a lot of coffee, made good contacts and, in due course, created measurable new business.

Finally, keep in mind the things people may obtain from your services. If they will:

- make more money;
- save money;
- save time, effort or hassle;
- be more secure;
- sort problems;
- exploit opportunities;
- motivate their staff;
- impress their customers;
- persuade others more readily (their bank manager or shareholders),

you will need to say so. And if they will do it quicker, easier, more cost-effectively or more anything else, say that too. If you believe you provide a worth while service, if you believe it is of real value, have the courage of your convictions and say so. If reading your promotion does not clearly show the reader you believe, why ever should they do so?

With all this in mind you can begin to get some real copy down on paper. There are two key aspects to this, the words (the tone, language and approach you use) and the structure into which you fit the words to complete the message.

Finding the words

The point about keeping it simple has already been made. It is worth repeating here. So use short words, use short sentences.

And short paragraphs.

Do not use too much jargon; at worst this will kill a message stone dead, at best it will dilute the message. But as Bernard Shaw said 'the only golden rule is that there are no golden rules'.

This means do nothing to excess. Sometimes you will need a longer word, a long sentence and some judiciously chosen jargon.

Two other approaches should pervade the text. First, it should be written from the client's, or potential client's point of view. As such, it will say 'you' more than 'I' and 'we'; probably much more. Count the times and especially beware of sentences – and thus points – that start with 'I' or 'we'. It is the quickest way to give the text an introspective feel.

Secondly, it must be positive. It should say 'this is the case', 'this will be what is done' and will rarely say things like 'I think . . .', 'Probably' or 'Maybe'.

Experienced direct mailers talk about 'magic' words, or at least words that inject a tone that should always be present. These include – free, guarantee, new, announcing, you, now, today, win, easy, save, at once – you must not overuse them or your message will become blatantly over the top, but do not neglect them either.

You must search constantly for ways of making your copy perform better. Again, the following is designed not only to float some examples, but also to show the approach you need to cultivate.

The guidelines that follow are reviewed in terms of 'do's' and 'don'ts', with no apology for any occasional repetition.

Don'ts
You should not:

- *be too clever*   It is the argument that should win the reader round, not the flowery phrases, elegant quotations or clever approach.
- *be too complicated*   The point about simplicity has been made. It applies equally to the overall argument.
- *be pompous*   This means too much about you, your firm and your services (instead of what it means to the reader). It means writing in a way that is too far removed from the way you would speak. It means following too slavishly the exact grammar at the expense of an easy flowing style.
- *overclaim*   While you should certainly have the courage of your convictions, too many superlatives can become self-defeating. One claim that seems doubtful and the whole argument suffers.
- *offer opinions*   Or at least not too many compared with the statement of facts, ideally substantiated facts.
- *lead into points with negatives*   For example, do not say 'If this is not the case we will . . .', rather 'You will find . . . or . . .' .
- *assume your reader lacks knowledge*   Rather than saying for example, 'You probably do not know that . . .' Better to say, 'many people have not yet heard . . .'
- *overdo humour*   Never use humour in fact unless you are very sure of it. An inward groan as they read does rather destroy the nodding agreement you are trying to build. A quotation or quip, particularly if it

is relevant, is safer and even if the humour is not appreciated, the appropriateness may be noted.

- *use up benefits early*   A direct mail letter must not run out of steam, it must end on a high note and still be talking in terms of benefits even towards and at the end.

Now some Do's

- *concentrate on facts*   This relates to the 'don't' about opinions; the case you put over must be credible and factual. A clear-cut 'these are all the facts you need to know' approach tends to pay dividends in professional services.
- *use captions*   While pictures, illustrations, photographs and charts can often be regarded as speaking for themselves, they will have more impact if used with a caption. (This can be a good way of achieving acceptable repetition, mention in the text and in the caption.)
- *use repetition*   Key points can appear more than once, in the leaflet and the letter, even more than once within the letter itself. This applies, of course, especially to benefits.
- *keep changing the language*   Get yourself a Thesaurus. You need to find numbers of ways of saying the same thing in brochures and letters, and so on.
- *say what is new*   Assuming you have something new, novel – even unique – to say, make sure the reader knows it. Real differentiation can often be lost, so in the quantity of words make sure that the key points still stand out.
- *address the recipient*   You must do this accurately and precisely. You must know exactly who you are writing to, what their needs, likes and dislikes are and be ever-conscious of tailoring the message. Going too far towards being all things to all people will dilute the effectiveness to any one recipient.
- *keep them reading*   Consider breaking sentences at the end of a page so that readers have to turn over to complete the sentence. (Yes, it does not look quite so nice, but it works.) Always make it clear that other pages follow, putting 'continued . . .' or similar at the foot of the page.
- *link paragraphs*   Another way to keep them reading. Use 'horse and cart' points to carry the argument along. For example one paragraph starts 'One example of this is . . .', the next starts 'Now let's look at how that works . . .'.
- *be descriptive*   Really descriptive. In words, a system may be better described as 'smooth as silk' than 'very straightforward to operate'.

Remember, *you* know how good what you are describing is, the readers do not. You need to tell them and you must not assume they will catch your enthusiasm from a brief phase.

- *involve people* First your people. Do not say '. . . the head of our XYZ Divison', say 'John Smith, the head of our XYZ Division'. And other people. Do not say '. . . It is a proven service . . .', say . . . 'more than 300 clients have found it satisfactory . . .'

- *add credibility* For example, if you quote users, quote names (with their permission), if you quote figures, quote them specifically and mention people by name. Being specific adds to credibility, do not say 'this is described in our booklet on venture capital . . .', rather '. . . this is described on page 16 of our booklet on . . .'

- *use repetition* Key points can appear more than once, in the leaflet and the letter, even more than once within the letter itself. This applies, of course, especially to benefits repeated for emphasis. (You will notice this paragraph is repeated, either to show that the technique works or perhaps to demonstrate that half-hearted attempts at humour are not altogether recommended.)

A final comment in this section concerns editing. Edit, edit, edit (more repetition). It is usually easier to start with more copy than you need and edit it back to the correct length, improving it as you go, rather than adding to a short draft. In addition, it may need going over more than once and time spent in 'fine-tuning' is often worth while. This is different from trying to incorporate the views of everyone else among the partners or on the marketing committee and it leads us conveniently to organisation.

Creativity and organisation

Partnerships are essentially democratic. Promotional activity is essentially creative. The two sit uneasily together. Everyone knows the story of the committee that set out to design a horse and ended up with a camel. On subjective matters, this effect is most pronounced. Take a simple example like the practice letterhead. Everyone may have different ideas of what is right, and on one level it is a matter of opinion. Yet what matters, all that matters, is how clients and prospective clients will see it. Will it strike them as up to date, effective, even novel, or will it end up as a compromise, various elements diluted so that every possible objection and view is accommodated internally, but any impact is lost externally?

There is no easy answer. But it does bear some thought. Such matters must be centred on one, or certainly fewer, people if decisions are going to be made that promote persuasiveness and are made promptly.

It cannot, for whatever reason, all be done internally then, support must be sought elsewhere.

Outside assistance

The design, preparation and particularly the writing of any part of the direct mail package is crucial, well worth some time and money being spent, and possibly some professional assistance.

The total process is perhaps more complex than might seem the case at first sight. The technicalities of getting things into print and choosing a printer are commented on in Chapter 4.

With an agency or freelancer on the 'creative' side, who will be concerned with design, graphics, copy etc., you are really seeking a partner in the implementation of a part of your marketing strategy. Again, look at what they have done in the past and for whom. Ask how well it worked, has that client come back to them for more, can you check personally with a satisfied client? It is important to make the right choice, and it may well be worth seeing a number of people. Your final judgement may well be influenced by those elements of the job with which you need most help; for example the fact that it is easier to find someone who will make a brochure look nice than someone who will ensure its overall message, that the words and way it is presented meet your objectives, and that it will therefore do a really persuasive job on those who see it. With direct mail copy this is perhaps the key (not that other things are unimportant!) and help with this may be useful. Only you can start the process, think through what needs to be said and perhaps do the first draft, so do not overestimate how much of the time of the job you can shed through delegating work to an outside agency.

In other areas you may need to consult list brokers (who can provide the names) and mailing houses (who physically get the shot into the post) – some companies do both. There seems little point in having your staff stuffing envelopes, when time is no doubt already at a premium.

Conclusion

Direct mail is an important element among promotional techniques, and has particular application for professional services firms.

It is used elsewhere. And it works. And it does not seem to antagonise recipients in the process. It lends itself to the kind of limited, cost-effective and continuous promotional campaigns professional services are finding increasingly necessary. This does not preclude wider scale use by the larger firms, since it is potentially useful at every level.

Direct mail therefore gives you the chance to better develop your firm. On the other side, an inevitable consequence is that an increased amount of promotion will be visible out in the market, perhaps contributing to a further increase in the prevailing competitiveness which faces professional services generally. As a result, while the client is presented with more information, more choice; the professional has more demanding clients, faces more new client situations in competition and sees established client relationships continuing to be more vulnerable than in the past. The degree of threat depends in part on the effectiveness with which existing client relationships are managed (see Chapter 7). By proper management you can make suggestions to existing clients before they arrive on his desk as direct mail from elsewhere and make him think 'Why didn't my adviser suggest that'.

Finally, while direct mail adds to the complexity of the promotional mix, and exhibits special factors to be taken into account in its use – as I hope this chapter has shown – it is in fact simply another promotional mechanism. For all the controversy that has, in some quarters, forerun its inclusion among the permitted techniques, for all the emotive reactions it tends to generate, it is, in intention, no different to other kinds of advertising.

It seeks to inform, and to do so persuasively. While it must of course do this in a way that is acceptable to its recipients, its ultimate objective is to produce more business. To do this it must be genuinely persuasive, creating anything else less is a waste of time and money. Ensuring it is persuasive needs an open mind, a creative approach and attention to detail. As has already been described, small changes, additions and nuance can make a real difference to results. We have also said for certain that even for those who perhaps at this stage disapprove of direct mail – it cannot be ignored. It is being widely used, it is proving effective and thus joins the other promotional techniques as a further element in the armoury that can be deployed to win more business and grow your firm.

Direct mail certainly presents the professional with an opportunity, and, as I said in the Preface, 'the trouble with opportunities is that they so often come disguised as hard work'. Those that take the time and trouble to understand it and use it will give themselves a slight, but significant, edge over those who do not.

EXAMPLE
The following examples provide interesting insights into the use of direct mail. Here I quote Ruth Webber, business development manager for the first firm at the time of the example, and now an independent consultant.

'Using direct mail or a mail shot is a concept that would not have been dreamt of by professional firms a few years ago, nor would it have been permitted by professional regulations.

Now, however, the firm without the glossy brochure is the exception, which itself calls into question its use as a marketing tool. Most firms decide they need a brochure and although the content and quality is important, more important still is how the piece will be used.

When I began working as in-house business development manager for Heery International, an American architectural and project management firm, mass mailing was very much the order of the day.

Following the system used by the US office, the London office sent brochures out in their hundreds, often addressing six or seven 'key decision-makers' in the same large firm. 'Go to the top' was the prevailing motto which meant the managing director was sent the brochure presupposing that if he passed it down to his subordinate responsible for hiring consultants, fear of ignoring orders would guarantee our appointment.

Whether the British are just contrary or the approach simply misguided, it did not work. I soon effected some changes in the method used to send out material and the basic guidelines are as follows.

- Send out brochures in small quantities so that they can be followed up with a brief phone call, to ensure arrival and gauge interest.
- Identify the most suitable person in the organisation, providing he/she has some decision-making responsibility. Do not just 'go to the top'.
- Keep mailing lists up to date, making on-going changes and carry out a complete overhaul at least every two years (hiring a student for this exercise can be quite economical).
- Where possible, target the material sent out so that it says something relevant about the sector to which you are addressing it. If the brochure

itself is standard, tailor the accompanying *brief* letter to suit.

A brochure may not always be the most effective medium through which to maintain contact with clients on a regular basis. A professional firm I met which recently had just spent £25,000 on producing what looked like a boxed set of LPs to commemorate their 25th anniversary. Inside were six brochures focusing on their specialisations, but the practical application of this expensive toy had not been considered. What would the recipient do with it? What happened when you only wanted to send out the most relevant one or two brochures?

An architectural client of mine started to produce a very good biannual review, containing new commissions and current projects with effective illustrations and photos. Copy was written by a non-technical person, to ensure appropriateness for the lay reader. The response from clients was excellent and it overcame the perennial problem of obsolesence, which besets brochures almost as soon as they have come off the press.

Many firms produce loose-leaf brochures which can constantly be updated, but again, considered from the recipient's viewpoint, these are less easy to read and sometimes awkward to file.

The key to a successful 'direct mail' programme is to work backwards, deciding first what you want to convey to clients, what they will be interested in, how you will use the material practically (there may be a variety of uses) and how easily they will be able to store it – a surprising number keep consultants' files, but a standard-size brochure has a better chance of being filed. Once these criteria have been decided upon, start progressing the design, but a word of warning – design by committee rarely works. Choose good graphic designers, brief them well and follow their professional recommendations.'

6 THE PERSUASIVE OPPORTUNITY OF CLIENT CONTACT
Making personal selling acceptable and effective

'We are all salesmen
every day of our lives'

Charles M. Schwab

In the past, there has been a strong feeling in the professions that professionals do not sell. They 'carry out client contact', they 'nurture personal relationships' and the business 'just sort of arrives'. So said the conventional wisdom, and truth to tell, very few, if any, people selected a profession as a career because they had a burning desire to sell things. Quite the reverse, perhaps.

However, times change.

As we have seen, attitudes to the whole 'business-getting' process have been changing, and attitudes to selling have been very much part of this. It needs to be done, and done professionally. A thorough approach is needed. In competitive times, and as I write this in mid 1991 we are certainly in such and perhaps likely to be so for some while, the need for the thorough approach is heightened. And never more so than in the whole area of persuasive communication. The precise manner in which we deal with clients becomes paramount. Small differences in approach can make the difference between success and failure. The whole process is inherently fragile. The fundamental techniques are important, their deployment more so. The approach has to be directed meeting by meeting, client by client. This applies to prospects, to chance meetings, to existing clients, and also method by method. It is no good being brilliantly persuasive one-to-one across the desk if you are unable to conduct business as persuasively on the telephone, in writing or in a competitive presentation.

As has been said, marketing should pervade all aspects of the business. Attitudes to what services are offered (and not offered), what fees are charged and so on are inherent to the marketing process. But the promotional techniques are the most visible, and are certainly a major element of marketing. No matter how well executed and how creative, they will, if successful, not produce any new clients themselves. What they will produce, if successful, is prospects – those sufficiently interested to say 'Tell me more'. The only thing that can convert that interest into agreement that will produce fees, is personal persuasive skills. This cannot be limited to the most senior in the firm, still less to only a few of them; it must be spread reasonably widely throughout the firm. Potentially everyone has a role to play.

It is this final, personal, part of the marketing process that this chapter reviews. It may appear to start with the basics. Indeed it does; but bear in mind the word 'fragile' used earlier, you need to be able to say not 'I know this', but to be sure that everyone in the firm who undertakes client contact which is designed to be persuasive, does so in a way which maximises the chances of success. And does so every time.

NOTE: The boxed **ACTION** points which appear in this chapter are designed to illustrate key points at which what is being done can be made more persuasive, more likely to *differentiate* from competition – and, often, to show how greater persuasiveness can be positioned so that it adds improved client awareness and service, from the prospect's point of view (rather than being seen as 'pushy').

As there are a number of elements to be dealt with in this chapter, we will start by reviewing the nature of the sales process, then turn to the face-to-face situation and then to follow-up activity and other communication techniques.

Fundamentals of success

Clients buy your 'professional competence'. Whatever they want done, from a straightforward project (are any entirely straightforward?) to a complex consultancy involvement, they want to be sure they are dealing with the right firm and the right people. And they will define this as the one with whom there is the greatest certainty of getting the job done right.

Put yourself in the clients' shoes for a moment. How do they know a good job will be done? In many ways the answer, if they have not used your firm before (and to a degree if they have), is simple. They cannot know. As has been said, intangible services are, by definition, untestable.

So, they seek a degree of measurement – prediction – from everything they *can* test. Among the things that contribute to this, the people rank high. Without doubt they will check out the people and, almost always these days, do this alongside checking one, two or more other firms.

Of course, you and your colleagues are good with people, you are professionally competent and, what is more, you are nice people to do business with. Surely if you create the right relationship their business will follow? Perhaps. However, is it just possible that the other firms being checked out have some pleasant and efficient people too? Some people will no doubt do business with you simply because they like you best. The majority, while getting on with their professional advisers may be important to them, will also weigh other things in the balance. They want you to be knowledgeable, efficient, reliable; they may want you to have expert knowledge of particular things; they certainly want to feel you understand them, their business and their situation and to act with that understanding in mind. And, if they get on with you as well, so much the better.

Now all the people in your firm may be exceptional, able to do the best job possible for a wide range of clients, but, as has been said, the client has to be persuaded of this fact. It follows, as night follows day, that the first chance (and perhaps the only chance) you will have of demonstrating your professional competence is when you are selling. Your excellence may shine through instantly when you start work but, unless it does so earlier, you may never start.

This fact, and the fragile nature of the sales process, both referred to earlier, makes it paramount that every element of persuasive communication – professional selling – is done correctly, with 'done correctly' meaning done in a way that will maximise the chances of people doing business with you.

A further point is worth adding to this explanation of why selling is so important. And that is productivity. Sales productivity, that is. People in professional firms are expensive (ask any client!). The opportunity cost of everything you do, other than doing or managing fee-earning projects, is considerable. If things are being done inadequately, two meetings where one should have sufficed, or if the success rate – the number of new clients in relationship to the number of prospects with whom you are in discussion – is too low, it becomes very expensive. Selling must be effective because it takes time, and costs money.

That said, let us now put selling in context. The flow-chart in Figure 6.1

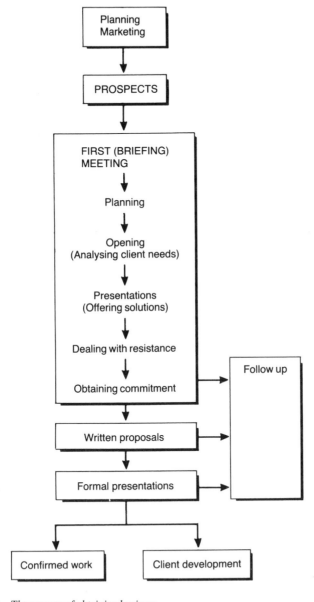

Figure 6.1   The process of obtaining business

shows the entire process of obtaining business, starting from planning and marketing activity through to individual contact with prospects and on, assuming success, to the client development which should always parallel and run beyond doing the work.

A number of things are clear from this picture. First, selling is a *sequential* and *staged* process. Occasionally one meeting may lead directly to business; more often a number of different interactions are necessary, building up the case and finally converting the interest generated into commitment.

Secondly, it is a *cumulative* process. In other words, each stage has to go right, the prospect can lose interest or drop out at any stage and at every stage he may well be making comparisons with how a competing firm goes through the process. Literally, if one stage is judged inadequate by the prospect, there may well be no chance to move on to the next stage at all.

Thirdly, these stages clearly involve different *methods of communication*, all of which must be handled with equal effectiveness. What is done must be equally persuasive, no matter whether it involves a simple one-to-one meeting, a telephone call, written communication (letters or longer, more complex proposals and so on), or a formal 'stand-up' presentation. Each method presents its own challenges, may demand somewhat different skills and none must be a weak link in the chain of communication resulting in definite business.

To a degree this means that selling is a complex process. None of the things that must be done are intellectually taxing, indeed much sales technique is based on common sense, but it must be carefully orchestrated to create the best approach. Habits and reflexes must be built up, and some aspects can only be refined through experience. It is certain that many professional people can make a good job of selling (some in the professions have become excellent and make many a salesperson elsewhere look to their laurels), provided the task is approached thoroughly, systematically and creatively. What is more, and this is a common fear, there need be no danger that increased use of sales technique appears so 'pushy' that it becomes self-defeating – 'switching-off' prospects and making what is done seem less than professional. Indeed I would hope to demonstrate that many of the techniques that can be applied will make the professional appear more helpful and more client-oriented.

The basis for the techniques involved is similar, regardless of method, and must reflect not only the sales objectives but also the way clients buy professional services. In addition, everything we will now deal with can be used in contacts with:

- existing clients (those already worked for and their colleagues in the same company);
- enquirers (those who take the initiative and make the first contact requesting information, advice or discussion); and, as appropriate, with
- intermediaries (those who can recommend your services to others). Every professional will have categories of intermediary that are almost as important as clients, these may include those such as banks, or other consultants.

The word 'prospect' is used to indicate people who might have a need for a firm's services, but are not yet clients.

It is to the client's thinking that we now turn.

The basis for sales technique

The core of what makes the basis for sales technique, is twofold and both elements start on the client's side of the relationship. First, we must consider the way in which people buy.

The buying process

Buying is simply an action that satisfies a need; that is a means to achieve objectives, a goal, ambition or end result. Conversely, people will not buy if they do not have a need, are not aware that they do, or they recognise it but not strongly enough to take action.

There are many kinds and combinations of need. These include single/ multiple; strong/weak; superior/subordinate; past/present/future; frequent/occasional; objective/subjective; individual/group; personal/ job-related and public/private needs. This must be recognised, as must the fact that different people will take the same action, but for different reasons, for example in booking a package holiday in Majorca. Conversely, different people will take different actions, but for the same reasons, as with different ways to impress the neighbours.

How do people buy? Some needs are satisfied by instinctive reactions, some by habit, others by conscious thought. However, decisions to act or not to act on the requests of other people are taken by the following thought process.

- I am important and want to be respected.
- Consider my needs.
- Will your ideas help me?
- What are the facts?
- What are the snags?
- What shall I do?
- I approve/disapprove.

Each step in the process must be taken before the buying mind will willingly move on to the next one. Some decisions can be taken at once, while others require a pause between each stage.

In buying professional services, decisions follow the same seven-step process, but execution of the process can be much more complex due to the nature of the client's business; the size of the organisation; the people and functions involved; their needs, and the degree of influence they have on buying decisions.

Selling is a process of need satisfaction and research shows two facts that are extremely valuable to sellers. First, that interviews are much more successful when the client states his needs. Secondly, as a result, they are less successful when his needs are only implied.

Nothing is successfully sold unless a client willingly buys. This is encouraged by offering satisfied needs as reasons for buying, i.e. perfect holes, not precision drills; reduced administrative costs, not computer programs. To follow the buying mind's seven-step process is vital to selling. There is a need to relate what is done in selling closely to the client's point of view; this can only be done if it is thought through carefully. In a word: planned.

A C T I O N
If you appear, indeed, are more attuned to the client's thinking than others, you will create a better, and easier, basis for everything you do.

Planning
The first rule about preparing to sell is simple – you must do it. Perhaps more business is lost because people believe that what needs to be done can be done 'off the top of the head' than for any other reason. Conversely, it seems apparent that successful salespeople, in any field in fact, are always those that do their homework.

Preparation may mean a moment's thought before your secretary shows a prospective client into your office; a few minutes with the file, notes etc.; or a couple of hours (or more) sitting round the table with colleagues to thrash out the best approach.

Such preparation allows you to ensure that:

- the meeting focuses on the individual prospect;
- you are more fluent and confident in what you want to do and can save time (a valuable resource for both parties).

The process of planning is similar whether you plan to see an existing client, a new prospect or if a really major project is in view. We will review these categories in turn, alongside the following checklists.

PLANNING FOR EXISTING CLIENTS

Here the need is to question what you plan to do, through the main stages involved in what follows:

- objectives;
- research;
- opening;
- presentation;
- close;
- equipment.

(See Sales Checklist 1.)

PLANNING FOR PROSPECT MEETINGS

The major problem in calling on prospects is lack of information, and often there is no previous relationship to which reference can be made, so the emphasis is, therefore, on pre-call research, finding out as much as possible in key areas, and planning how to get things off to a good start.

This only formalises the 'thinking first, acting second' principle to ensure that subsequent discussions with the 'prospect' (whether existing client or enquirer) proceed purposefully. (See Sales Checklist 2.)

PLANNING FOR A MAJOR PROJECT

Where a major project is possible, there are additional considerations to be borne in mind. Major sales are time-consuming, complex, risky and expensive. The rewards for success and the penalties of failure can be enormous (e.g. computer installations). Such purchases often mean big

Sales Checklist 1: Call planning – existing clients

	Yes	No

1   *Are my objectives:*

stated as client needs?

commercially worth while?

consistent with our policy?

achievable within our resources?

measurable?

timed?

2   *Have I done enough research on:*

the person to be seen?

the client's situation?

recommenders?

influencers?

supporters?

their needs?

competition?

3   *Will my opening:*

put him at ease?

get him interested and talking?

explore his needs?

establish his priorities?

4   *Will my presentation:*

offer him desirable results from his point of view?

prove my case to his satisfaction?

explain complex points simply?

show how his needs can be met?

5   *If he raises objections:*

have I considered what they might be?

have I got answers which will satisfy him?

are they related to his needs?

6   *Will my close:*

get a commitment?

match my objectives?

make it easy for him to agree?

leave him feeling better than before the call?

7   *In terms of equipment:*

have I identified what I will need?

have I identified what he may need?

have I got it with me?

have I decided how to use it?

Sales Checklist 2: Call planning – prospects

Yes   No

1   *Objectives – see Sales Checklist 1.*

2   *Have I done enough research on:*

	Yes	No
background information on this prospect?		
—published sources?		
—prospect sources?		
—other sources?		
background information on his industry?		
—published sources?		
—prospect sources?		
—other sources?		
background information on his competition?		
—published sources?		
—prospect sources?		
—other sources?		
possible needs?		
major needs?		
future plans?		
whether there is an obvious need for my services?		
whether it has sales potential?		

See Sales Checklist 1.

3   *Will my opening:*

	Yes	No
fill gaps in essential knowledge?		
—buying process?		
—decision makers?		
—industry situation?		
—company situation?		
—organisation?		
—needs?		
—competition?		
—his?		
—ours?		
impress him about me?		
impress him about the company?		

See Sales Checklist 1.

4   *Presentation – See Sales Checklist 1.*

5   *Objections – See Sales Checklist 1.*

6   *Close – See Sales Checklist 1.*

7   *Equipment – See Sales Checklist 1.*

Sales Checklist 3: Planning a major sale

A 'no' answer to any of the questions should be resolved before proceeding.

		Yes	No

1 Pre-call analysis

1.1 Do I know enough about this prospect and his industry?

1.2 Is anything extra needed?

1.3 Do I have some idea of his possible problems and needs?

2 Survey of client situation

2.1 Have I identified the decision-maker?

2.2 Do I know his possible problems and needs?

2.3 Is there agreement in principle to proceed?

2.4 Have they agreed to let us survey their operation?

3 Identification of client needs

3.1 Have I identified all the individuals/departments who will be affected by a purchase/non-purchase decision?

3.2 Do I know their needs?

3.3 Do they recognise the importance of their needs?

3.4 Have I got all the facts to justify my solution both operationally and financially?

3.5 Have I involved all those who will be affected?

4 Development of solution

4.1 Does my solution meet the various needs?

4.2 Will it meet the priority needs?

4.3 Will it cause any major problems for the clients?

4.4 Will it cause any major problems for us?

4.5 Is it likely to be accepted?

5 Operational and financial justification

5.1 Do I know where my solution will have greatest effect?

—buying/accounts?

—production?

—marketing and sales?

—R and D?

—personnel?

5.2 Can I quantify the effects?

5.3 Do they offer significant improvements?

5.4 Have I calculated and produced the relevant figures?

6 Verbal agreement

6.1 Does everyone accept the operational and financial arguments?

6.2 Any problems?

6.3 Problems resolved?

7 Written confirmation

7.1 Do I know who should receive/read my formal confirmation?

7.2 Do I know which method of confirmation will be most effective?

7.3 Does it contain everything needed by the readers to gain their acceptance?

8 Commitment

8.1 Should I present the written confirmation?

8.2 Having presented, did I get acceptance?

8.3 Did I answer all questions/objections?

8.4 Has the commitment been implemented?

changes to a prospect's business, involving both operational and financial analyses, and the willing agreement of many people in different functions.

Success in these situations, therefore, requires involvement in the prospect's business, contact with all who affect the final decision, identification of their specific needs, and satisfaction of the operation and financial requirements. While no two major sales situations are the same, the similarities are numerous enough to produce an eight-stage approach:

- pre-call analysis;
- survey of client situation;
- identification of client needs;
- development of solution;
- verbal agreement;
- written confirmation;
- commitment.

Each stage contains a number of key points that have to be covered (see Sales Checklist 3).

Finally, in planning, there is the need for the longer term view, a 'client strategy' for those major clients, which in most firms produces a significant proportion of total fees and, hopefully, profit. Such clients, because of their complexity and power, are different in nature as well as size. They are not like all other clients, only bigger. This can rapidly be demonstrated by considering the effect of losing one. It is, therefore, vital that the relationship with them proceeds purposefully over a long period and this normally means planning at least a year ahead. Thus, the elements to be considered in developing a major client strategy of this sort include:

- contacts in the client organisation;
- contacts in the practice;
- assignment analysis last year, including trends;
- competitive activity, and relative strengths and weaknesses in terms of service, fees and terms, and 'presentation';
- next year's objectives;
- overall strategy statement;
- detailed action plans
  — contacts to be made

— objectives of calls
— support required
— timing and deadlines.

Current trends continue to indicate that major clients and the way they are managed will, in future, form an increasingly important part of many firms' work. To manage them well, the professional will need a broad appreciation of business; planning skill and systems; co-ordinating ability; financial techniques; and negotiating skills.

Observation shows that planning tends to be a weak area. Strengths can be maximised in face-to-face situations by thorough planning, so that the possibility of client rejection caused by unforeseen errors is reduced to a minimum.

Using the seven-step buying process discussed earlier, the thorough planning of a sales approach can be turned into a real and effective approach.

As a final plea not to forget or underestimate the necessity for planning and preparation consider the following story (reproduced from *Everything you Need to Know about Marketing* by Patrick Forsyth (Kogan Page) about the nature of buyers:

It is any buyer's job to get the best possible deal for his company. That is what they are paid for, they are not actually on the salesmen's side, and will attempt to get the better of them in every way, especially on discounts.

This is well illustrated by the apocryphal story of the fairground strongman. During his act he took an orange, put it in the crook of his arm and bending his arm squeezed the juice out. He then challenged the audience offering £10 to anyone able to squeeze out another drop. After many had tried unsuccessfully, one apparently unlikely candidate came forward, he squeezed and squeezed and finally out came a couple more drops. The strongman was amazed, and, seeking to explain how this was possible, asked as he paid out the £10 what the man did for a living. 'I am a buyer with the Ford Motor Company', he replied.

Buyers are not really like this; they are worse.

If you worked in the motor trade you would recognise this instantly, but a serious point is made; when people wear their buying hat they are not on your side. They are concerned with *their* situation and needs, and they are getting more and more professional at going through a process which gets them, as they see it, what they want.

ACTION

Preparation in all its forms is often skimped so, while pressure of work (not least client pressure) may make it difficult, it is a very worth while investment and an important, easy step towards positive differentiation to make sure it happens.

Clearly, with these basic tenets in mind we need to consider the dynamics of the face-to-face meeting, so we will turn to this next – leaving other methods of communication such as telephone and written elements, which utilise common techniques, but deploy them in a different way, until later.

Face to face

So, having thought about the process, and what we are going to do regarding a particular meeting, the next step is to run the meeting. And, run the meeting is right. It is important to see it as something to direct, with yourself in the driving seat.

ACTION

Resolve to get hold of the meeting, ensure you are in the driving seat. Run the kind of meeting you want, and clients find they like – preferably like better than they do any competitors', and you will give yourself a head start.

The simple procedure of, for example, suggesting an agenda can help you get hold of the meeting. An agenda that suits you, but that makes sense to the client, and is certainly phrased that way, 'It might be most helpful to you, Mr Client, if we were to take . . . first, then . . .'. This is an excellent example of what was mentioned earlier, sales technique coming over to the client as helpful and focusing on his needs. They are at liberty to amend your suggestion, but you are likely to end up following broadly your suggestion.

Thereafter, the meeting will fall essentially into four parts:

- an opening, predominantly concerned with analysis of client needs;
- a 'presentation' of your response to those needs, offering solutions;

- dealing with resistance (a less clear stage, since objections can come at any time);
- obtaining willing commitment to proceed further.

What that final 'willing commitment' is to, or at least what it might be to, must be borne in mind from the start of the meeting. In some meetings the aim is to agree to do business; in others to agree to a next, firm, stage along the way – another meeting, a proposal or whatever; in others it is just to obtain more information or an introduction to a decision-maker. Clearly, the more tangible a step forward is achieved the better, and having it in mind throughout the meeting, makes it more likely to occur, as you wish.

Now, we will consider the four stages in turn.

Analysing client needs

Client attitudes vary at the beginning of interviews. They can be friendly, hostile, indifferent, interested, helpful or defensive, and the opening of an interview is therefore a crucial time for both parties.

Remember the first two steps in the buying process.

- I am important and want to be respected.
- Consider my needs.

These two steps make the professional's objectives at the beginning of an interview very clear:

- to make the client feel important in their eyes; and
- to agree to the client's stated needs.

Successful selling is particularly dependent on this stage in the buying process being well handled. Exploring, identifying and agreeing to the client's needs correctly makes them want to hear the proposition. Subsequently, making it attractive reduces the possibility of objections and thus obtains more voluntary commitment.

Remember that people act to relieve a felt need. Where the need is low, the solution has a low impact, where the need is high, the solution has a high impact, either positively or negatively, depending on the way it is offered. Sometimes, clients will volunteer their needs and priorities. More often, needs have to be explored, identified and spelt out before they can be agreed and priorities set.

ACTION

It is not putting it too strongly to suggest that this is a 'sheep and goats' factor in selling. That is, those who find out more about client needs, really find out, and are seen to do so by the client, have a head start on everything else that follows. *It can be the first step to beating competition.*

So how do we go about it?

Exploration can be carried out either by questions or statements, or by a combination of both questions and statements. Questions are initially safer and more productive, but they have to be carefully and correctly used. The questioning technique most likely to bring results utilises four basic types of question:

- background questions – for example, 'What's your unit cost per item?';
- problem questions – for example, 'Are unit costs a problem?';
- implication questions – for example, 'What effect are high unit costs having on the rest of the business?';
- need questions – for example, 'What would you like to happen as far as unit costs are concerned?'

used in sequence.

Open or closed questions can be equally successful, but open questions (that cannot be answered with 'yes' or 'no') encourage the client to talk and produce more information.

The type and combination of questions used is very important. Experience shows that asking fewer background questions but focusing them better, asking more problem questions, amplifying problems by asking implication questions and converting problems and implications into need questions works best and forms a logical sequence.

By contrast asking a relatively large number of background questions, fewer problem, implication or need questions, and introducing solutions after the stage of asking background questions works less well.

The reason for this difference in the success rate is very simple. The first follows the client's buying sequence, the latter makes professionals talk about themselves, their firms and their services which distances the approach from the client.

Each type of question has an equivalent approach based on a statement, where the same sequence can be used as with questions, namely Background – Problems – Implications – Needs, and statements can be most confidently used when the accountant already has a thorough understanding of the client's situation. Thus, they are more often used after questioning or during subsequent meetings.

Clients with strongly felt needs will often buy with very little encouragement. Many clients, however, are satisfied with existing solutions. They will maintain the status quo unless something causes them to become dissatisfied. Professionals faced with this situation must, in fact, create some dissatisfaction before the client will consider a change. This must be done without criticising the client's previous decisions, which may well make him defensive. This can most readily be done by showing that due to factors outside his control, the situation is unsatisfactory. Many outside factors can be used in this way: other people's actions and attitudes; the behaviour of materials, products or systems; market forces and local, national or world-wide events; natural phenomena like the weather and many others.

Clients will normally have a mix of needs and they will rarely be equally important. The next stage, as a client's needs are established, is to identify and agree their priority. Questions that will establish this must, therefore, be included in the early stages of conversation.

This early stage is vital, since, as the old saying has it 'You get only one chance to make a good first impression'. Not only are clients making judgements on competence and approach at this stage, but the success of all that follows is dependent on the information base being established. What precisely is done next will be based on this information, and is the first step towards an approach that will differentiate us from our competitors and secure the business in competitive situations.

Offering solutions

Once needs are identified and priorities established, the next step is to show how satisfaction will come from the specific services or recommendations that are offered. Again the action springs from the appropriate stage of the buying process.

The client's mental demands are as follows.

- Will your ideas help me?
- What are the snags?

This means that the professional has four objectives: to make his ideas understandable, attractive and convincing, and to get feedback that the first three have been successfully achieved.

Each of these elements must be considered in turn and they then have to be deployed together in a cohesive and effective conversation.

Making ideas understandable

Three main factors affect this, they are as follows.

Structure and sequence
What you present at a meeting should always be structured around the client's needs, e.g. 'so in choosing a system, your first concern is compatibility, your second is simplicity, and your third is productivity. Let's look at the compatibility aspect first, and then deal with the others . . .'.

It is also important to conclude one aspect before moving to the next, and to take matters in a logical order.

VISUAL AIDS
People understand and remember more when information is presented in visual form. Charts, diagrams, slides, pictures and brochures can all strengthen the clarity of the presentation. In using them follow the basic rules, keep them hidden until they are needed, keep quiet while they are being examined (people cannot concentrate on two things at once) and remove them after use to avoid any distraction. Clients like it too if some of the material has clearly been produced uniquely for your meeting with them, perhaps by incorporating the client's name or logo somewhere.

JARGON
Every company and industry has its own language or jargon and professional services are no exception. Some jargon can be useful, if pitched at the right level, but overall the presentation must use the client's language. This means using words and terms which you are certain the client understands and avoiding words or terms which can be misinterpreted in any way, e.g. 'our service is cheap'.

ACTION

In a technical business, the aspect of making things understood, clearly understood, can be easily overlooked (you may feel you need some help in making things more persuasive, but surely not simply in explaining the firm, its services or a particular approach.) Make sure you really do explain clearly. At least as many prospects are lost solely because they are confused as because they are inadequately convinced. Check if you are not sure.

Making ideas attractive

People buy things for what they will do (benefits, that is desirable results from the listener's point of view) not for what they are (features).

Professional services can do many different things for clients, but not all clients want the same things done. Thus, only those benefits which meet the listener's needs should be mentioned and it is the process of selecting and matching items from the total list of benefits to an individual customer's specific requirements that makes a particular idea, or solution, appear attractive.

There are normally three types of benefit which can be used: benefits to the listener in his job; as a person; or benefits to others in which he is interested, and the choice will depend on the listener's needs and priorities.

This benefit-oriented basis of description in talking with clients is vital. It is another 'sheep and goats' factor. The most successful professionals do not sell simply their services – they sell benefits; that is what clients want to buy. But what, exactly, are benefits? This is worth a moment's careful consideration.

Benefits are what products or services do for the customer. It is not important what they are, but what they do or mean for the customer. To take an everyday example, a person does not buy an electrical drill because he wants an electric drill, but because he wants to be able to make holes. He buys holes, not a drill. He buys the drill for what it will do (make holes) and this in turn may only be important to him because he wants to put up shelving as he needs more storage space.

Realising this not only makes selling more effective, but also easier. You do not have to try to sell the same standard service to a lot of different people, but meet each person's needs with personal benefits.

Benefits are what the services you sell can do for each individual client –

the things he wants them to do for him. Different clients buy the same service for different reasons. It is important, therefore, to identify and use the particular benefits of interest to each. What a product 'is' is represented by its 'features'. What a product 'does' is described by its benefits.

If this is forgotten, then the things which are important to a client will not always be seen as important from the professional's viewpoint, particularly, if as is likely, he has had little or no sales background. The result can, understandably, end up in a conflict of priorities, thus:

Client	Professional
1. Himself	**1. Himself**
Satisfaction of his needs,	His firm
e.g. minimising tax, saving	His services
money, improving cash flow	His ideas
2. His needs and the benefits which satisfy them	**2. His services and making this client buy it**
3. This professional	**3. Benefits to this client**
His firm	
His services	
His ideas	
4. Buying from this person	**4. Client's needs**
	Benefits which satisfy
	this client's needs

The client is most unlikely to see things from the professional's point of view. Everyone is, to himself, the most important person in the world. Therefore, to be successful, the professional has to be able to see things from the client's point of view, and demonstrate through his words and actions that he has done so. His chances of success are greater if he can understand the needs of the people he talks to and make them realise that he can fulfil those needs.

This is essentially achieved by the correct use of benefits. In presenting any proposition to a client, even simply recommending a service in reply to a query, you should always translate what you are offering into what it will do.

Often a firm grows introspective and service-oriented (this is then all too often reflected in brochures) and gradual service development can reinforce this attitude by adding more and more features. It is only a small step before everyone is busy trying to sell services on their features alone.

When competitive firms' services are almost identical in their performance – at least from a prospect's viewpoint, it can be difficult to sell benefits, since they all seem to offer the same benefits. Choice, then, often depends on the personal appeal of some secondary factor. But even then, there must be emphasis on the benefits in those features, rather than on the features themselves. Features are only important if they support the benefits that the customer is interested in.

Deciding to concentrate on describing benefits is only half the battle, however. They have to be the right benefits. In fact, benefits are only important to a client if they describe the satisfaction of his needs.

Working out the needs, and then the benefits, means being 'in the client's shoes'.

To know what benefits to put forward, you must understand the needs of the client, and the potential clientele. Firms often have more than one decision-maker, therefore, it is essential to pinpoint your contact within the hierarchy in order to relate to them accurately.

To do this it is useful to analyse services in terms of features and benefits. Thus an accountant might contrast:

Benefit	Feature
provides a quicker, more certain analysis with less disruption of the accounts department	computer-assisted audit

Such an analysis (and it is a useful exercise to work this out point by point), will help differentiate between features and benefits. It is a useful ploy to present the benefits first; where features lead, i.e. 'We can offer a computer-assisted audit', the client response (mentally if not spoken) can too often be 'So what?'.

An analysis can be produced for each service or for a service range, and can be presented within a firm to help everyone learn just what is a feature and a benefit.

Note that not all the needs will be objective ones; most buyers also have subjective requirements bound up in their decisions. Even with technical services the final decisions can sometimes be heavily influenced by subjective factors, perhaps seemingly of minor significance, once all the objective needs have been met.

By matching benefits to individual client needs, you are more likely to make a sale, for the benefits of any service must match a buyer's needs. The features only give rise to the right benefits.

By going through this process for particular services and for segments of your range, and matching the factors identified to client needs, a complete 'databank' of information from the client viewpoint can be assembled.

With the competition becoming increasingly similar, more buyers quickly conclude that their main needs can be met equally well by more than one firm. Other needs then become more important. If, for instance, a buyer needs tax advice, he is likely to find a number of firms which will offer the service required, all of which will cost practically the same.

The deciding factors may then become people, availability, service, specialist knowledge and so on. The professional must therefore look at the 'features' contained by the firm as a whole and be ready to convert them into benefits to clients – in the same way as we can practise finding benefits for the full service range.

All aspects of the 'features', whether to do with the services themselves, the manner in which they are provided by the firm or its staff, are sources of benefit to clients. Such factors include:

- price/fee levels
- availability of service or staff
- credit
- expertise
- specialist knowledge
- speed of action
- training assistance
- quality/objectivity of advice
- time firms have been established
- reputation, location, philosophy, size policies, financial and international standing
- the character, style and manner of its staff

Each item listed above could be a source of benefit to potential clients and help convert them into an actual client. By 'thinking benefits' and by seeing things from the clients' point of view, you can increase the contribution made to producing new business and increasing the firm's profitability.

Knowing how and why clients view your services as they do, is a prerequisite to improving all the specific communication areas reviewed here and to making your own use of them become more effective.

ACTION

Talking benefits is always a basic component of an effective sales approach; it translates the case into clients' terms, and makes it absolutely clear you are seeing things from the client's point of view. Check you are doing it justice; all the briefing and much of the thinking about the firm, and its services will be introspective, and may prompt an introspective view and approach, unless you do so.

Making ideas convincing

If benefits are claims for the service, such claims may have to be substantiated, as sales claims – about anything – are always viewed with some scepticism. This can be done by describing the features which produce them, or by reference to third parties.

Third party references must be used only to support your case, and not as arguments in themselves. If a specific third party is named, it should be one respected by the listener, and should face similar conditions to those of the client. A third party should not just be mentioned, but also linked to a description of the particular benefits and need satisfactions that they obtained.

Thus, the statements.

'I conduct practical workshops to develop presentation skills in senior staff.'

'I conduct . . . and have run such events for X and Y [where X and Y are appropriately chosen firms].'

'I conduct . . . for X and Y. In the case of Y, we were able to incorporate rehearsals of actual planned client presentations, which they were convinced then went better as a result.'

are progressively more powerful. If a specific example of business gained can be added to the third, so much the better.

The example that follows shows the correct linked use of the benefits and features.

EXAMPLE

Simple statement   B–F

For example, 'You will get more assignments if you use Benefits that match the client's needs.'

Comparison statement   B–F–WA*–NE*

For example, 'You will get more assignments if you use Benefits that match the client's Needs. Vague or unrelated Benefits have a low impact.'

Sandwich statements   B–F–WA–NE–F–B

For example, 'You will get more assignments if you use Benefits that match the client's Needs. Vague or unrelated Benefits have a low impact; but by carefully selecting Benefits that have a strong appeal you will get more business and get it sooner.'

*WA–Wrong Action
*NE–Negative Effect

Obtaining feedback

To ensure that progress is being made towards the ultimate objective, accurate feedback is necessary all the time. It is then possible to be flexible and readjust as the conversation proceeds. By observation, by waiting and listening to the client's reply, and by asking for a comment, feedback can be assured, and monitoring questions like the following can constantly be answered:

Am I discussing your Needs?
Is this a problem?
Is my proposition attractive, clear and convincing?
Have I overlooked anything?

This ensures that the client's needs are being satisfied, keeps the client involved in the discussion, and prevents problems developing later on.

Presenting one's case is simple and successful if one follows these basic rules:

- take one point at a time;
- tell the client what it means to him in terms of results;
- show him what it is or means;
- provide proof where necessary;
- check progress by obtaining constant feedback.

> ACTION
> Obtaining feedback, maintaining a two-way aspect to the
> conversation (yet maintaining control) is crucial. Some of it is as
> simple as making sure you listen. 'Pardon?' Listen, really listen and
> use, and be seen to use, the information you are given to tailor your
> case. Anything else will seem like the 'standard patter'.

Even so there can still be certain problems.

Dealing with resistance

Instinctively considering possible disadvantages in contemplating an action is a natural human reaction. In selling, such considerations pose resistance, though the tendency for this to occur can be reduced. Resistance is more frequent and stronger when needs are insufficiently explored, solutions are offered too soon, or benefits and features are presented too generally.

Some objections are not inherent in clients, but can actually be created by the person selling.

Resistance has both an emotional and rational content. Emotionally, the client because defensive or aggressive, rationally, he needs a logical answer; these two elements have to be tackled separately and sequentially if resistance is to be overcome. How? First by keeping your emotions under control, by listening, pausing and thinking, acknowledging his comment – a sort of 'sparring' technique designed to lower the temperature.

Next, rational answers must be provided. It helps to turn the objection into a question, to establish the client's need behind his resistance. Why is he asking this? Is it an excuse? Delaying tactics? Perhaps he does have a point? An apparently straightforward comment such as 'It is very expensive' may mean a wide range of different things from 'it is more than I expected' to 'No', from 'It is more than I can agree' (though someone else might) to 'I want to negotiate', and so on.

Although, 'What are the snags?' is an instinctive part of the buying process by the time the client reaches this stage he may be sufficiently attracted by the proposal to pass on without raising objections. It pays to concentrate on resistance prevention rather than resistance cure. Agreement on stated needs, and careful selection and presentation of need-related benefits, reduces both the frequency and strength of resistance.

EXAMPLE
A management consultant, sitting down for a follow-up meeting with a client to discuss proposals recently submitted in writing, was immediately challenged on cost. 'Before we get into this at all,' he was told, 'you must understand that we have to get the best possible price for this project.'

In a considered fashion he closed the folder in front of him and responded to the effect that 'if it is the lowest price you want, we may as well not go on, as I know our proposals will not be the cheapest.'

The client immediately changed tack, 'The proposals were very interesting', he did want to discuss things. The meeting proceeded on a rather different basis. This is less technique than sheer confidence. And, selling needs that too, albeit based on experience and sound judgement.

ACTION
You should rarely be caught out by objections you have not foreseen, at least in general terms. Thus, handling them effectively is another result of good preparation. There will always be some, however, that demand you are 'quick on your feet'. An apparently unexpected objection, well handled, can be impressive, and taken as a display of competence.

Obtaining commitment

Knowing that the objective of all selling is to obtain client commitments often obscures the need to remember how clients arrive at the point of commitment. Clients only willingly take buying decisions after they have recognised and felt needs, and are convinced that their needs will be satisfied by implementing the proposal. Thus, the best chance of success lies in doing a good job before the client reaches the stage of asking himself 'What shall I do?'.

Attempts to get commitment (closing) without first having created desire for the proposal will normally be seen by the client as pressure tactics. The bigger the decision, the greater the pressure, and the stronger the client's resistance.

Closing does not cause orders, it merely converts a high desire into orders and a low desire into refusals. Even when a desire is high, however, the client may not volunteer a positive commitment. Similarly, the client may want to make a commitment, but there are several variations of it, and the professional wants one particular kind. It is in these situations that closing skills are valuable; such skills concentrate the buyer's mind on the advantages to be gained from the buying decision itself.

There are certain behaviours, questions and comments indicating a general willingness to buy that can provide 'buying signals'. Tone of voice, posture, hesitation, nodding, questions on details, showing acceptance in principle, or comments expressing positive interest are all examples. These can be converted into closes, being careful not to oversell when the client wants to make a commitment.

Although this is the crunch point and it can sometimes be avoided because of the unpleasant possibility of getting a 'no', the commitment must actually be asked for: the only question is exactly how it is put. There are various approaches. Here are some examples.

Direct request

For example, 'Shall we go ahead then and start getting these improvements in service levels?' This should be used in situations where the client likes to make his own decisions.

Command

For example, 'Install this new system in each regional office. It will give you the information you want much more quickly and help you to make more effective decisions.' This can be used where the client:

- has difficulty in making a decision; or
- has considerable respect for you.

Immediate gain

For example, 'You mentioned that this year the company really needs to improve productivity. If you can give me the go-ahead now, I can make sure that you see specific results within three months' time.' This could be used in a situation where, by acting fast, the client can get an important benefit, whereas delay might cause him severe problems.

Alternatives

For example, 'Both these approaches meet your criteria. Which one do you prefer to implement?' This could be used where the professional is happy to get a commitment on any one of the possible alternatives.

'Best solution'

For example, 'You want a system that can cope with occasional off-peak demands, that is easy to operate by semi-skilled staff and is presented in a form that will encourage line managers to use it. The best fit with all these requirements is our system 'X'. When's the best time to install it?' This should be used when the client has a mix of needs, some of which can be better met by the competition, but which, when taken as a whole, are best met by your solution.

Question or objection

For example, 'If we can make that revision, can you get the finance director to agree to proceed?' This should be used where the professional knows he can answer the client's objection to his satisfaction.

Assumption

For example, 'Fine. I've got all the information I need to meet your requirements. As soon as I get back to the office I'll prepare the necessary paperwork and you'll be able to start by the end of next week.'

Concession

Trade only a small concession to get agreement now or agree to proceed only on stage one.

So far so good. The answer at this point may well be 'Yes'. But no matter how well a case is presented and questions handled in selling professional services, the prospect will invariably have some objections to making a decision. Sometimes these objections are stated, but often they are reserved and come in the form, 'I'll think about it'.

When this happens, simple closes may only irritate the prospect and the way forward may be unclear. Yet it is a key stage to get over, and this can be done by listing the objections:

'I agree you should think about it. However, it's probably your experience also that when someone says they want to think about it it's because they are still uncertain about some points. In order to help our thinking on these, let's note them down.'

Then make a list with room for more objections than he has, do not write any down until each is understood, and do not answer any – yet. Flush them all out and be sure there are not more to come. This enables an additional closing technique to be used. 'If I'm able to answer each of these points to your complete satisfaction, can we agree we're in business?' This is the *conditional close*. Each point listed is answered in turn, crossed off the list, and the prospect's agreement with each checked, then the close is not repeated, but assumption is used to conclude matters: 'Fine, we're in business'.

Having made a commitment, a client may need reassurance that he has done the right thing. Therefore, always thank him, confirm that he has made a wise decision, touch once more on what will come from it, conclude and leave promptly.

When the client has been satisfied on the first points in the buying process, a close, emphasising the need satisfaction that a commitment will bring, will naturally convert desire into action.

Good selling can often make formal closing unnecessary: 'Make him thirsty and you won't have to force him to drink'.

ACTION

Some of the business will go to those most prepared to tie it down positively. It can be awkward actually to say 'Right, when do we start?' (probably because we know they could say 'no'), but not asking – or saying 'Please think about it' leaves us open to more positive thinking competition.

Of course, the commitment given may not be to do business, and the necessity for 'steps on the way' has been referred to previously. The next section looks, briefly, at the important question of follow up.

Follow up

If every new client sprang from one, self-contained meeting, the sales process would be much easier. But, as was explained earlier, it is not like that, as you will know only too well, one contact leads to another. A meeting, another meeting, a proposal, a telephone call; they follow each other and must maintain both the initiative and the interest.

Follow up must start immediately after the first contact, and many a job has been lost by default because of poor follow up. Accurate follow up is always necessary to correct misunderstandings, carry out promised actions and to show keenness for the client's business. After each call, building goodwill is important, making the client feel it was a worthwhile contact, even if his commitment was not made, that the time spent was a valuable investment in the future. Follow-up action should be automatic and made immediately after each call, while ideas are fresh. A record of what was promised should be made as a prompt to the next action. It may take a conscious effort to make sure that the logistics of the business allow the follow up that is necessary; 'production' responsibilities have to be phased in with selling, and often demand priority.

There is not a great deal to be said about technique here, since it is much more a question of discipline and system. For example, make sure that you attempt to fix the next meeting, if appropriate, before you walk out of the current one. Do not put off those, necessarily awkward, telephone calls, when the prospect needs prompting to tie down the next stage. Leave it, and the moment passes. It gets more difficult, not easier; and, in the end it may become impossible. If so good prospects can die, by default, through neglect.

So far we have considered the process and the techniques involved, and have done so on the assumption that the contact is predominantly face-to-face. Indeed it may be, and because this is what most people are used to it is to some extent the easiest to deal with within the sequence of events.

There are, however, other methods of communication and they are just as important. If there is any danger of them being taken for granted, or handled in an unthinking manner, then they can represent weak links in the cumulative chain of events and, at worst, can reduce the success rate unnecessarily. In the next section we examine these other methods.

Other communications methods

If we are not face-to-face with the prospect, what are we doing? Well, we may be on the telephone. We may have to write to them (either a letter, or something inherently more complex, a proposal for instance); and, worth a mention although it is still face-to-face, we may be asked to make a formal presentation (that is, on your feet, with a group of clients – their board perhaps – using visual aids and with much less feeling of security than sitting comfortably at a desk, especially if it is our desk).

In this, the final section of this chapter, we will look at these in turn. The intention is to focus on what parts of the methods need a different approach from face-to-face communication, but many of the principles that make for effective – persuasive – communication remain the same regardless of method. Some of the points made are, unashamedly, basic, even obvious, you may feel. The point is, however, do they make a significant difference to your chances of success? By now you should be persuaded of the importance of getting every element of this fragile process as right as possible. These final details can again prevent the wrong impression being given, or make sure business does not go by default.

First, we will look at the ubiquitous telephone.

Telephone contact

Any telephone conversation is simply two-way communication, albeit using a particular medium. It is surely not difficult, after all some people talk on the phone for hours and hours. On the other hand, like any communication, there may be a good deal hanging on it. Any problem will dilute the chances of success. And the problems of 'voice-only' communication are considerable, and in some cases prohibitive. Try describing to someone how to tie a necktie for example – without any gestures or demonstration. It pays, therefore, to consider all the factors that can make vocal communication successful, and not underrate it as 'simply a telephone call'.

Such factors are perhaps best reviewed in terms of how you use the telephone itself, your voice and manner, obtaining and using feedback, and planning. The telephone distorts the voice, exaggerating the rate of speech and heightening the tone. You must talk into the mouthpiece in a clear, normal voice (if you are a woman, it can help to pitch your voice lower.) It is surprising how many things can interfere with the simple process of talking directly into the mouthpiece: smoking; eating; trying to write; holding a file or book open at the correct page and holding the phone; sorting through the correct change in a call box; allowing others in the room to interrupt; or allowing a bad-quality line to disrupt communication (it is better to phone back). This is all so obvious, yet so easy to get a little wrong, thus reducing the effectiveness of communication.

Voice and manner
Remember that on the phone you have to rely on your voice and manner in making an impression. None of the other factors of personality are perceptible. Here are some suggestions to help you.

Speak at a slightly slower rate than usual.
Speaking too rapidly makes it easier to be misunderstood and also

mistrusted, although speaking too slowly can make the listener impatient or irritated.

Smile. Use a warm tone of voice.

Though a smile cannot be seen, it does change the tone of your voice. Make sure you sound pleasant, efficient and perhaps most important, interested and enthusiastic about the conversation. Enthusiasm is contagious.

Get the emphasis right.

Make sure that you emphasise the parts of the communication that are important to the listener, or for clarity. You only have your voice to give the emphasis you want.

Ensure clarity.

Make sure you are heard, especially with names, numbers etc. It is easy to confuse Ss and Fs for instance, or find 15 per cent taken to mean 50 per cent.

Be positive.

Have the courage of your convictions. Do not say: 'possible', 'maybe', 'I think', or 'that could be' (watch this one, professionals are apt to be far too circumspect).

Be concise.

Ensure a continuous flow of information, but in short sentences, a logical sequence and one thing at a time. Watch for and avoid the wordiness that creeps in when we need time to think, e.g. 'at this moment in time' (now), 'along the lines of' (like).

Avoid jargon.

Whether jargon is of the firm (e.g. abbreviated description of a department name), the specialisation (e.g. technical descriptions of tax regulations or legal procedures for instance), or general (e.g. phrases like 'I'll see to that immediately' – in five minutes or five hours? 'Give me a moment' – literally?). At least check that the other person understands – they may not risk losing face by admitting you are being too technical for them, and a puzzled look will not be visible. Jargon can too easily become a prop to self-confidence.

Be descriptive.

Anything that conjures up images in the mind of the listener will stimulate additional response from someone restricted to the single stimulus of voice.

Use gestures.

Your style will come across differently depending on your position. For example, there may even be certain kinds of call that you can make better standing up rather than sitting down, such as debt collecting or laying down the law perhaps. (Really! Try it, it works.)

Get the right tone.

Be friendly without being flippant. Be efficient, courteous, whatever is called for.

Be natural.

Be yourself. Avoid adopting a separate, contrived, telephone 'persona'. Consider the impression you want to give: Mature? Expert? Authoritative? In command of the detail? Try and project just that.

Your intention is to prompt the other person into action. You should speak naturally in a way that is absolutely clear. Here are some useful additional rules.

Be courteous.

Always be courteous.

Be efficient.

Project the right image.

Be personal.

Use 'I' – say what you will do.

Be appreciative.

'Thank you' is a good phrase (but not gushing).

Obtaining and using feedback
Talk *with* people, not at them.

As a first step to encourage response, form a picture of your listener (or imagine them if you know them) and use this to remove the feeling of talking to a disembodied voice.

Remember to listen.

Don't talk all the time. You cannot talk and listen simultaneously.

Clarify as you proceed.

Ask questions, check back as you go along – it may appear impolite to ask later.

Take written notes.
Note down anything, everything, that might be useful later in the conversation or at subsequent meetings. Get the whole picture and avoid the later reaction of being told 'but I said that earlier', which can indicate that your credibility is suffering. Do it as you proceed, not at the end of the call.

Maintain a two-way flow.
Do not interrupt, let them finish each point – but make sure, if they are talking at some length, that they know you are listening. Say 'Yes' or 'That's right' to show you are still there.

Concentrate.
Shut out distractions, interruptions and 'noises off'. It may be apparent to your listener if you are not concentrating on him – it will appear as lack of interest.

Do not over react.
It is easy to jump to conclusions or make assumptions about a person you cannot see – resist this temptation.

'Read between the lines.'
Do not just listen to what is said, but also what is meant. Make sure you catch any nuance, observe every reaction to what you are saying.

Planning
Because we are attempting to gain agreement or commitment, planning the call is important.

This does not mean a lengthy period of preparation, though certain calls may be well worth planning more formally, but it does mean that the brain must always start working before the mouth! Making a few notes and a few moments' thought before dialling is usually well worth while. This kind of planning will help you:

- overcome tension or nervousness;
- improve your ability to think fast enough;
- prevent side-tracking (or being side-tracked);
- make sure you talk from the listener's point of view;
- assess your own effectiveness.

Above all it will help you:

- to set clear and specific objectives designed to gain agreement and a commitment from the other person.

Planning is necessary even to cope with incoming calls (at least those that follow a pattern). It is designed to make sure you direct or control the conversation without losing flexibility, and react to others accurately, without being led on by them. Plan to make difficult calls early and do not put them off – they will not get easier, rather the reverse.

Never think of any call as 'just a phone call'.

How you sound

People considering their effective use of the telephone should know how they sound to a listener at the other end of the line. This is not difficult to organise; a standard cassette recorder or dictating machine on which you can record your own voice is all that is necessary. The result will be very similar to what you might hear on the telephone.

Practise by talking and playing back your words. More usefully, rehearse any particular important, or repeating, call which you know you have to make.

Better still, get a friend or colleague to hold a conversation with you so that you hear yourself, on playback, responding to questions and conversation that you were not expecting.

If you have not done this before it is likely that even a few minutes of self-analysis will show you a lot, and allow any specific weaknesses or habits to be improved.

One key reason for telephoning is worth examining further.

Making appointments

A call designed to gain commitment to a discussion with a prospect, someone, perhaps, who has seen a brochure and asked someone to call, needs specific thought and a systematic approach if an appointment is going to be reliably secured.

Before you even dial the prospect's number, you must have at hand the following:

- all client information available to date, including any 'personal hints', which can help avoid gaffes such as the wrong pronunciation of someone's name;
- information on your availability;
- a checklist of the information you ideally want – other services being used by the client, their preferences, size of company, or whatever is relevant.

The next step is to get through to the right person. The best way to do this is to ask for who you want, confidently. If asked, give your name and/or your firm's name, but no more. If you speak to a secretary, offer a suitable alternative, e.g. 'Can you make an appointment, or would you prefer I spoke to Mr Smith?'. You will not always succeed, but such an approach will certainly help.

A structured approach will have a greater chance of success than attempts at 'one-off' conversations. The following steps are advisable.

- Check that you are through to the right person.
- State your name and firm.
- Give your reason for calling.
- Ask for any additional information that will be needed, or will be desirable, at this stage.
- Give reasons for the appointment (rather than some other means of proceeding) in terms of benefits to the client. The best reason is to find and mention something they will see, touch, have demonstrated – something that can only be satisfactorily carried out at a face-to-face meeting.
- Speak of the meeting as 'working with the client', e.g. 'If we meet we can go through the details together and make sure we come to the right solution'. This prevents them feeling they are allowing you to come and 'do something to them'.
- Mention the duration of the meeting. Honestly. There is no point in pretending you only need 30 minutes if you actually need an hour. At worst you may arrive and find they have only exactly the 30 minutes you asked for on the telephone available.
- Allow a reasonable lead time, for the client. They are less likely to refuse an appointment for 7–10 days' time than to refuse an appointment for tomorrow.
- Offer an alternative – 'Would 3.00p.m. Thursday afternoon be suitable, or would you prefer a morning, say Wednesday morning?' – with the first option more precisely stated than the second.

Now and again resistance will be met, but you can then employ an objection-handling technique. The 'boomerang' technique is particularly useful for 'turning' an objection. For instance:

Prospect: 'It's not convenient – I haven't the time.'

Professional: 'It's because I know you're busy that a short meeting may be useful. It will give you the opportunity to hear how we go about things and see whether scheduling more time to discuss the project is worth while.'

When you have got them back on the track again, and sounding even tentatively agreeable, you can 'close' again as fast as is polite – with the appointment as the objective.

If it is impossible to make an appointment, you can still get something from the situation by getting new information for the records. Having 'won' the conversation and 'negotiation' to that point, they will often be in the frame of mind to allow you some concessions, and may be quite willing to give information about future plans, changes or the names of others in the organisation you could contact etc.

Finally, if you are visiting the prospect (which they may prefer, particularly for a first meeting) do ask about location – a sentence or two may save you hours of searching. What about parking? Do they have a car park?

If they are visiting your office make sure they know exactly how to find your premises – confirm this in writing (send a clear map if you have one) and inform others internally (including the receptionist) as necessary, making sure they know how important the visit is to the firm.

This can be an awkward kind of call to make, you may be conscious that there is an element of 'push' to it, but a systematic approach will make it easier to conduct and more acceptable from the other end.

Written contact

The problem here (to an extent this is similar to the telephone) is that too much is written on 'automatic pilot'. Too much can then be the reiteration of a formula for producing a particular kind of document which, on examination, has little more rationale than being 'the way it has always been done'. Written material needs some thought. Take letters, for example.

Letters
Letters last. Unlike telephone calls (which are not often recorded), they stick around to be re-read and reconsidered. They need to look neat; think with what trepidation you start reading something that is illegible or untidy.

No matter what the subject of the letter is, you want to be sure that your letters will (a) command attention, (b) be understood, and (c) be acted upon (it is this last that differentiates persuasive communication from simple factual communication). If they are to do this, you have to take some care in preparing them; in this age of dictating machines and rush and pressure, it is too easy to just 'dash them off'.

PREPARING PERSUASIVE (SALES) LETTERS

Before you even draft a letter, remember the sequence of persuasion, and in particular remember to see things through the other person's eyes. Then ask five questions:

(1) For whom is the letter and its message intended? (This is not always only the person to whom it is addressed.)
(2) What are their particular needs?
(3) How do our ideas or propositions satisfy those needs – what benefits do they give?
(4) What do we want the reader to do when he receives the letter? We must have a clear objective for every letter, and these objectives must be clear.
(5) How does the reader take this action?

Questions 4 and 5 are frequently forgotten, but they are very important. It should be perfectly clear in your own mind what you want the recipient to do, and very often this can be put equally clearly to the reader; but having achieved this, you can lose the advantage if lack of information makes it difficult for them to take the action you want.

A very important part of a letter is the first sentence. It will determine whether or not the rest of the letter is read. People seldom read a letter in the same sequence in which it was written. Their eyes flick from the sender's address to the ending, then to the greeting and the first sentence, skim to the last – and then, if the sender is lucky, back to the first sentence for a more careful reading of the whole letter. So the first sentence is about the only chance we have of 'holding' the reader, and it should arouse immediate interest. But gimmicks should be avoided. They invariably give the reader the impression of being talked down to. So how can we achieve the best opening?

Make sure the start of the letter will (a) command the reader's attention, (b) gain interest, and (c) lead easily into the main text. For example:

- ask a 'Yes' question;
- tell them why you are writing to them particularly;
- tell them why they should read the letter;
- flatter them (carefully);

- tell them what they might lose if they ignore the message;
- give them some 'mind-bending' news (if you have any).

The body of the letter runs straight on from the opening. It must consider the reader's needs or problems from his point of view. It must generate interest. It must get the reader nodding in agreement, 'Yes, I wish you could help me on that'.

Of course you are able to help. In drafting a letter you should write down what you intend for the reader and, of course, list the benefits, not features, and in particular the benefits which will help solve that problem and satisfy that need.

You have to anticipate possible objections to your proposition in order to select your strongest benefits and most convincing answers. If there is a need to counter objections, then you may need to make your letter longer and give proof, e.g. comment from a third party, that your benefits are genuine. However, remember to keep the letter as short as possible.

Your aims should be the following:

- to keep the reader's immediate interest;
- keep that interest with the best benefit;
- win him over with a second benefit (or more);
- obtain action at the end.

In drafting you can make a (short) summary of the benefits to the reader of your proposition. Having decided on the action you are wanting the reader to take, you must be positive about getting it. It is necessary to nudge the reader into action with a decisive final comment or question, just as we advocated in face-to-face contact.

A WORD ABOUT LANGUAGE

Remember our intention here is to prompt the client to action rather than demonstrate your 'Oxford English', (though it is nice to be grammatically correct). You should write much as you speak.

The following are some useful rules: be clear; be natural; be positive; be courteous; be efficient; be personal; be appreciative. Just as we said earlier about language on the telephone. It is perhaps doubly important in writing, where a 'civil service' style can take over all too easily.

Throughout the whole process bear in mind exactly who you are going to be communicating with; in other words have their characteristics very much in mind.

Is it someone you know well? Where a good mutual understanding exists, you can get straight to the point without too much preliminary. Is it someone with the same understanding of the topic of discussion as you? In this case, no elaborate explanation is necessary. It is someone more senior, older or more important than you? Perhaps, someone who will expect, or appreciate, a little respect? Are they going to be difficult? (Do we know this or are we assuming it?) And if so do we need to be that much more careful, polite or circumspect? There are few rules here, but most problems occur not because we cannot handle the situation, but because we have not taken enough time and trouble to think it through, and adapt our approach to the circumstances.

ACTION

Always consider carefully just what a 'sales letter' actually is. Many kinds of letter have a sales connotation and need to be persuasive. Some may see them as 'administrative', as a surveyor or architect may see certain letters about technical matters on a project, or as an accountant may see the so-called 'management' letter sent after an audit – some see this as the final stage winding up the project, and see no need for any sales orientation in it, while others see them as the first communication of a new period, and by reviewing matters, and flagging action for the future, it takes on a very clear sales role. This kind of view reminds one of the difference between the person who sees the glass of water as half-empty or half-full – a sales orientation sees opportunities everywhere.

Proposals

The proposal is a tool to help close the sale successfully. By itself, the proposal will not get the order; proposals do not sell, people do, but the proposal can and must help. Furthermore, it must act on its own, and bridge the gaps when no one is personally involved. As such it must not be a weak link.

A proposal is more complex than a letter. It has to command attention, be understood and is designed to be acted upon. It must put across clearly the technical information necessary – a process that must be done to match the client's point of view. Before pen is put to paper it is necessary to think clearly about the intentions of any specific proposal. For whom is the proposal, and its message, intended? (This is not always only the person to whom it is addressed.) What are their needs? How does your position satisfy those needs – what benefits does it give?

What do you want the prospect to do when he receives the proposal? There must be clear objectives for every proposal, as follows:

- it must be commercially worth while;
- it should be stated in terms of client needs;
- it should be realistic and achievable;
- it must be specific, clear and appropriately timed;
- it must be capable of evaluation with a yes/no answer.

Lastly, how does the prospect take this action?

It is necessary to select a 'shape' for the proposal that will ensure it makes sense to the prospect and can be made persuasive, one that makes sure the proposal will:

- be well organised, with the flow of information easy to follow;
- be put in sequence, so that the prospect will agree each point progressively;
- highlight critical areas of particular interest to the prospect;
- summarise all previous agreements;
- state all the facts that the decision-maker(s) needs;
- summarise all previous agreements;
- be easily understood – by all those who may read it;
- position your organisation in an appropriate role.

There are essentially two approaches, a letter proposal or a formal proposal. A letter is more appropriate to some situations than a formal proposal and vice versa.

In general, the complexity of the sales situation and the prospect's business methods will be a guide to determining which type of proposal to use. It can either be a *letter proposal* which summarises the critical elements of the recommendations for the decision-maker in a letter. Attachments that document the solution or provide extra information can be added.

The letter proposal is appropriate when:

- a more detailed proposal is not required;
- recommendations can be clearly presented within the scope of a letter;
- it is necessary only to summarise what has already been agreed upon;
- all prospect concerns are solved;
- there is no competition for the work.

The other type of proposal is the *formal proposal* which is a more detailed approach to presenting recommendations. A formal proposal is appropriate when:

- recommendations are complex;
- recommendations will be perceived as high in cost;
- the decision-maker is dependent upon recommenders and influencers to help make the buying decision and it is clear that their involvement is important;
- the decision-maker or some of the recommenders and influencers have not met personally.

PROPOSAL CONTENTS

Each likely section of a proposal is now commented on in sequence.

(1) **Introduction**   Remember that it is a sales document; the opening must command attention, gain interest and lead into the main text. First impressions are important, so the first sentence must not be wasted.

The introduction may need to establish the background, state the purpose of the letter/proposal, and refer to previous discussion/ agreements.

It can also include a title page (with the client's name, an index, terms of reference and credits).

(2) **Statement of need**   This describes the scope of the requirement and makes it clear that the writer understands what is necessary, and how it will be decided upon.

Ideally, it does no more than confirm in writing what was originally asked for and added to during the survey visits.

It has the value of emphasising the identity of views between client and professional, showing the client that you understand what he wants and does not want from an external adviser or expert.

EXAMPLE

Details of client needs for an accountant's audit proposal that could be stated individually might include such factors as the following.

- **It complies with existing statutory requirements.**
- **It is unqualified and will satisfy shareholders when published.**
- **It improves investors' confidence by safeguarding shareholders' interest with an independent viewpoint.**
- **It helps the client get credit from banks and suppliers.**
- **It gives him security by having generally accepted accounting principles giving 'correct' financial information.**

- It uses control mechanisms proven in his industry, giving him confidence in the production of correct results.
- It shares the burden of audit responsibility, by protecting management while also controlling their audit activity.
- It allows the situation to be under the client's control at all times.
- It gives a minimum of disturbance to his operation and customers.
- It does not overload staff.
- It avoids the necessity of costly databanks and in-house experience by ready access to the accountant's skills, especially in tax and accountancy.
- It gives information which can be adapted for various user needs, e.g. ownership, management and personnel.
- It gives cost-saving suggestions from familiarity with the organisation, e.g. systems, taxes etc.

(3) **The solution**   This describes the suggestion not just in terms of technical details (features), but also in terms of advantages and benefits. If possible, it should be made exclusive, i.e. the benefits offered cannot be duplicated by competition.

There is no more effective way to ensure a reader's attention than to ensure that the content of the proposal is totally directed towards him and his needs. Everything which the proposal contains must not only be relevant to the prospect, but its relevance must also be explained and he must agree.

A standardised, or unthought-out approach, may become confusing or present a programme which hardly refers to what was formally established, and certainly does not deal in depth with the prospect's real needs one by one.

It is easier to make these points than to determine how they should be phrased. Advantages must be translated in a way that stresses benefits, so that the implications are apparent, by using a phrase like 'which means that . . .'. Features of the approach, method or services are less important than the benefits – what it means or will do for the prospect. Using these factors together in the sequence benefit feature will present the most powerful argument, and avoid the comment 'so what?' (This concept was reviewed more fully earlier in this chapter.)

In addition, reference to timings can be made at this stage.

(4) **Costs**   All costs need to be stated clearly, but related to the benefits of the suggestion, plus any intangible factors.

Quotes must be alive to going rates for similar jobs, and to the prospect's views and perception of fees. The prospect must be convinced that he will get value for money. Since some prospects will only read this section, it should start with a short summary of the benefits of using the firm.

Attempts by the prospect to establish individual scale rates should be resisted if possible, since these may be misleading, particularly if:

- the firm tends to work more quickly and efficiently than others;
- it is usual practice to absorb certain start-up costs on the basis of expected recurring work.

Even if no fee estimate can be given in the proposal, a range or a top figure may need to be worked out. This is in case of pressure at the presentation meeting, where dissatisfaction may ensue if the prospect receives no indication at all. Do not disguise any costs, but do support them with benefits.

Proceeding to set out the associated areas of manpower and the implementation timetable may help to move the reader positively away from the costs. It may be useful to amortise costs – to spread them over months or project stages. For instance – to illustrate value.

A C T I O N
Another element that is increasingly necessary (and asked for) is CVs of those who will be involved on a project. It should be clear that these should be tailored – as the rest of the proposal is – you should resist the temptation to send out the standard versions, they may well need some editing to ensure they emphasise the appropriate aspects of staff experience and expertise to each individual prospect.

---

(5) **Closing statement**   This can refer to any attachments, for example, literature/samples. It should create a sense of urgency, so that the decision-maker will act promptly and should close, i.e. ask for the commitment, making it clear what the next action is to be.

A summary of why this proposal is right will help those key executives who are very busy and who need a precise statement of the facts to help them make a decision, and those key personnel to whom the proposal was not presented. Repeating the benefits after the costs section means that a reader is left with final impression of benefits rather than only the price.

Such a summary might include:

- a review of the origin and scope of research effort;

- an outline of the key findings on what is wanted;
- a summary of what is offered and how that meets the prospect's criteria for external support.

It might finish with a summary of tangible and intangible benefits.

In a formal proposal, each section should have its own page, a table of contents will make it clearer and the letter accompanying the proposal (if it is posted rather than presented) must not be a formality, but should add something to the case – perhaps strengthening its urgency or specifying further action. For example:

- it might give appreciation of being asked to work, reassuring the prospect that he was right in contacting the firm;
- it might emphasise that the proposal represents the mutual conclusions of the prospect and the proposer;
- it could close by indicating who can be contacted or promising to contact in the near future, and suggesting a timetable of action.

Style and language are important too. The document should be attractively laid out, grammatically correct and well typed. It should look formal, efficient, individual and clear.

EXAMPLE

A firm of planning consultants had invested in a high-quality desk-top publishing facility to ensure they could produce high-quality proposals (and other documents). This included the ability to include four-colour illustrations. And, they had plenty of illustrations to use; every past project resulted in plans, diagrams, visualisations and photographs being added to the store of impressive examples of past work.

Writing proposals was regarded as important, but tended to be a hectic process, hemmed in by client pressure and deadlines on current projects. A formula had been evolved, mechanically, of dropping in illustrations – examples of recent work – almost on a ratio basis, that is so many pages of text, so many illustrations.

It looked good, but no logic or explanation was apparent to the client. Choosing particular examples, captioning them, and positioning them within the text of proposals to exemplify particular factors took a little longer, but made the documents more powerful in their persuasive role with clients.

Layout is especially important: it should not be squeezed into one, 10 or any particular number of pages. Headings and paragraphs will ensure clarity and emphasis; <u>underlining</u>, or CAPITALS or **bold type** will get the attention you want.

So will indenting.

The suggestions regarding language and so on in the section on letters apply equally here.

ACTION

Proposals are important, time-consuming and too often a weak link. Have a look at the last few that have gone out within your own firm, check that you are really happy that they do a persuasive job and, if they need fine-tuning, give your future proposals just a little more thought.

In Figure 6.2 you will find a checklist that can be used either to help compose a suitable proposal, or to check how a past one is likely to be regarded.

EXAMPLE

An example, which links back to what was said earlier about research, concerns a firm providing consultative services. A low success rate on major competitive pitches prompted them to commission research among those who had rejected their proposals. This produced useful information.

But first we should mention a firm which had conducted a 'perception survey' to ascertain what their clients and others thought of them. The survey looked at this in various specific ways; what sort of size, position and quality were they seen as having, what range of services and so on. The survey produced detailed results, many of which showed very different perceptions from what partners thought existed. This led to many detailed changes in the way the firm promoted itself. It is, in fact, all too easy to operate on the basis of what – in effect – we *hope* is the case rather than of fact.

Now to the main, more specific, example of a survey which was designed to help uncover the reasons why one of the key *ad hoc* service divisions of a major firm had lost a string of competitive pitches over a two-year period. Research conducted among target clients who had, in fact, rejected the firm uncovered many clues.

First, there were some general factors relevant to the firm as a whole, of which the firm was, perhaps, not sufficiently well aware.

	Yes	No

Does our proposal satisfy the key client requirements?

Does the covering letter:
Announce the submission of the proposal? ☐ ☐
Emphasise that the proposal represents mutual conclusions? ☐ ☐
Thank members of client's organisation for their time and effort? ☐ ☐
Suggest a timetable and action plan for closing the sale? ☐ ☐

Does the title page indicate:
The title of the proposal? ☐ ☐
For whom it is prepared? ☐ ☐
Name of company submitting the proposal? ☐ ☐
The date? ☐ ☐

Does the table of contents:
Indicate the beginning page for each of the elements in the proposal? ☐ ☐

Does the introduction:
State the causes for the proposal to be written? ☐ ☐
Review the client's goals and benefits sought? ☐ ☐
State the origin and scope of any survey work? ☐ ☐

Does the situation analysis state:
What is the current level of performance with the client? ☐ ☐
What changes the client wants to bring about and why? ☐ ☐
Why these changes cannot be brought about under existing conditions? ☐ ☐
What is sought from 'the outside', i.e. us? ☐ ☐
What is the priority order of requirements? ☐ ☐
Our understanding of the client's decision-making criteria? ☐ ☐

Do the terms of reference:
Summarise our understanding of the scope of the work, the objectives,
relationships, expectations, and constraints? ☐ ☐

Does our proposed solution:
Show how we can help them within their priority order of needs? ☐ ☐
Show our competence in those areas, with examples and proof? ☐ ☐
Explain the service we will offer? ☐ ☐
Explain how it will confer benefits on the client against their priorities
of need? ☐ ☐
Identify the functions that may be involved and how they will be
co-ordinated? ☐ ☐
Stress how the proposed solution will help achieve the client's goals? ☐ ☐

Is there a plan for implementing the solution to:
Identify the implementation procedure? ☐ ☐
State any contraints on implementation? ☐ ☐
Specify the sequence of activities? ☐ ☐
Identify review points requiring decisions or support from the client? ☐ ☐

Does the statement of fees:
Identify the key benefits? ☐ ☐
Phase the cost of stages if appropriate? ☐ ☐
Specify exactly what is and is not included in the cost? ☐ ☐
Leave room for re-negotiation of currently unforeseeable cost? ☐ ☐
Specify timing of payments and repayments? ☐ ☐

Does the conclusion:
Highlight the key requirements? ☐ ☐
Restate the main benefits to be gained? ☐ ☐
Stress the main differentiation of ourselves from competition? ☐ ☐

What Appendices are essential:
Financial? ☐ ☐
Technical? ☐ ☐
Case histories? ☐ ☐

Figure 6.2   Proposal checklist

- In an environment where the professions are marketing themselves to an increasing extent, some of the client's competitors had effectively 'sold' themselves in advance of their final meetings.
- As with the world of advertising some years earlier, the era of the beauty parade had now arrived; the firm was less often the only choice, more often it was one of three to be chosen and sometimes even one of six, eight or 10 at the first hurdle to select a shortlist.
- Many potential clients, partly through the marketing activities of some firms, were now more aware of the many options open to them. Sometimes they would be stimulated by an approach, entertain the firm marketing itself, review their 'usual' firm and invite a big-name client in as a 'control' with little real chance of gaining the business.

Secondly, there were particular factors relevant to the firm, the first of which was presentation skills where standards and style were also reviewed and addressed as another part of the project.

The other significant element was the written proposal: this is one of the few tangibles which the target client sees; this indeed is the only information available to any other decision-makers who may not have been present at the presentation. It is crucial and can be a weak link.

While this is not the place to examine all the requirements of a good proposal document, key factors emerging in this research suggested the following.

- *Do not* begin with six or eight pages which literally play back the brief.
- Even more, *do not* merely change the odd word or reverse the position of sentences.
- *Do not* focus your thinking and your recommended plan in only one or two pages in the middle.
- *Do not* end with six or eight pages of irrelevant case histories which even lack any statement of benefits to their recipients.

All these are worth nothing. I would like to say that the firm clearly benefited from these findings, but within months a proposal the firm produced unfortunately reflected the above '*DO NOT*' headings precisely, even to the extent of eight pages of case history drawn from only one market and one in which their prospective client did not operate.

It transpired that the individual author of the proposal had not been exposed to the findings of the research. This suggested a final rule, which should be adhered to in many research projects:

- *Do not* pay for good external research consultancy unless you intend that

all of your relevant departments and key individuals will be exposed to the findings and able to benefit from them.

Both examples are intended to show the potential for practical results flowing from research which can more than justify the cost.

Presentations

There are, of course, different kinds of presentation. Some may be promotional, an opportunity to address a conference or a spot during promotional events, often called 'client seminars'. Some are speculative, such as the 'beauty parade' when the presentation comes first in the cycle of sales events. All can make you vulnerable.

In every case your competence is on display, and what the quality of your future work is anticipated to be is judged, in part, directly from the effectiveness of your presentation. People do not say 'that was a poor presentation', but 'I think that is an unsuitable person'.

To complete the sequence we have been pursuing, we will take a follow-up presentation as an example. That is we will assume there has been a meeting, and that following that written proposals have been submitted and now the next meeting is to present the content, formally, to a group at the client's premises.

It is beyond the scope of this book to review every aspect of present-ational skill, though it should be noted that it is a necessary skill and one that (almost) everyone can develop to some degree with training. The essentials are worth a moment's thought, however, and to do this we will go back just a little in the sequence.

Proposals, however good, can only do so much on their own: they need presenting. The evidence is that, while this may happen rarely at present, particularly among the smaller firms, it is a growing practice that makes sense for clients especially if competitors are presenting their offerings.

The moment to agree this, to sell it, is at the end of the survey meeting. Finding out how many copies of the proposal document are needed (which may also provide additional information about decision-makers – if you have seen two people and they ask for three copies, who is the third one for?), and setting a date, time and perhaps other details (attendance, location), will allow planning for the meeting that will best help secure the business.

The ability to make effective presentations is an essential executive skill not only in selling to prospects, but also for in-house selling at executive meetings, and in making recommendations following an assignment. However, it is an unnatural social act for many people made more difficult by familiarity with a polished television performance.

EXAMPLE
The following provides a warning against allowing the whole process to become a routine, slavishly followed rather than creatively applied.

A firm of architects received an enquiry from a national organisation. They had meetings with them at their London headquarters, they put in proposals, they were successfully shortlisted and invited to make a formal presentation to a committee (the organisation was a charity, administered as an association rather than a company).

They planned, to some extent, their presentation and tailored an element of it from a stock of 35mm slides showing past work. Arriving at the prospect's office for the 30-minute presentation and asking where in the room the electric points were located, they were met with blank looks – and the secretary, showing them into what was a charity for the blind, said something to the effect that as most of the committee were blind, slides were not terribly appropriate.

Two minutes later the committee arrived, and a presentation based on slides had to be made without them. It could have gone better.

Somehow no one spotted this, the thinking was too hasty, too much along tramlines. The reflex was 'presentations mean slides'. If such a dramatic error can be made, preparation of everything to ensure nothing – albeit less serious – is missed, is vital.

In addition, many presentations are further complicated by the client trying to follow a proposal while listening to the presenter explaining something different.

The objective of the presentation must be to:

- present the people, clearly and understandably;
- get feedback, avoid monologue and gain agreement;
- present the solution credibly to convince them; and
- handle objections, to satisfactorily answer questions and objections.

USING THE PROPOSAL
The presenter should prepare his copy of the proposal with notes, examples and headlines to guide his talk. Since competitors will be saying mostly the same things (for example, 'We pride ourselves on our good service'), and because just reading the proposal is not enough, it must be turned into an aid to presentation.

Key elements of the presentation are now commented on in sequence:

PRESENT CLEARLY

Take a structured lead:

- by suggesting a format and timetable for the meeting, for example, that you go through the proposal together with discussion after each subject and cut-off times of two hours;
- by handing out and showing briefly the contents of the proposal, but suggesting that it will be more productive if you study it together, section by section, starting by ensuring that you have the facts right; and
- by following the proposal and reading aloud parts of it without re-writing it.

USE PREPARED AIDS

- use prepared aids as visual paragraph markers for ideas;
- keep words to a minimum;
- ensure uniformity of size, colour and layout; and
- introduce the aid, talk it through and remove it.

USE YOURSELF AS A PRESENTATIONAL AID:

- be enthusiastic – if you are not convinced, they will not be;
- stand or sit upright but with varied positions;
- use hands to emphasise rather than distract;
- look at individuals and change expression; and
- carry voice pitch, tone, pace and duration.

USE LANGUAGE AS AN AID TO INTEREST:

- use questions as well as statements;
- use metaphors, similes and analogies;
- use examples to paint pictures;
- repeat and summarise frequently before, during and after.

Remember that the proposal is the main aid; it is wasteful to reinvent the wheel.

GET FEEDBACK, AVOID MONOLOGUE
Know your 'man':
 M̲oney
 A̲uthority
 N̲eed

CHOOSE A STYLE OF DELIVERY
- Will you address the decision-maker or the audience in general?
- Will you use a formal stand-up or low-key discussion style?
- Will there be a greater or lesser involvement of a team?
- Will there be a liberal or selective use of aids?
- Will you make use of client language/jargon?

Check for feedback by involving the prospects continually, to get their agreement before moving on. Get them nodding early on, refer to the situation, to matters clearly agreed:

- watch faces and body movements for reactions;
- ask questions to ensure agreement on the need to introduce each main point;
- do not move on if people are still worried;
- summarise frequently;
- make notes of points of agreement and disagreement; and
- watch the time (an accurately timed session is, in itself, impressive).

PRESENT CREDIBLY
The presentation is the occasion when the prospect and his team are able to judge the human side of your suggestions, so he will be using the opportunity to assess your complete capability for:

- doing what you have said;
- doing it better than competitors;
- integrating with his own staff; and
- not causing extra work or problems.

You must pick your team and agree roles, so that there is no confusion during the meeting. Deciding exactly who attends from your side, and how many, is important, as is the link between that and who will do the work.
 Give proof:

- build up the team's credibility;
- demonstrate how your firm has been successful;

- allow individual experience to shine (without boasting);
- use expressions like 'in our experience . . .';
- work in examples of how you have worked in the prospect's industry;
- illustrate your argument with published references;
- quote convictions and agreements already made by the prospect; and
- above all, talk throughout in terms of benefits.

Experience of having successfully worked in a company like his before is often what the prospect is looking for. If you do not have this experience how close do you come?

- Ensure that the decision-maker and all his advisers are present.
- Ensure that they are pre-sold and looking forward to your presentation.
- Avoid presenting anything new that may create resistance.
- Emphasise the points that have already been agreed with the decision-maker and his advisers.
- Reinforce your message with simple, graphic visuals.

Proposals represent the summation of the effort with the prospective client, and the commitment to him. This does not mean that large amounts of information should be submitted just to look impressive, but it does mean it should be carefully thought out and well organised.

A well prepared and presented proposal increases client confidence – essential when selling professional services – and increases the possibility of success.

The need for formal presentation at this stage is increasing as clients become more and more inclined to check out any appointment very carefully. It is a key element in differentiating one firm from another, and one that may demand some training within the firm.

ACTION
Spend time improving, if necessary, presentational skills and remember that it is all too possible for a poorer, but better presented service, to be bought in preference to a better, but less well presented, one.

If all these methods are handled as well, with as much attention to detail, and as persuasively as face to face meetings, then the basis for a good success rate in pulling down the business will be secured.

A final point regarding selling. Those who are, by their position – or by inclination – not involved in marketing activity may feel it is 'someone else's responsibility'. It is not that they believe it should not happen, only that they should not be the ones to do it.

This does not apply, however, to selling; everyone (certainly practically everyone) is involved. The switchboard operator, answering to a new contact, is, in a direct way, selling. The many working on client assignments, seen only as fee-owners, are regularly able to spot opportunities for selling and their manner and performance influence the client's perception of the firm and their likelihood of responding to 'cross-selling' of the range of services.

Very few, if any, firms have full-time salesmen. The 'production' resource and the sales resource in a professional services firm are the same people; the professional staff. If you and your colleagues are not selling – and doing so effectively – for your firm, no one is doing it.

Selling is now, quite simply, one of the 'stock-in-trades' of the professions, as important as much of the technical knowledge that is highly prized, was won only through extensive training and has to be regularly updated.

The successful professionals of the future must recognise this, and take steps to equip themselves for the sales fray. The brief review contained in this chapter will be a helpful part of the process for some; courses, and above all practice, will also form a vital part.

Indeed, you may even come to like it. It is always satisfying when a prospect says 'yes' and becomes a client. It can be even more satisfying when this is not just fortuitous, but when you can look back over the whole process and say 'I made that happen'.

7 SYSTEMATIC CLIENT DEVELOPMENT
How to make them loyal for life

'Life is what happens while you
are making other plans'

John Lennon

A retail store, in America, has a sign at each cash point which says 'WARNING – Customers are perishable'. So they are, clients too; neglect them and they rapidly cease to be clients.

EXAMPLE
I applaud the firm who explained to me what they called the LYBUNT system. It involved a series of simple, logical card index cards and formats to ensure contact – sales contact – was regularly kept with clients whilst work was in progress and beyond. A system they felt was essential to their on-going success.

And LYBUNT? It stood for 'Last year, but unfortunately not this'. We perhaps all know the feeling.

Client Development is a key area of marketing for professional services. A high proportion of on-going work may well come from existing, or recent, clients. But – guess what? – it will not just happen.

For larger firms and major clients, quite a number of processes are involved and some are, to a degree, complex. The essentials are crucial for everyone however, so, if some of the detail of this chapter seems to be suggesting a sledgehammer to crack a nut, do not make the mistake of rejecting the process. Client development is essential to every firm. Only the degree of detail necessary will vary.

But while the concept of client development is often accepted as necessary and desirable, precisely how this process can best be initiated, managed and controlled within the firm's overall business and marketing plan remains a largely unsignposted trail.

EXAMPLE
One firm where I presented the idea of a client development system to their annual partners' conference felt this was an idea with real merit and left committed to action. A year later, asked what progress had been made, the senior partner reported that they 'had had three meetings to discuss exactly what sort of system should be instigated'. But no action. We all know the feeling.

So the specific objectives of this chapter are to provide appropriate and implementable guidelines – 'signposts' – in this key area. As a result of this, it should be possible to form clear links between the overall marketing planning process described in Chapter 2, and the activities and control processes necessary to translate marketing strategy into action in respect of client development.

Before going further, client development should be defined; it is the management of client relationships in such a way as to hold existing business, maximise the likelihood of identifying opportunities for further work and progressing them to the point of agreement for more work to be done. It is an on-going process and an additional dimension to the management of client work, not an alternative to it.

The marketing role of client development

Links to marketing objectives and strategy

Any firm approaching the implementation of a client development programme must recognise that the preceding stage – evaluation of clearly defined overall marketing objectives and strategy choices by those in the firm – must be done *first*. The planning forms 3–12 in Chapter 2 provide the minimum desirable overall planning framework for the firm. If notes are recorded under these headings, this will provide the necessary coherent framework of reference, within which client development activities can take place. By adopting this systematic approach the firm can make optimal use of the key resources of time and money; and ensure its ultimate selection of which market segments – and which 'development opportunity clients' – form the potential market from which profitable growth can most likely be achieved.

Marketing objectives reviewed

In that they have deep significance to the evolution and implementation of the client development process, the six major marketing objectives available to a firm are worthy of a brief review. They are:

- **To increase market share** In a static or low incremental demand market this can only be done by 'conquest' selling – that is, winning business from other firms.
- **To expand existing markets** This involves focusing on selling the fullest range of the total service portfolio to existing clients. It also implies that very close cooperation and communication must exist, or be fostered, between those working on different service areas in the firm.
- **To develop new services for existing markets** This can involve either the revision ('re-packaging') of existing services and/or the introduction of completely new services. This is one of the growth routes already adopted by many larger firms, who have progressively added needed services to their 'historic' service offerings.
- **To develop new markets for existing services** This is not always easy. However, new services may be what a new client tries first, giving him confidence to buy other, more central, things later on. This means that additional, if more fundamental, business can be won by a progression from a 'service portfolio expansion' approach.
- **To develop new services in new markets** This is an example of true diversification and, as the highest risk marketing objective, has been traditionally eschewed by many firms. Competitive pressures and the need to retain good staff by offering high 'challenge' and personal development opportunities may force a review of this attitude in future.
- **To improve the profitability of existing operations** In mature markets, where little incremental demand exists, many firms must, in the short term at least, seek higher returns from greater productivity and cost-efficiency of their operations. It is perhaps self-apparent that if firms have pursued this route to the ultimate, and profitability still remains at a less than satisfactory level – then more 'offensive' marketing objectives are called for. These are the only logical alternatives to business shrinkage resulting from static or declining profitability.

The link to promotional activity

The plethora of promotional activity has already been covered in Chapter 4 of this book. In terms of client development, and whatever permutation of marketing objectives are selected and pursued, promotional activity divides into two main areas.

Marketing communications

In the broadest sense, the primary objectives of all marketing communication, i.e. advertising, public relations, seminars etc. are (a) to create an enquiry or 'opportunity to do business' with new clients, and/or (b) to remind existing clients of additional services on offer from the firm, and/or (c) to reinforce continuing usage of existing services. No matter which of these primary objectives are set for the various elements of the communications mix, only face-to-face selling will ultimately determine whether or not marketing objectives are actually realised.

Face-to-face selling

The primary focus of all promotional activity is face-to-face selling, which is the most appropriate, relevant and effective form of promotion for any firm offering professional services. By definition, professional services are people-intensive; the people are the product, and must form the final link in the promotional chain.

Attitudes to client development

The greatest opportunities for profitable business development lie in building from the existing client base. Like any promotional activity within the profession, it must be conducted ethically and, perhaps even more important, in a manner that is acceptable to clients – otherwise any effect will be wasted. But, in this respect, an opportunity only exists when all members of the firm working on existing assignments with clients are organised, prepared and equipped to look for it!

The only situation in which such opportunities can subsequently be pursued, prioritised and capitalised on, is through personal contact with client decision-makers and influencers.

If opportunities are not to go by default, then it is vital that all members of your firm, at whatever level, share the attitude that, in working for, and communicating with existing clients, *two* priorities exist:

1) to perform to the highest technical standard on current work, so that

a client re-books that similar work with the existing firm as their supplier, wherever that type of project is required on a 'repeat' basis; but also

2) that this should go together with 'opportunity search', i.e. the planned identification of current needs which are not being met by the firm, or its competitors, and changes in the client's market environment or operating or organisational policies which will give rise to new needs, which can be satisfied either by existing services, or the extension/development of services within the firm's capabilities.

Why are client development opportunities missed?

Opportunities are missed! In which firm can it be objectively said that an opportunity has never been missed; that no client has brought in somebody else to do something you could have done?

The reasons for this include:

- over-reaction to adopting a 'selling' stance;
- lack of insight that 'opportunity search' is a vital activity;
- lack of awareness of other services which the firm offers (this is often despite a firm conviction within the firm that everyone knows about everything in the range of services!);
- lack of persuasive communicative skills;
- focusing on the 'urgent' (today's task) to the exclusion of the 'important' (creation of tomorrow's business);
- lack of clarity on the firm's business development needs;
- lack of a coherent sales development plan for existing clients within the framework of clear overall business development objectives.

Managing the client development process – overview

Although all are important reasons perhaps the final two listed above are the fundamental causes and the first five are the resultant effects in relation to the key question – why are opportunities missed? This suggests that a systematic framework for managing the client development process must be followed. A suggested staging for this is as follows.

Stage 1   Develop and communicate clear overall marketing objectives and strategies specifically in relation to business growth.

Stage 2   Decide where in market segment and client terms these objectives could be met.

Stage 3   Develop/initiate a thorough review of the existing client base to highlight where opportunities may exist (situation analysis).

Stage 4   Decide where clear opportunities do exist (account development strategies).

Stage 5   Focus attention on client development priorities through evolution of specific sales plans.

Stage 6   Allocate specific priorities to individuals working on current client assignments (who does what by when.)

Stage 7   Evaluate and control the development process over the plan period.

Stage 8   Analyse where significant variances in planned versus actual performance lie.

Stage 9   Take corrective action where and when necessary.

Stage 10   Feedback results and experience gained into the *next* marketing plan.

Initiating the client development process

So far, I have referred at several points to the importance of the management of the client development process taking place as a planned element of the overall marketing plan. We now turn to the key questions, and resultant specific approaches and formats which are necessary to implement the client development management process, at Stages 3–10 in the systematic approach outlined above.

Organisation

Key question 1 – How well are we organised in relation to client development?

Where do responsibilities lie?

One of the key organisational problems to be solved by a firm offering professional services and operating with the objective of growing the firm through client development is how to allocate the appropriate amount of the 'production' and 'sales' resources to each function.

The 'production' and 'sales' resources tend to be the same people and this becomes a more difficult problem in the smaller firm where, overall, there are fewer people.

In most firms, client development is regarded as everyone's responsibility. If this approach were to be adopted in a 'raw' state, or applied literally rather than systematically, the only predictable result would be, at best, unplanned client development and, at worst, utter chaos.

In the early stages of business development, therefore, the responsibilities can best be clarified by considering the overall client development process in three component parts, as follows.

The overall marketing planning work

This includes data collection on markets, analysis and decisions on objectives and strategies, and construction and communication of overall plans and systems.

Because of the objective and policy-forming nature of these activities, some firms have successfully allocated this area to a 'practice development' person. He, as it were, wears this 'particular marketing hat' and, while he may not personally do everything, he has a key role in initiating and controlling activity.

In most firms, the success of this overall part of the client development process depends heavily on the goodwill, insight and frequency of communication between senior members of the firm. This is particularly vital if marketing objectives of developing additional business via increased/ new services to existing clients are being pursued, and if some services are separately organised from other main services. Forms 3–12 in Chapter 2 provide a review of the range of planning documents likely to be useful, within this area of responsibility.

The implementation work

These are the 'selling-on' activities in relation to existing and new clients which must be carried out by the whole firm within the framework of the overall marketing objectives. Because of the increasing range of services offered, some firms have set up 'project teams' for the largest existing or potential clients to provide the full range of skills and experience necessary to make progress, and ultimately to satisfy client needs.

At an overall planning and implementation level two factors seem to aid success. First, that responsibility should be concentrated rather than spread. Thus, if a new service is to be successfully launched and subsequently grown within, say, the existing client base, it is more effective to commit an individual or small group to that action. As a result, internal publicity or 'knowledge-building' about the service itself and its potential benefits to clients can be most effectively pursued. And from this process, external 'applications' (markets and target clients) can most readily be identified. Implementation then rests with those staff who have the greatest knowledge of, and the best relationships with, the decision-makers in the 'target' clients for the new service.

Secondly, that the development activities are, wherever possible, defined, quantified and timed at the planning stage. However, this definition must specify the links between the results required and the development activities or clients.

Specific account plans
The third is translation of the two preceding marketing planning processes into specific account (client development) plans. In this context 'account plans' are the quantified and qualified client-based action programmes through which the firms' overall marketing objectives will be ultimately achieved. Precise guidelines and formats which clarify and exemplify the account planning process will be dealt with in subsequent sections.

Responsibilities beyond development of current client opportunities

Beyond the development from the current client base, responsibilities will need to be allocated in relation to new/prospective clients who are the by-product of either:

- referrals from existing clients;
- enquiries resulting from marketing communication activities, i.e. advertising, PR, seminars etc.;
- previous clients who have not used the firm's services for some considerable period of time.

In general terms ultimate responsibility for turning enquiries into sales will always rest with senior partners. There are several factors which necessitate this, as follows.

1) By nature of their management role in the total practice development process they are inherently in the best position to examine whether the potential assignment:

- provides an acceptable 'fit' between the current or planned services offered by the firm and the client's requirements;
- they are in the best position to forward the enquiry to other senior managers into whose discipline area the potential project may fall, if it is not their own.

2) Being involved in the initial stage allows them to check later whether the new business enquiry resulted in subsequent fee income.

3) They should also be in the best position to judge whether specific individuals have the technical competence, selling skills and time available to pursue rigorously and efficiently the most potentially desirable business opportunities.

In practice, many firms adopt a systematic allocation of responsibilities, where initial vetting and any necessary qualification of an enquiry coming into the firm by letter or telephone is done by senior people, and at the earliest possible stage the enquiry is then delegated to the individual at 'operating' level who can best pursue it. While delegation of that pursuing should be to one person, on whom responsibility for making sure it happens rests, this does not mean that others will not be involved in the follow-up process. Sometimes 'team' selling is necessary and appropriate. Senior people should remember the difference between 'managing' an account and 'directing' it. A background role may be important and will always include acting as backstop to make sure sales opportunities are not missed.

Enquiry progress form

An enquiry is a crucial starting point from which new business can result either from prospects or new clients. Such contacts are too important to be allowed to go by default. A form, perhaps one you design (or adapt) specifically for your firm or even your department, bestows the proper importance on the enquiry. It should act first as a record; with copies being passed on as necessary (not least to build up the information you need for ratio analysis). Secondly, it acts as a checklist; to prompt whoever is taking the enquiry to ask the right questions. Items like the job title of an enquirer, important to help ascertain where he is in the decision-making hierarchy; or whether and by whom he was referred to you, useful to evaluate promotional activity, may easily be overlooked.

Last, and by no means least, such a form can be used to ensure an enquiry is progressed promptly and efficiently; specifying and recording action. The last entry on such a section should always be the *next* action you decide upon. While it may not always be possible, indeed necessary, to complete all the form, everything beyond the basic information may help; that is, it may increase the chances of a sale ultimately being made successfully.

A reference number can be used to tie in with other systems within the firm.

Such a form can either be designed solely to record the enquiry – as in Figure 7.1 – or it can be linked to subsequent stages documenting:

- details of initial enquiry;
- subsequent action;
- result for the firm – as shown in Figure 7.2.

In both cases NCR-type carbon sets of form facilitate communication.

ACTION
Compare any form you use with Figures 7.1 and 7.2 and make sure it is doing the complete job you want.

Continuing sales attention

Earlier the key organisational problem of deciding how the 'production' versus 'sales' resources could best be organised and committed was discussed. Often these responsibilities are vested in the same individual, and line reporting relationships and the nature and flow of the day-to-day workload can either facilitate or impede the effective allocation of effort necessary to develop business while performing current assignments to the highest standards.

As with so much of marketing there is no magic formula, but two main approaches are being adopted in firms providing professional services to help alleviate this potential dilemma.

The first, referred to previously, is that where new services are introduced with the initial objective of selling these into existing clients, specific responsibilities for building internal awareness of the service and external client opportunities for it rest with an individual or a small group. Outside the professions, this relates closely in principle to the 'brand or product management' function found particularly in consumer goods organisations.

It has the essential merit of pre-selecting the appropriate service for its correct client market, in relation to overall marketing strategies.

ENQUIRY PROGRESS FORM

To:
Ref No: From:

Enquiry taken by:	Date:	Company:
		Address:
Source of enquiry:		
Stated need:		Tel. No:
		Contact name:
		Position:
Comments:		Nature of client:
		Additional information:
Action taken:		
Action promised (inc. timing)		

Subsequent progress:

Date	

	Resulting fee	Value	Date
		Job Number	

Figure 7.1   Enquiry progress form 1

BOOKED/REFUSED

Description of assignment:

_____

_____

_____

_____

_____

Refusal reasons:

Price ☐   Reproposed ☐

Competition ☐   Age ☐

Other _____

Date:

Company name

Value [ ]

Location [ ]

Ind. class [ ]

Work type [ ]

Job no [ ]

Staged booking [ ]
Amount o/s

Other ref. nos. _____

Client A/C [ ]

Engagement partner
(project manager)

PROPOSAL

Description of work:

_____

_____

_____

_____

_____

_____

_____

_____

_____

Company name:

Location	

Value £

Ind. class [ ]   Group

Work type [ ]

New client   Yes/No

ENQUIRY PROGRESS FORM

Source of enquiry ☐

Advertising ☐   Existing client ☐

Public relations ☐   Personal contact ☐

Centres of influence ☐   Seminars ☐

From: _____   via associates ☐

Referral: ☐   From: _____

From: _____

Other: _____

Stated need: _____

_____

_____

ACTION: BY WHOM _____

BY WHEN _____

Company: _____

Address: _____

_____

_____

Tel. No:

Contact name:

Position:

Industrial classification:

Comment:

Figure 7.2   Enquiry progress form 2

Secondly, 'relationship management' principles (about which much of the remainder of this chapter is concerned) with their ongoing review of client reactions to completed work, and resultant or emergent opportunities, are an inherent part of the client development/assessment process over time. This process can be most appropriately undertaken by the staff directly involved with the client, who also initiate contact with more senior personnel or other specialists as and where appropriate. It is also evident that in some firms at least, efforts are being made to move beyond historic 'blind alleys'. For example, a letter which only reflects areas historically worked on, but goes no further to highlight or examine current or potential needs for additional professional services which the firm can provide, is allowing opportunities to go by default. Appendices to such letters, an agenda for client review meetings which prompts discussion on future needs etc., are effective methods of cost-effectively moving transitionally from 'today's assignment' to 'tomorrow's business development'. Ensuring the thinking exists which produces this degree of fine-tuning of actions in a way that makes them an integral part of client development is crucial in any firm.

Information systems

Key question 2 – Do our client information systems help the business development process?

Overview

Client information systems in many firms are limited to a simple historic database listing clients' addresses, contact names and similar primary details, recorded either on client files, individual record cards or, increasingly, in computer systems. In many cases, important though it is in its own right, this information deals only with the direct operating information specific to a particular project, i.e. contacts at senior and line level within the client firm.

However, for any firm seeking business growth through client development, three critical areas will need to be examined:

- Do existing records give sufficient qualitative depth, so as to aid future business development opportunities, rather than simply provide a past record of work done?

- Do the information systems themselves provide, to the firm as a whole, sufficient depth of information to avoid 'reinventing the wheel' by being able to access historical projects similar to the one being addressed, thereby reducing the work involved in new client assignments and/or give insight to relevant service-related solutions?
- Do they aid the business development process by providing cross-market or cross-disciplinary links to enable the firm to highlight industry trends and issues? This will help prepare 'start of the art' business advice and informed new business presentations, to either existing or new clients, which demonstrate reasonable understanding of the issues the client is facing in his markets.

While no panacea or generally applicable solution to these questions would appear to exist – providing all things to all firms – certain implications are clear, namely:

- using client information systems in a purely historic context;
- collecting and recording narrow assignment-related information;
- storing information in a manner which is difficult to access, will not, itself, provide any direct help to the business and its client development process.

If systems are to provide a real basis for client development, comparison of what is currently known about clients with what specifically needs to be known to opportunity-spot now or in the future – a 'gap' analysis – forms a logical starting point. This type of analysis should be conducted at two levels within the firm. First, by senior people as an integral part of the marketing planning process, and secondly by assignment managers in relation to specific clients, particularly at the opportunity search stage of account planning.

What information is needed

Collecting data and organising it is a most challenging task which requires both good judgement and sound method. Good client files are the most critical element for sound planning. In this context 'knowledge is power'.

Specifically, the following information should be available on 'priority' clients.

GENERAL/HISTORICAL

- history of their company;
- ownership;
- subsidiaries, if any;
- organisation structure;
- corporate objectives
- problem areas – current;
- problem areas – potential.

FINANCIAL DATA

- profit and loss, balance sheet data;
- key financial ratios;
- comparisons of ratios on an inter-firm, inter-industry basis;
- creditworthiness;
- payment history etc.

MARKETING DATA

- client's key markets and trends, evolution etc;
- competitors active in his markets;
- profiles of buyers, influencers, etc. in his markets;
- product range/width/depth;
- future market/product plans;
- distribution routes;
- pricing policies;
- communications activities;
- sales force organisation/methods;
- market position;
- market share;
- environmental factors likely to affect his markets;
- legislation affecting his operation.

COMPETITIVE DATA

- Which other professional service firms do they, or have they, used?

HOW DECISIONS ARE MADE ON PROFESSIONAL SERVICES

- Who decides?
- Who influences?
- The decision-making process.
- The basis on which decisions are made.
- The time-scales involved.

KEY CONTACTS
- names;
- titles;
- ages;
- needs
  —personal
  —job
  —departmental/others;
- ability to buy;
- authority to buy;
- best time to meet;
- attitude;
  —constructive
  —supportive
  —positive
  —critical.

Sources of information

The above information will clearly, in the main, be built up and added to as the needs and priorities for business development clarify over time. But whether for an initial, or subsequent 'developmental', or review meeting with a prospective or existing client, a sound base of up-to-date information is crucial to credibility. Any client can lose faith in uninformed suppliers, quite apart from any personal insult they may feel.

Background knowledge also provides a supplier, particularly of professional services, with another most precious commodity – personal confidence. This communicates itself to clients and builds credibility. In this context, the following sources are worthy of consideration:

- colleagues/senior partners/client records and files;
- local/trade/national press;
- industry/trade shows and seminars;
- directories/yearbooks/agencies —
  Jordan Dataquest
  Intercompany Comparisons Ltd
  Financial Times Yearbook
  Dunn and Bradstreet
  Who Owns Whom
  The Directory of Directors

Kompass
investment houses
Economic Intelligence Unit
local authorities
chambers of commerce;
- the prospect/client himself—
annual report
share prospectus
internal PR publications
organisation charts
industry contacts.

This information-building process does not just happen – it must be planned and reviewed regularly. The above list is essentially illustrative and there are other sources of information which can be tapped with a bit of research, effort and creativity.

Storing and retrieving client information

Based on the numerous information needs and sources available, the problem is less one of acquiring information than how, by whom and where it should be recorded and accessed.

A useful start point is to divide information into the following broad categories.

Operational information
This will be needed by staff working on current assignments, business development projects etc. As, by its nature, this type of information will tend to be used at 'point of contact', i.e. on client's premises, it needs to be:

- concise, e.g. Kardex or A4 size;
- coded, rather than explicit, in confidential areas;
- secure at all times.

Long-term or strategic information
This will be needed by staff working at the firm's offices, and will tend to be more permanent and comprehensive in nature than operational information. By its nature this will include correspondence, annual account plans, proposals, reports, client background information etc.

Increasingly, many firms are regarding much of this information as transposable where appropriate on to computerised record systems. Clearly, policies must be established so that while information is accessible for sales planning and development purposes – it is also secure from unauthorised or unnecessary access.

By its nature this is a decision area which cannot be generalised – every firm must make its own decision to fit its specific environment and priorities.

Some firms in professional services are tackling at least some of the inherent problems mentioned by establishing a third client information base, which is looked at below.

A job experience database

The primary objective here, beyond issues of security versus accessibility, is to provide the cross-industry, cross-discipline information links referred to earlier. This is particularly relevant in professional firms where the following situations may exist.

- Previous/contemporary industry knowledge and experience can be a key 'differentiating' factor in winning or growing business in a competitive climate.
- 'Re-inventing the wheel' may occur. For everyone this can have a potentially costly effect on time spent and fees lost or incurred when on any assignment new methods and approaches are developed from scratch, rather than on the basis of what has been previously done or originated. If a good starting point is missed, a job may immediately become less profitable.
- Trends at an industry level need to be monitored by senior partners in an 'opportunity search' client development context.

The job/experience database form shown in Figure 7.3 illustrates an input/summary which is equally applicable to manual or computer-based systems. Clearly, a master-file or index would need to be added to ensure overview and access. In large firms with regional offices linked by computer it can be accessed from several points.

Categories of information held might include:

- work type classifications;
- project/job codes;
- industry sector;
- industry code;
- client name;

JOB REF:
_____

CLIENT:
_____

NATURE OF ASSIGNMENT:

_____

VALUE:
_____

STAFFING:

_____

SUMMARY OF WHAT WAS DONE:

_____

PARTICULAR PROBLEMS ENCOUNTERED:

_____

NEW APPROACHES USED OR MATERIAL DEVELOPED:

_____

RELEVANCE TO OTHER COMPANIES/INDUSTRIES:

Figure 7.3   Job/experience database form

- summary of what was done;
- problems encountered;
- new approaches used/material developed;
- relevance to other companies/industries.

This approach has the additional merit of providing 'core' information at a number of stages of the marketing planning/account planning process and can also be cross-referenced back to original enquiry/progress forms of the type illustrated earlier.

This summary provides the end-view or 'review' stage of progress with specific clients to a total process which started with a 'preview' at an enquiry stage.

Fundamental client information principles

In conclusion two principles are worthy of restatement:

(1) 'Gap analysis' – measuring the difference between the information available versus information needed is a key first step to making information bases future-oriented, i.e. focused business development, rather than passively historic.
(2) The problem with information of this type is potentially one of 'overload' – given multiple requirements and sources – rather than 'shortfall', but the decisions on how, where and with whom this information is stored and how it can best be accessed, must be addressed and answered.

It has been said, with some truth, that 'if your system works well, it is obsolete', so constant review is necessary to refine and develop the agreed system, and make sure it remains relevant to current operations. Without this systematic approach, your excellent system of today will inevitably deteriorate into a future 'filing system' or archive.

New business selection

Key question 3 – Can we clearly and objectively select new business opportunities?

Overview

Though the prime concern of client development is by definition with existing, known clients these must originate somewhere and before moving on we will look in this section at how new business originates.

There are three fundamental routes by which new business is created or 'arrives' in the client portfolio of a professional firm, namely:

- building business in existing clients (developmentally);
- enquiries from potential clients (reactively);
- solicitation of business from potential clients (proactively).

As previously discussed, the first two rely essentially on selling skills, i.e. seeking and capitalising on opportunities to expand business from the current base and handling new enquiries from the initial to commitment phase efficiently and effectively. The latter, third, new business route is essentially a 'proactive' rather than developmental or reactive method.

All methods of marketing communications, i.e. advertising, PR seminar etc. will be the fundamental method by which totally new clients can be accessed. Given that the ultimate objective of marketing communications is to create an 'opportunity to do business', i.e. an enquiry, this will then fit into the second area or route by which new business can ethically be created and progressed.

But, irrespective of the route taken, certain fundamental principles apply to new business selection. As far as possible it should be planned activity, should be subject to vetting of specific opportunities at a relatively senior level, and should be a controlled process. This latter principle is patently a by-product of the first two.

The search for new business opportunities should be planned so that:

- opportunity stimulus exists, preferably on a regular, phased, basis;
- future opportunities (market sectors, professional service areas, specific clients) are examined and assessed for development at the planning stage, wherever possible;
- guidelines and definitions of what constitutes desirable and acceptable new business are established and communicated as an integral part of making the firm's plan known to anybody involved in the next period's client development process. This will avoid time-wasting advances in directions not fitting with the firm's overall plans.

It should be vetted so that:

- any new business opportunity of significance, in fee terms, can be assessed against the firm's plan and how it would utilise resources;
- the 'fit' with the firm's overall objectives and strategies can be assessed;
- the opportunity cost of pursuing an unpredicted opportunity against planned client or market development can be evaluated;
- trends can be assessed in the new business area.

It should be controlled so that:

- resources and effort remain focused on activities within the scope of the original plan.

(It is accepted that all of these steps are based on an arguably, optimistic scenario, in which sufficient opportunities exist from which to select. But to ensure that this state does prevail is, after all, the purpose of this chapter as a whole.)

It is without doubt worth re-emphasising that new business selection and review is made much more systematic and objective, and much less 'hit and miss', if a solid business plan – and marketing plan – exist in the first place. A review of the business/marketing planning process is largely the subject of Chapter 2.

Selecting worthwhile potential clients – currently and in the future

Using the preceding overview as a 'thinking frame' is the first essential step. However, there are specific questions which must be posed, discussed (and answered!) and criteria set within each firm as follows:

- Overall, do we know what constitutes a 'worthwhile' new client? And more explicitly
- Do we know if it is really likely that a particular prospective new client will agree to buy a significant amount of our services, measured in fee income, either now or in the future?
- Have we the resources to cost-effectively meet his needs?
- Does the nature of his need, or the complexity of his business, require a major investment of time/staff available?
- Can the scale/rate of likely fees be cost-justified to him?
- Does this client's 'buying history' (with you or other professional firms) imply a significant opportunity?
- Would gaining this client create a desirable knock-on effect in his or other industry/market sectors? Is it a prestigious and influential account to have? (Beware, judgements here must be very pragmatic.)

- Will the cost of the 'inputs' in time, staff, work load and terms be significantly less than the 'output' in revenue terms?
- If not, will the costs involved in gaining experience here be immediately recoverable by creating opportunities for the firm elsewhere in the market?
- Does this prospective client/enquiry offer significantly higher opportunity than other prospective business currently under review?
- Do we have the services which he needs currently available?
- If not, how urgent is his need? And if it is not urgent – but a major opportunity exists – should we develop our capability to meet his need?

No such list of selection criteria can ever be exhaustive – but these questions represent the 'filter' questions posed by many professional firms. Equally, not all of them can be answered instantly – often further qualification with a client, and/or a period of internal discussion is necessary. Both of these steps – when needed – are vital, if only to avoid accepting or rejecting business opportunities without due consideration. Equally, the review process should not take too long – even the most desperate client has limits to his patience! This means establishing filter or vetting standards at an early, rather than a later, stage in the business planning process.

Strategically, two questions should always be asked when a significant opportunity exists.

- Does this opportunity conform to our current strategic plan?
- If not, is pursuing and accepting it strategically justifiable?

It is self-evident that these two questions can, and should, only be finally answered with decisions at a senior level within any firm.

The link with promotional activity

In selecting new opportunities, there are two main links with promotional activity, the first 'causative' and the second 'preventative'.

- The **causative** link assumes that all promotional activities – whether by marketing communications or personal selling effort – are targeted effectively, and that key business development areas have been segmented realistically.

    Further, that correct methods of promotion – non-personal or personal – have been identified and used within the context of the total

communications 'mix' available, and that the service 'offer' matches the promotional objectives, in type and benefit.
- The **preventative** link assumes that resources and action are subsequently committed only to opportunities produced by promotional activity, i.e. in the market segments identified in the original promotional plan.

This has two implications – first, by its nature it is a way of measuring promotional activity by results, against objectives, rather than cost or expenditure committed or incurred. And, secondly, the source of any enquiries which happened by 'accident' rather than by 'design' can be examined to see whether more effort or expenditure on promotional activity in that area can turn 'accident' positively into 'design'.

A good example here is at least one professional services firm who now systematically use public seminars as a promotional route, among other purposes, because of new business which arrived originally by 'accident' from this source.

Establishing client relationships

Key question 4 – Have we clearly identified the relationships wanted with, and by, key development accounts?

Establishing and management of client relationships

Not only is the market environment characterised by high competition, but the work of professional service firms is, at least in some areas, being perceived as 'commodities' by clients. With performance standards which are in many cases perceived by clients as 'technically' the same whoever may supply professional help, establishing and maintaining positive client relationships can provide a key 'differentiation' opportunity for many firms. In this context a firm's most precious assets are its relationships with its potential or existing clients.

There is little doubt that decision-makers mentally position potential and existing suppliers of all services and products within a spectrum which might be represented as follows:

Client perception totally negative	**Client perception totally positive**
Expressed attitudes	*Expressed attitudes*
'They're only interested in fees'	'They're interested in our total business'
'Simply another supplier'	'They stand out from other suppliers'
'No different than the rest'	'They are different – positively!'

While this obviously represents an extremely polarised view of client perceptions and attitudes, it highlights the truth of the old saying, 'You don't have to be different to be good, often being good is different enough'.

Differentiation is critical and is less a matter of gimmicks than efficient and creative client orientation. Specifically, therefore, the following points on relationships are important:

- **positive** relationships based on mutual trust, credible performance and good relationship management by supplier firms will inevitably win more business at the potential sales stage, and preserve more business at post sales stage; and
- **negative** relationships where mutual trust is lacking, performance appears at best average and poor relationship management exists, will inevitably not win business at the potential sales stage, and will most certainly cause the client to ask competitor firms to propose for the current supplier's business.

It is axiomatic that most firms will want to be positioned positively rather than negatively in this 'perceptive' area. But, as with other areas of the client development process, it won't just happen – these relationships must be planned, managed and reviewed constantly, by all staff who have contact, developmentally or operationally, within client companies. Maintenance and enhancements of client relationships do not so much depend on an annual lunch with a senior partner, good manners, public relations, charm, diplomacy, window dressing and manipulation – rather on the insight that:

- any relationship with a client can, perhaps inevitably will, decay over time;
- managing the relationship progressively and consistently is much more effective than trying to pull a neglected relationship back from the edge of the abyss down which the client's fees are about to disappear!

Attention to client relationships is akin to preventative maintenance on a car.

In a demanding, and increasingly competitive, professional environment, technical competence alone is clearly no longer enough – creating a sense of mutuality, growing the business partnership is a vital extra dimension.

Benefits of well-managed client relationships

Truly effective client relationships where high trust and solid relations exist, pay off in two key ways.

- The **work** performed can usually be done with less inherent obstacles in the way – in the sense that information, comments or support from the client and his staff are without doubt given more readily and willingly to someone regarded as a 'working partner', than to a perceived 'third-party supplier'.
- The **sales** process – gaining further work where the client needs it, adding services which are of true value to the client, or repeating regular assignments – is inherently easier. Any of us talk more openly about present problems, other needs we have, where priorities may change in the future and so on – to people we trust and have a mutal relationship with, than with somebody who is simply 'doing their job'. Referrals to other clients are also more readily given to somebody who is valued beyond simply their technical competence.

Managing client relationships – practical steps

Managing the client relationship implies conscious actions to control and expand the 'account', a process of 'selling-on'.

This process involves three stages:

- establishing the relationship;
- managing the relationship;
- reviewing the relationship.

Establishing the relationship

This starts at meetings preceding the 'sale' of a project. The process here is built on pre-meeting research. Prepared information can make it clear to the client that knowledge and interest in his industry and business are important to you; and using such information as a base to discuss in depth where his problems, needs and priorities really lie and then basing subsequent proposals on his priorities enhances the relationship at this stage. The first meeting represents a significant opportunity to begin to stand out from the crowd.

Selling techniques deployed at this stage should and can enhance the building of a relationship and in fact provide the first opportunity with a new contact to demonstrate professional competence. In other words, the way selling is conducted should be instrumental in positioning the firm and individuals in the right role for the future.

Managing the relationship

This can be effected in a number of ways, some of which may appear obvious, but are worth re-emphasising:

- Send 'thank you' letters on client acceptance of assignments:
    - to emphasise the time which the client has previously committed to you in the decision-making stage;
    - to reinforce the implementation of the project;
    - to maintain a sense of mutual urgency.

- Ensure that any project is proceeding in the way that both parties agreed:
    - to ensure it is on time;
    - to ensure it is within cost parameters;
    - to prevent frustration or dissatisfaction;
    - to pre-handle any problems or complaints;
    - to turn 'promises' into 'realities';
    - ideally checking at prearranged review points.

- Monitor and report the results of your actions/activities:
    - to keep the initiative;
    - to create new opportunities;
    - to keep in contact with the decision-maker(s);
    - to re-emphasise the benefits of your work to the client.

- Expand your contacts in the client firm:
    - to increase awareness of his total activity;
    - to brief, where ethical, other executives on past/present activities and benefits to them.

- Keep *au fait* with the client's industry and business:
    - to help you identify other recommendations;

— to confirm the client's confidence in you an an interested and informed 'business partner'.

- Read the client's publications:
  — to identify additional client priorities or needs.

- Try to attend internal meetings of key clients:
  — to present your services on subjects under discussion;
  — to keep clients informed of any of the firm's activities which might be of interest.

- Invite the client, or his staff where appropriate, to your functions:
  — to cement the relationship.

- Try to get involvement in the client's planning processes:
  — to advise objectively where emerging priorities from his side coincide with developing services from yours.

- Establish a key client monitoring system:
  — to record past and current activities;
  — to plan future activities together.

If you find that such actions have no benefit, or seem inappropriate to you or the client's business, you will obviously think twice before carrying on with them, but many of them do have positive value in building and growing the client relationship. Other ideas must be created to keep the process fresh in the longer term.

A form is useful to decide/plan what steps should be implemented – and what the results over time have been, in the relationship management process. While it is unlikely that every one of these actions should (or can) be actioned with every client with equal emphasis, assessing the value and impact of them is a key stage from which many firms will potentially benefit. It is a good idea to make sure there is on every client file a document that records sales action taken and which, like the enquiry form, ends with the next action that it is intended to take in order to progress the business. Once such action has led to a specific request to discuss some particular project being made, then the enquiry procedure can take over.

The intentions of such a form are again to act as a record, a checklist and prompt.

It is not possible to specify how these forms should appear in every firm or department. However, Figures 7.4 and 7.5 are examples of two which are intended to act as blueprints from which other, more individual,

To:	From:	
Ref. no:		**CLIENT REVIEW FORM**

Work being carried out:	Client:
	Address:
	Tel. No:
Project manager:	Contacts: Name Position
	1.
	2.
Completion date:	3.
	Type of organisation:

Follow-up sales action:

Date	

Work proposed:	Value £
☐ Agreed ☐ Refused – Reason	

Figure 7.4   Client review form

CLIENT			PERIOD	

POSITIVE ACTIVITY PLANNED	R/E*	BY WHOM?	WITH WHOM?	WHEN OR FREQUENCY (IF APPLICABLE)

*Regular or exceptional?

Key points – Why this strategy and activity?

_____

Success criteria	Results

Figure 7.5   Relationship management programme

forms can be developed. They major on the sales *action*, but could alternatively be linked to a checklist of service range.

ACTION
Consider having a 'client review form', a formal system that will prompt sales action by recording future actions, not just what has been done. If this exists and is consistently used, at least for major clients, it can pay dividends.

Whatever combination is selected, one of the most effective methods for 'selling-on', which is the ultimate objective of relationship management, is to conduct formal, timely reviews with the client's senior management.

Reviewing the relationship
This starts by researching, through discussions with colleagues or staff involved, or in discussions with client staff, results obtained by them from current or previous work. During such activities identify satisfaction levels, results obtained by the client firm, other priorities and problems – and thus highlight any new requirements. A process of collating these findings, discussing priorities with the key client contact and other interested parties, getting their current 'view of the world' and presenting further recommendations at a formal review can now be made mutually productive. In some firms this is already an adopted process, following or during internal reviews of current or completed projects.

Formal client review meetings will be at their most productive if structured along lines such as these:

- Review and compare achievements of the past period:
  — original objectives set;
  — solutions proposed;
  — work undertaken and completed;
  — benefits obtained by the client;
  — discrepancies, if any, between objectives and results with reasons.

- Present new proposals:
  — needs and priorities which the client currently has;
  — solutions, i.e. ways you can help;
  — benefits and results which the client will receive.

- Present an implementation programme:
  - objectives;
  - actions and milestones;
  - review points.

- Gain commitment from the client to the next step.

Working systematically in this way allows the potential both to check relationships, and client perspectives and perceptions, turning new clients into retained clients, retained clients into growing clients and, therefore, aids in making time invested on client development activities most productive.

Relationship management reviewed

It is realistic to emphasise here that not all clients – and not all professional projects – require the same degree of relationship cultivating and effort. These decisions are judgemental and will be different, even by degree, for every firm. However, whatever effort and investment is made in cultivating the client relationship, it should be made in a systematic and regular way. This means that any firm interested in developing client business must be sensitive and alert to the risks involved in simply letting relationships evolve by *laissez-faire*. Opportunities can too easily go by default, and competition is increasingly vigilant.

For a client, agreeing to do business with a firm offering professional services is only a first step. How the total relationship develops after this point, as well as pure technical performance, affects deeply his decisions 'next time around'!

'Business partners', if that is his perception, rather than 'simply another professional', are valued and retained, rather than easily substituted or replaced. Being seen as a 'business partner' is dependent on good relationship management. Just hitting it off well with the client is no longer likely to be sufficient.

Planning and executing client development strategies

Key question 5 – How well do we plan and execute client development strategies?

Planning at the client level

At several stages so far it has been emphasised that, even assuming a clear commitment to the principles of client development, 'it doesn't just happen – it must be planned'.

But it is also worth stressing that planning – and executing the plan, i.e. making it happen – can't take place in a vacuum. By its very nature and because of its critical importance – new business creation via coherent client development strategies must be a part of an integrated and complete process.

It must be integrated in three directions.

- **'Downwards'**, in that an overall business and marketing plan must first exist, if only so that client planning in relation to business development has a corporate framework in which to operate.
- **'Upwards'**, in that, if reasoned new business development plans at the client level are generated at the right stage, they become an 'input' at the formative stage of the firm's overall business plan, i.e. an estimate of potential from existing clients forms a key part of forecasted business growth.
- **'Sideways'**, in that, at a time when firms are expanding their involvement in additional disciplines and thus the 'service portfolio' on offer and, at the same time, expanding geographically in many cases, i.e. new offices or special divisions for individual service areas – client development plans should, by their nature account for the total business development potential for that client on a cross-discipline, cross-geography, etc. basis. 'Sideways' integration alone provides a superb communicational/opportunistic basis on which individuals in different disciplines and/or different locations can co-operate and 'synergise' on business development opportunity searching and knowledge sharing. This is possible because there is a common core on which the plan centres – the client, rather than the technical discipline involved.

This background provides the basis on which the key question of 'How well do we plan and execute client development strategies?' can, at the first stage at least, be answered, i.e. is it objectively an integrated process:

- downwards?
- upwards?
- sideways?

If the answer is yes – senior people should still ensure that it continues.

Integration of planning is, frankly, challenging and time-intensive – better to restress internally from time to time the inherent benefits than to have to act as a 'doctor to an ailing patient' if integration is decaying.

If the answer is no – consider the risks inherent in 'planning in a vacuum'. Even the best overall business plan is not capable of operation if client development activity 'on the ground' is not happening. Conversely, the best client plan can ultimately become a form of 'guerilla warfare' if it is working in spite of, or at cross-purposes to, the overall business plan. This can cause potential irritation or lost opportunity across disciplines, offices geographically separated etc. Many firms have learned these lessons the hard way, but those with clear, integrated plans for client development now have an advantage over those operating on a more *ad hoc* basis.

For which clients should detailed development plans be created?

The purist would say, 'Every single one'. The realist would say, 'If that is possible – certainly', but in practice, 'Prepare detailed (and that is the key word) plans for, at the very least, all major clients'.

If the realist's view is to be adopted then definitions of major/key/developmental clients are called for; these clients are those which:

- produce high volumes of business or potential;
- require a high level of attention or commitment of the firm's staff, at all levels;
- have possibly high potential for other services which the firm can provide.

Additional 'indications' are that they exhibit some or all of the following characteristics:

- any one client that accounts for in excess of, say, 5 per cent of the firm's overall business, measured on a time/fees basis for each of the firm's services;
- clients whose level of business with the firm is such that losing it would have significant effects on the firm;
- clients who have an obvious potential to grow to these levels of business and importance;
- clients who are major opinion-formers (and therefore affect other client relationships).

How do such clients differ from other clients?

In practice, the answer here will vary from firm to firm, but some indications are:

- they require a lot more attention through visits etc.;
- they provide the opportunity for larger potential sales and more risk;
- in dealing with them, the firm will tend to be in a more 'competitive' situation (and the client knows it!);
- more decision-makers or influencers;
- more chance of the firm coming up against organisational politics;
- the decision-making process can be complex;
- the firm will have to maintain overall client satisfaction, i.e. in several departments or divisions;
- more and better information will be required.

In other words they are different, not just in size but in nature, and most emphatically, therefore, more detailed client planning will be required for them.

Detailed planning for major clients

It has already been made clear that plans at the client level are extremely important – the real implication of what has been said previously here is that the client plan forms the 'operational dovetail' to the strategic business plan of the total firm.

Because it can be a time-intensive process, there is still evidence in the profession, and indeed in the wider business world beyond that, of resistance to a client planning process in detailed form. Two frequent areas of critical comment can be summarised in statements like these:

'The more detailed it is – the more it operates as a strait-jacket to us.'
'Developing our business is essentially opportunistic – unpredictable events cause additional needs which we can meet and, therefore, why write a predictive plan for something that can't be foretold?'

These comments are understandable. But, on being stated they contain, paradoxically, the very answer to the comments: that substituting the words 'defined parameters' for 'strait-jacket' emphasises the need to define the logical limits within which development activity can freely take place – without conflict with the firm's overall plan.

Business development is, to no small degree, 'opportunistic'. But planned activity, if it includes true insight into what may happen in the client's own markets and operations for the next year(s), centres on ensuring that predicted changes in his needs or priorities, are, wherever possible, linked to timely and logical action plans. Not least, this ensures that your presence is felt as a 'business partner' as and when the changes occur. Thus, the plan brings together opportunity and action on the planner's part and to his, and the client's, mutual benefit. As was indicated earlier, opportunities only exist when they are seen to be, and coincide with solutions a professional service can provide.

A well-reasoned client plan ensures that people, money, time and support facilities are used to best advantage. This is of vital importance in obtaining business from major clients, since more often than not a team of people will be involved. Without a detailed plan the problem of co-ordinating their activity would be considerably greater. In addition, without a plan it is difficult to ensure that the correct priorities are allocated, or that minor, but still important aspects of the firm's activities are not overlooked.

Planning – not just plans!

Dwight D. Eisenhower, who was responsible in 1944 for the biggest movement in history of men and material, once said: 'Plans are nothing; planning is everything'.

The important thing which Eisenhower highlighted was that a fixed, rigid plan was useless in itself; the important aspect was the planning process. This covers analysis, forecasting, objective setting, strategising and programming.

The client plan, which is of course concerned with the future, must be flexible in its construction so that it is able to adapt to changes, since the future cannot be predicted with a high degree of accuracy. Thus, a plan defined from forecasts is useless if it is seen as a set of actions which must happen. The planning process is as important as the plan, which should in any case be more like a route map than details of one road.

Formalised approaches to client planning

A formal plan serves as a framework for day-to-day decision-making and provides a method for follow-up and evaluation of how client development activity is progressing.

The planning process should supply answers to the following questions:

- Where are we now? (Analysis)
- Where are we heading? (Trend analysis, forecasting)
- Where do we want to go? (Objective setting)
- What is the gap? (That can or must be filled)
- How do we get there? (Strategic and action plans)
- How are we progressing? (Controls)

The answer to the last question (monitoring actual results against the planned results) is, of course, an input to the others over time. In practice, any good planning process is always continuous.

Planning consists of four distinct phases which we will now examine.

Where are we now and where are we heading?
This phase is concerned with a situation analysis – a process of putting together the history of the performance of all services, market climate etc., and the identification of future opportunities and threats, and present strengths and weaknesses within each major/key client.

Where do we want to go?
This phase encompasses the following.

Assumptions	those conditions in the client firm or market which cannot be quantified and for which we have to assume a certain posture.
Statement of objectives	these are the goals which have been identified for the client plan and should be quantified specifically in areas of: — value/mix of professional services; — share of business; — profit, where the directive of fee income less attributed costs can be deducted.

What is the gap and how do we get there?
This phase encompasses the following.

Basic strategy	defines the specific approaches we will take (major courses of action) to achieve the objectives of the plan.
Specific actions	these will define: — what needs to be done (detailed actions); — when it needs to be undertaken and completed by;

— who is responsible for those activities;
— where appropriate, the costs of that activity, e.g. notional or fee cost of a senior partner's involvment.

How are we progressing?
This phase addresses itself to the controls and review procedures – these are the mechanisms for monitoring actual performance against planned performance and initiating corrective action when things do not go according to plan.

The client plan is a formal statement of the support effort for a specific client. Developing the plan involves the following steps.

- Situation analysis of the client company:
  — opportunity and threats identification;
  — strengths and weaknesses analysis.

- Objectives within this client situation:
  — including assumptions about those conditions which cannot be quantified.

- Strategy statement:
  — encompassing the main strategic actions to be pursued.

- Actions plans:
  — including costs or budgets for the activity where appropriate;
  — time-scales for the activity;
  — support required

- Control and review procedures:
  — with other firm's personnel, 'internally';
  — with the client, i.e. formal, 'external reviews'.

First step – situation analysis
The first major section of the plan is an examination of the present situation – your 'trading performance' with the client and the present and future business environments in which both the client and therefore, you as suppliers of professional services, are operating. The situation analysis section itself can be usefully divided into four sections – an account profile, normal forecast, opportunities and threats, and strengths and weaknesses analysis. This encourages a systematic situation appraisal by the person responsible for originating the plan.

SECTION I — THE CLIENT PROFILE

This sets out a profile of the client company showing:

- your present business volumes, expressed as fee income, and services used;
- your present share of the business by service and 'usage' area;
- a description of the trend by service and 'usage' areas;
- a cost analysis identifying all costs directly incurred in dealing with the client, e.g. attributable promotional/support costs, personal cost estimates against fees generated, fees attributable as costs of other's time etc.

A quantitative analysis of the particular client will now exist, in terms of fees/usage by service or service groups, and the relative costs incurred, together with a picture of trends and some indication of share of customer business in relevant service areas.

SECTION 2 — NORMAL FORECAST

The client profile should be followed by a forecast of the firm's 'sales' to this client under 'normal conditions'. This is what might occur, assuming no major changes in the marketing environment or marketing strategies of the firm.

Clearly, the preparation of this forecast requires close liaison within the firm at a senior level, and reference to client records of past activity. Detailed client knowledge, i.e. from the uniform client information/research base is essential.

The forecast would have to be revised if quite different environmental conditions are expected or strategies are planned, e.g. economic growth, legislation, competition and changes in the firm's or this client's activity.

The current and probably future 'sales' picture will by now exist. However, the picture is a forecast and not yet necessarily agreed targets or objectives. It is the answer to the question 'Where are we heading?'.

SECTION 3 — OPPORTUNITIES AND THREATS IDENTIFICATION

The normal forecast section should be followed by a section in which the person developing the plan identifies the main opportunities and threats facing his firm.

The opportunities and threats describe outside factors facing the client and supplier of professional services, i.e. the firm. They are written so as to suggest possible actions that might, by implication, be warranted.

The main opportunities and threats for the future are likely to be identified from the following areas.

- **Economic factors**, if it is, say, an industrial client, will his markets grow or decline? If he is exporting, will exchange rates, import quotas changing etc. affect his business, financially or organisationally? And, as a result – will such factors affect his needs for our services, thus limiting or expanding the use of our services?
- **Technological factors/changes**, e.g. a client entering a market for computer systems may need additional services in business planning, the raising of venture capital, additional management accounting systems. As a corollary, a client whose business may be eroded by a competitor entering his market with a substitute or replacement product may need management consultancy services, or – at worst – assistance from an insolvency firm and/or legal adviser.
- **Political/legal factors**, e.g. effects on the client of likely changes in, say, product liability legislation, which will affect his products detrimentally – he may need additional help in inventory management, insurance or contract preparation.

The above list is simply intended to illustrate what analysis of opportunities and threats can provide if it is used as a 'thinking frame'. With major/key clients in volatile markets, or who are organisationally complex, discussion and sharing of views with colleagues within the firm can be a useful and desirable process. This is 'sideways', 'downwards' and 'upward' integration in its most practical and potentially potent form!

As the above examples illustrate, an opportunity only exists for the firm if it can be met either with the expansion of a service currently used, or the use of an additional service, within the firm's current or planned portfolio.

Because of this, it must be relevant to follow and dovetail the opportunity/threat analysis with a strengths/weaknesses analysis. It is only then that a changing future situation for this client can be truly categorised as an opportunity, a threat or simply a future event which has no effect for your firm – or is someone else's opportunity!

SECTION 4 – STRENGTHS AND WEAKNESSES ANALYSIS
In this section of the plan the quality of the firm's offering to the client is evaluated. This will enable the value to both parties to be determined. As a result, an extra dimension is added to the quantitative picture of 'sales'

and profit, which will be required to determine an effective strategy to achieve the objectives.

A simple format is to divide the firm's offering into three main component parts:

- 'product' – services;
- fees and terms;
- 'presentation' and support;

and assess them against the competition in each of the areas of the client's operation where a buying influence exists. Again, good knowledge is required – of client buying influences and needs, and of competition (generally and *vis-à-vis* this client).

The first step in the strengths and weaknesses analysis would be a **service analysis**. The depth of detail will vary from service to service (or range), and client to client, but the aim is to identify strengths and weaknesses *vis-à-vis* competition as seen from the client's point of view, using a concept of value analysis.

The second step would cover **fees and terms**. A similar exercise should be carried out for these. In looking at fees, the supplier should be aware that his service will be of varying importance to different clients, and different areas of his operation will be viewed differently (not only fees but the total terms of business should be compared).

This is becoming an area in which many firms are benefiting from a market-based approach to fees charged and, indeed, what fee levels are tolerable, i.e. 'sensitive' or 'insensitive' in the client's view. For example, some fees may be a 'market sensitive' area, i.e. a client may turn to other firms if fees appear to rise dramatically in relative terms to, say, last year, or those charged by others. On the other hand, fees charged for, say, the origination of inventory management systems, which bring stock costs dramatically down or ensure they are kept under control, may be perceived as tremendously high in value by the client. In such cases relatively higher fees may well be perfectly acceptable. This is certainly true of any service area which makes savings for the client.

The third step would cover **presentation analysis**. The term presentation is used to refer to all the other factors associated with the supplier's offering, besides the service itself and fee levels/policies.

Examine all the elements of support provided to or needed by the client and compare your standards against the competition as seen from the client's needs. This will include such things as:

- advice on legislative changes;
- specialist seminars on topics of regular interest;
- seminars of an *ad hoc* nature, perhaps topical;
- the firm's links with intermediaries (others who the client may need to work with, in some cases, in a way which overlaps with your services);
- documentation, i.e. standard business forms;
- access to specialists or senior partners, overseas offices of the firm etc.; and so on.

The steps following a situation analysis – the client plan itself

Client plans will vary in depth or requirement, formats which are most suitable and degree of precision needed, from one firm to another.

This notwithstanding, some explicit guidelines on the client plan generation process, terminology and areas of potential difficulty are useful, if only to establish a framework for discussion within your firm. (Experienced planners may choose to skip this part – but why not review it anyway – after all, experience itself can change over time!)

Ingredients of a client plan

Given that situation analysis is a precursor and will provide detailed insight into the 'forward situation' the firm will face, plans subsequently generated should have the following three ingredients.

OBJECTIVES

Objectives are essentially end results in key areas. These should be as clear and concise as possible and should concentrate specifically on what the firm expects to achieve with this client in the plan period. General or modifying remarks that fail to further define the objectives should be avoided.

A useful 'acid test' is to ask whether the objectives are 'SMART', that is:

Specific   stating precisely what will be achieved by the plan, evident in a form that is;

Measurable   in other words that control area performance standards etc. can be applied where required;

Achievable   within the resources available;

Realistic fitting the overall business plan of the firm (essentially 'Should we be doing this?', as opposed to 'Can we achieve it?');

Timed specifying how effort and support is spread effectively throughout the year's client activity, times/dates exist for key activities, and that deadlines or review points exist.

STRATEGIES

These essentially define the 'route' which activity will take. Strategy is the vital link between objectives and action programmes, the frame into which activity fits.

Strategies should concentrate on those major elements of the programme which will be directly responsible for enabling the firm to achieve its desired goals. Statements should not go into minute detail about the activity in question. These are covered in the plan of execution or 'tactics'.

ACTION PROGRAMMES

These essentially define the detailed steps necessary in pursuing. Precise detail on who does what by when are needed here.

Action programmes are, by nature, tactical – they define the 'week-to-week' events by which the strategy with the client will be followed, in order to achieve the stated objectives.

Special techniques

Detailed and comprehensive client planning may involve certain special techniques, for example the following.

- **Statistical forecasting** Specifically in answering the question 'Where are we heading?' (trend analysis). This is essentially the mathematical extrapolation of past sales figures into the future on the assumption that all the variables will remain the same.
- **Sensitivity analysis** Specifically in the area of defining scientifically likely reactions to fee levels etc. This is often causally linked to the overall technique of 'value analysis'.

Specialist help should be sought if these two and, indeed, other techniques are used, where the firm's, or indeed the planner's own, knowledge is less than required.

The client planning process reviewed

The overall development of major client plans should be an annual process and involves the following:

- forecasting 'sales' and profit objectives;
- analysing strengths and weaknesses of the firm's 'offering' in the client's eyes;
- developing a major client strategy;
- identifying the main activities to be carried out to ensure that the objectives are achieved.

Unless meaningful plans are drawn up, the activity towards key developmental clients will tend to become uncoordinated and the results are likely to be less successful. Experience shows that those firms who carry out this planning activity most effectively mobilise their resources more efficiently, are more likely to maximise the revenues and profits they achieve, and have a more mutually rewarding relationship with their major customers.

For the plans to make maximum impact they should be:

- specific, listing detailed activity;
- easily measured, quantified wherever possible;
- succinct, easily read and understood;
- directive, showing clearly what is required from each individual (or department) concerned;
- a basis for commitment by the individuals involved to achievement of the objectives.

The link to records/systems

In addition to guidelines given earlier about information systems, some comments on how client development plans, and planning, link to records/information are worth making.

Because detailed client plans are 'information intensive' – a tremendous amount of factual data needs to be reviewed, fed into or generated at the planning stage – information gathering should be done over time. Those who have suddenly to find the often detailed information required when 'the plan' is due (or late) will appreciate this point. As an adjunct to this, it is clearly valuable to have record systems which both record factual data over time – progressing as and when it is collected and providing the information easily – in the form needed, at the planning stage.

Several firms, through insight or 'remembered pain', have made client planning systems essentially 'rolling' plans and formats, i.e. details of what has been achieved, costs involved, opportunity/threat analysis etc. is regularly reviewed and updated throughout the year. This has four effects.

- The client plan and record systems at client level are automatically linked and the format/content of both can be reviewed together.
- The client plan is under progressive review during its operational stage.
- The 'state of affairs' shown in the client record is always firmly up to date.
- Next year's plan, particularly in the information area, takes far less time, in that a minimum of 'reinventing the wheel' is called for (or finding out from scratch where the spokes of the wheel have been buried!).

Involving the client in the process

Client development should not be viewed as something 'done to' the client in isolation. Involving the client in the process makes sense from two major directions, both philosophically and practically.

Philosophically, because it is, after all, not simply your future as a supplier you are planning, it is the client's too. If professional services are going to have an impact on his future, perhaps his input is desirable.

Practically, because a client may well have gone, or be going through, a similar planning process – and, therefore, have readily to hand data or views on his markets, financial requirements, opportunities etc. Consider the potential time to be saved if you could tap into his views and plans for the future. The planning stage also provides a superb opportunity to review with major clients the year that has gone and the period ahead. In this sense, it is a logical point for formal review, at which future links may be formed, and is a tremendous 'opportunity generator'. Mutual planning discussions also help forge, or re-forge, the 'business partners' approach described on page 243.

Control and evaluation

Key question 6 – Do we effectively control and evaluate client development activity, in relation to the overall business plan?

Making sure the client development process takes place

Detailed planning for major/key clients must be, by its impact on client
development activity, an exhaustive process. Particularly if being done
for a number of clients for the first time in depth it can be, as many can
readily confirm personally, an exhausting process, both physically and
mentally!

As with all major endeavours, once the planning process has been
completed, there is an understandable tendency to sit back and 'relax a
while'. And here is the point at which many a good intent starts to go
astray. Planning is the first step, actions as planned, must follow, or the
whole process will become an irrelevant and costly 'theoretical exercise'.
This is worth considering in particular if first steps are being taken in this
area, perhaps initiated by the marketing plan. If a lot of effort is expended
to no good effect, then the credibility of all such activity will take a knock.
It may, therefore, be worth linking first steps to fewer, really key clients,
where certainty of follow-through should ensure results and set the scene
for increased activity thereafter.

The purpose of control, the point of evaluation, is to ensure first that
what has been planned is happening and secondly that what is happening
is being compared to the original plan.

The by-product of control and evaluation is to make the planning
process dynamic to ensure it is happening. You will need to feed consistently into the client planning system fresh information to keep both
the plan and the client information ('data') bank as up to date as is
necessary.

This dynamic process can be pictured thus:

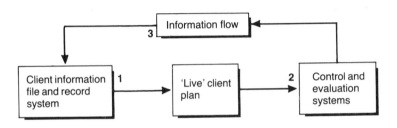

At point 1 – The client information file and record systems provide data for the client plan.

At point 2 – What is happening during the plan's 'operational' phase is being assessed.

At point 3 – The results of control and evaluation are being fed back as 'updates' to the client information system and record file, which itself provides an accurate base on which the next plan is written. And so on.

This, at a glance, emphasises the positive, as opposed to the very common, punitive nature of the control process. Frankly, it is a fundamental insight which is often overlooked. More philosophically, controls are a 'friendly policeman' rather than a 'sentencing judge'. The ultimate purpose is to ensure that efficiency (required results) is never overtaken, in a hectic life, by effort in the wrong direction.

Methods of control and evaluation

Applied methods for control will vary in their precise nature from firm to firm, particularly in the detail required in planning. This detail, as a judgement area, should itself include definitions of the details of control points in the client development process, but several guideline points can be usefully made, in terms of the nature of controls in the client development process.

Some key questions to ask follow from these initial points. First, the control process is the assessment by 'variance analysis' of whether key performance standards are being met, i.e. the formula:

$$\text{Actual result} - \text{Standard} = \pm \text{Variance}$$

In this context, the formula is answering the question posed earlier (in relation to the client planning process, 'How are we progressing?').

This, of course, reinforces the fact that for control to be possible, performance standards have to be stated in the initial plan.

Secondly, controls provide guidance through feedback on how well the individual responsible for the actual achievement of the planned client development process is performing. On a broader front, controls also provide those managing the personnel working on client development activities with explicit feedback on how well they are motivating 'their people'. In most firms success is a co-operative effort and the results of this, positive or negative, can be pragmatically measured here. This itself suggests that future resources in management support, additional promotional expenditure, training etc. can be committed more objectively, through a two-stage process of:

- measuring what has happened;
- asking/discussing 'why?' if significant negative variances exist.

Thirdly, control and evaluative standards can be of three distinct types, all of which are inherent in a well-thought-through process, as follows.

'Absolute' standards

These include such features as total revenue produced by the year end from the client, total costs attributable, total attributable profit, revenue producing hours spent, non-revenue producing time spent etc. These types of 'absolute' standards have a primary strong point in their favour – they provide just that, an 'absolute' measurement of what has happened. These results serve as the 'facts', the prime standards achieved (or not, as the case may be). But these types of standards also have an inherent weak point which is that history cannot be changed! They measure what has happened, but it is by then usually far too late to redress any negative balance, except in the future, for example, via next year's plan. Absolute standards alone or predominantly applied, are inherently risky in the critical area of client development activity/plans.

'Moving standards'

These provide a more useful standards basis. If client development results are monitored by those managing the activity, on a monthly, weekly (or sometimes even daily) basis, variances can be identified more readily, and trends in the variances will allow future problems to be predicted and, where the right corrective action is possible, avoided.

For example, client A's plan might call for a new project following another to be agreed ('sold-in') by October latest, so that work could commence in November. But if this does not happen because the person responsible has been tied up on an overrun project at client B, then either:

'(1) someone else could be sent, if suitable, to talk with client A'; '(2) someone else could be sent to release the person tied up at client B'; or '(3) if there is no one else – at the very least, it will be known that the estimated fees from client A are in jeopardy'. In this case plans need to be laid showing how to 'replace' this revenue some other way. This example, if lengthy, also makes a further point, in that 'moving' standards can be further refined if a third type of standard is applied.

'Diagnostic' standards

These can help identify why performance is varying from plan and are defined by asking the question 'What affects the achievement of success?'. For the person managing those responsible for client development work, these are particularly useful, in identifying the actions that staff themselves must take, which, in turn, lead to achievement of objectives set. Fundamentally, there are only four standards in relation to 'sales' activity for professional service, as follows:

- What clients are staff meeting on development 'calls'?
  Are these the right clients, or kinds of clients?
- How many clients are the subject of specific development 'calls'? Are these as against plan, in numbers terms?
- Is contact frequency appropriate? Are you staying in touch, as and when opportunities predicted arise?
- What is actually done by staff, in a face-to-face development 'call' with clients?

All of this can be summarised as, 'Are we as a firm, and as individuals, doing the right things, at the right time, at the right frequency, with the right clients to ensure our business grows according to plan?'. This is the essential link which binds client development activity to the business plan for the firm as a whole. This argues for one more repetition of our basic theme that 'client development won't just happen – it must be planned'. Control is an essential part of this process.

The following checklist of key control questions may prompt internal discussion.

- Have we defined the key areas of activity that need to be evaluated?
- Have we defined what is 'success' in each area?
- Have we identified the factors that will affect success in each area?
- Have we established appropriate criteria for evaluating environmental, client and the firm's performance?
- Do we know the sequence of likely causes?
- Does our information system provide data to compare against the success criteria?
- Do we have a systematic approach to variance production analysis and corrective action?

These answers can provide a powerful guide to the quality of existing plans, at both the firm's and at each major client's level. If there are no answers, or the answers are unsatisfactory, then action is necessary sooner rather than later. The only alternative is to leave client development, and thus the growth of the firm, exposed as a hostage to fortune in the hostile and increasingly competitive market for professional services.

Guidelines on client development

In the early stages of this chapter six key questions were proposed to those in firms concerned with managing the client development process. They bear repeating here on two counts.

- First, addressing these questions is fundamental to making the challenging process of client development a planned process, rather than just hoping or expecting that it will happen.
- Secondly, on the grounds that there will be at least one reader who will travel by the least lengthy route from start to finish, that is, from the opening paragraph, to this summary, without dwelling or glancing too deeply at the intervening thousands of words. That reader – if any of the following questions provide a moment's disquiet in terms of the quality of your answer to them – should go back and read the guidelines in that area at least. If client development is important to your future, and your answers give you pause for thought, haven't you just added one more element of potential risk to what is an already challenging future for the profession as a whole?

The six key questions are these.

- How well are we organised in relation to client development?
- Do our client information systems help the business development process?
- Can we clearly and objectively select new business opportunities?
- Have we clearly identified the relationships wanted with, and by, key development accounts?
- How well do we plan and execute client development strategies?
- Do we effectively control and evaluate client development activity, in relation to the overall business plan?

Looking to the future there is little doubt that the professions face an increasingly hostile and competitive market environment, from a number of directions. Competition from 'within' the profession is intensifying. The large firms, in particular, are taking a much more overt, 'proactive' approach to business growth – adding more services to their existing portfolios, for example. This is probably a powerful route to growth – by creating client experience and satisfaction with the experience.

This, combined with many clients' wishes to reduce, rather than increase their suppliers in numbers, means that other firms providing more limited services are, by definition, under increased scrutiny by the client, and increasing competition as a result.

In addition, competition from 'without', i.e. the work being under-taken by overlapping specialists (accountants and banks, for example) is growing in scale and nature in that these organisations are also reacting to fierce competitive pressures in their own, more traditional markets.

In addition, clients are becoming more demanding and, as many firms will bear witness, are no longer content to view services such as audit on a 'sitting tenancy' basis – clients will shop around and will demand value for money in terms of that often ill-defined 'something extra'. Clients are also more aware of what other professional firms offer, both qualitatively and quantitatively.

For many firms, this scenario means that repeat business, or business just walking in the door, is not an automatic process. Existing business has to be defended and new business has to be won. That is the future, and whether that leaves the reader feeling besieged or encouraged, is the most telling point of all. For those firms who have planned the develop-ment, who are ensuring that it happens, the future looks pretty good from where they sit. Albeit that there is always an element of risk, the planning and execution of carefully considered client development at least reduces the risk to an acceptable minimum.

The process described here should not be rejected as overkill. It will take time, particularly first time round, but it will not take a dis-proportionate time in terms of the size of business provided by major clients, the potential inherent in them and, perhaps even more important, the impact of losing them.

It is too easy with the pressures that exist on time to ignore or shortcut the process, and perhaps other elements of marketing also, the imple-mentation of which would add a new dimension to your firm's growth. As John Lennon put it, 'Life is what happens while you are making other plans'. The danger is that your direct competitors may not be so complacent, may take more of an initiative and reap the benefits. A final word here reflects a repeating theme of this book.

Client development is a vital part of the marketing process that con-tributes directly to a firm's success. It must be planned and controlled. It will not just happen, it demands initiation. That is both a challenge and a marvellous opportunity. These guidelines are designed to help in a small way to make client development contribute to at least some professional firms' futures – and thus to their planned business growth.

8 AFTERWORD
What next?

There was a time when no detailed understanding of marketing was necessary in the professions. Indeed, in many, the use of most of the techniques it involves was not permitted.

Now, however, marketing is, for better or for worse, a part of the on-going activity of any firm. The question is not whether you should do it, but how can you make what you do – in its many and changing details – appropriate and really effective.

With the acceptance phase largely over, the task of implementation comes next, and many are now struggling to get to grips with the techniques which are involved and are now permitted. This implies a broad range of activity; assessing what services to offer; taking a marketing view of fee levels; experimenting with sales techniques – and co-ordinating the complex range of activity that makes up the promotional 'mix'.

More and more people have discovered that initiating activity in these areas provides real opportunity to increase their firm's growth, development and profitability. Some are proving very good at it; in some cases to no one's greater surprise than their own.

BUT (there is always a but). Vidal Sassoon is credited with saying, 'The only place where success comes before work is in the dictionary'. Success for a professional services firm is no doubt dependent on many things; paramount among them is the quality of the service given and the work done. And I need not point out to readers that you need to work at that.

You need to work at marketing too. It does not just happen. And it is constantly dynamic and always subject to market and competitive pressures. There is no one right way to do anything in marketing, from designing an advertisement or direct mail letter, to setting up a marketing database. The best way today, tomorrow and next month will each be different and differently interpreted by different firms. The whole purpose is to differentiate and that must be done creatively and continuously.

An understanding of the many techniques involved and the co-ordination of them is essential, and it takes time. However obvious it may appear, this cannot be overstressed. Implementation of marketing takes time. In a fee-paying business, where the same people are the production resource and the promotional resource, how that time is made available, when and who does what, is crucial. Even in firms taking a real initiative with marketing this often remains a problem, seemingly with no easy answers.

For those who tackle the process successfully, making real plans, laying responsibility, understanding and using the techniques appropriately – albeit with some experiment along the way – there will be new business enquiries available. For those who pick up enquiries skilfully, in a truly sales-oriented way, there will be new clients signed.

In a business where the feeling has traditionally been that 'nice guys don't sell', who can honestly say they do not get satisfaction from a client, or better still a new client, giving his final approval to a project? If you do not at present, or have not thought of it in that way, try it. There are more and more people in the professions who do, and more and more firms are working hard to make sure it is a feeling that occurs to them more often.

For those who do all this and then not only turn in first-class work, but also manage and develop their clients purposefully, there are real opportunities for the future. Whoever wears the 'marketing hat' has considerable responsibility, and if successful, can take potentially a great deal of credit for what the firm can achieve in the future – though the achievement, of course, will affect the whole firm.

The 'BUT' mentioned above is thus one that can be surmounted. If the time is put in, if a constructive view of implementing the various techniques and processes outlined here is taken, then marketing can make a real difference.

Marketing is by no means a panacea. The trick is to make sure it works for you.

A marketing checklist

Without devaluing the importance of anything else commented on in this book, below we set out what are perhaps the key overall questions to ask in order to be sure that the way your firm operates is really marketing oriented.

- Have you reviewed/analysed
  your market?
  your channels of access to the market (intermediaries etc.)?
  your competition?

- Are you *sure* you know how clients/non-clients perceive you?
- Are your financial objectives clear?
- Is your range of services clearly defined?
- Is your fee structure worked out and easy to deploy?
- Are you in touch with all key decision-makers?
- Is your promotion mix (public relations, advertising (including direct mail) and sales promotion) well organised, co-ordinated and likely to be effective?
- Is the personal selling role planned, organised and effective?
- Is all of this summarised in a clear marketing plan that links to the structure, staffing and intentions of the firm?

If, in attempting to answer the above within and around your firm, you show up gaps, pose more questions, or prompt discussion or argument, then there may be more to organise if you are to get the most from what you are doing in marketing and maximise its effectiveness.

ACTION

There is an old Chinese proverb to the effect that 'a journey of a thousand miles begins with a single step'. If reading this book has prompted even a few intentions to action (you may like to check back over the '**Action boxes**' before you put it to one side), then list them all, time a few and start with – at least – one or two. There is then much more likelihood of real action following. And there seems to be a good deal of evidence that some firms are achieving a competitive edge, not because they are taking more clever and creative action than their competitors, but because they are taking sound basic action in an area where their competitors are not taking any.

You can start by filling in Figure 8.1.

Date	Action	Those involved

Figure 8.1   Action plan-making marketing work

APPENDIX

1992 – is it an opportunity for professional services?

New opportunities are on the way. For some years we have been subjected to a steady stream of propaganda (and this is not too strong a word) about how 1992 represents a momentous change for us all. Our private and business lives will be changed for ever. Controls will disappear, standards will be harmonised, costs will fall, investment will be stimulated, incomes will rise and all will be well with the world (or at least with Europe).

What has been made less clear is exactly when all these opportunities will be here and how one can make sure of being in a position to benefit. That change is coming is clear, and it is not coming to help specific firms – in professional services or any other field of activity. The inefficient, and those who are not prepared, may be in for a shock. There will be losers as well as winners.

Those who will be successful will already be taking the longer view and planning for the future. Specifically they will:

- have identified the sequence of planning activity necessary;
- highlighted marketing activity which will require planning;
- assigned appropriate management responsibility at all levels.

Professional service firms may need to know about the single market, both on behalf of their clients (an accountant may be asked to help a client set up European subsidiaries; a lawyer may be asked about distributor agreements; a designer may find that the brochure he is producing must have versions in three different languages) and for their own development.

We will concentrate here on the latter. '1992' is not an event, it is a progressive change. The difficulty is with planning for something new, where no past experience can help, and much information is lacking. Before we can move forward we must anticipate where we want the process to take us.

Much of what we need to take into account demands a crystal ball. Some, about a third, of the EC Directives which will create the format of operation for many markets, are approved. The majority are not, and other major issues such as the harmonisation of VAT remain to be decided. (This is not the place to review the detail of what the single market means in technical terms, though you may find it worth while to seek out a suitable reference on this aspect.) Any plan must be based therefore on 'likely scenarios' of how all this will turn out.

What can you be clear about? Competition will increase, prices will come under pressure, the logistics of pan-European organisation will present problems. With these, and other factors, in mind your firm must decide its strategy.

The amount of analysis and discussion that will be required should not be underestimated. Practically, among a plethora of details, certain factors are the key.

- **Positioning** This must be based on regular monitoring of where the firm stands in relation to its markets and existing key clients. This may need research, and in positioning you must aim for the common ground. So much is written about the differences in Europe, but the firm's differentiation must major on common need, which research shows are the main criteria on which buying decisions are made.
- **Focus** The very fact that Europe represents a diversity of opportunities is a danger. If it is tackled on too wide a front, then nothing may be done sufficiently thoroughly to ensure an impact is made. Any firm needs to focus its efforts in a way that carefully selects the priorities and builds on these progressively. Deciding what will *not* be done (at least initially) is as important as what will be done.
- **Sales** The activities that will produce the business must be a priority. The main factor here for professional services is time. Time spent on the ground, with collaborators, with potential clients. Whether this is done from the UK, or a team and an office, put together in a new location, the investment is considerable, not least because local competition is in a better position to put weight behind their competitive effort.

Those who are ahead of the game, able to co-ordinate their efforts in terms of marketing, finance and personnel across national boundaries, make formidable competition. That is not to say that a niche cannot be carved out in Europe; it can, and some are doing this already, but it needs a powerful commitment.

Someone, to continue a theme, must wear 'the European hat'. Senior management must identify market focus, think through the organisational and personnel implications and, at the most senior level, base all this on a clarity of purpose about the long-term intention and strategy. Only then can the work of operational people, both in planning and implementing any move into Europe, make sense.

It would be wrong to conclude a book such as this with no mention of Europe, and the cautionary note we have adopted in our comments is based on observation of problems encountered by some (see **EXAMPLE**, below).

EXAMPLE

An apparently key opportunity for development of business in Europe is via loose associations of one sort or another with national businesses in various countries and cities.

One firm, seduced perhaps by visions of a letterhead listing associates in Brussels, Stockholm and Rome, or whatever, spent a great deal of expensive senior management time on setting up a network of such arrangements. This involved research, finding people to contact; making contact; travel to meetings all round Europe; the thrashing out and agreeing of terms of reference and contracts, and so on, and so on. Months later, with a suitably amended letterhead, they sat back waiting for the enquiries to come in. The one or two that did were time-consuming to progress and came to nothing.

The moral is one that has been repeated a number of times, 'it does not just happen'. Not only is such a network costly in time and effort to set up, it needs an on-going investment of both for it to have any chance of success. Communication has to flow, people have to meet, projects have to be initiated. 'Out of sight, out of mind' as the old saying has it, and it is compounded in this case by the fact that everyone in such an arrangement seems prepared to spend much more time taking than giving.

Of course, there are opportunities. As this book goes to press 1992 is upon us. Yet, 'the change' is by no means complete, the picture of what it will mean still unclear in total. That is why the theme here is one that focuses on planning. There will no doubt be work that can be done in

Europe on an opportunistic basis. That is fine. It can produce both revenue and experience; and one thing can lead to another.

Those who really build a truly additional business ahead of others, however, will be those who make an early start (if that is still possible), who set clear objectives, plan for the longer term and match their plans with a commitment of resources, not least people. Then the rewards can no doubt be worth while.

Europe, and the changes its development will bring, is perhaps a classic example of opportunities being hard work. And, as I write, I have just been asked to go to Poland; and that is, no doubt, part of yet another opportunity.

INDEX